T0270990

This book examines the development of employers' human resource management and industrial relations policies in Britain. It adopts a broad historical perspective, beginning with the inheritance from the nineteenth century and coming up to date with modern human resource management policies. It focuses on how managers organise the employment relationship, how they control work relations, and how they deal with trade unions and industrial relations. The author examines these in the context of the market within which the firm operates, and the strategy, structure, and hierarchy of the modern industrial enterprise, developing a theoretical approach which emphasises the effect of these factors on management choices.

The book shows that historically British employers tended to adopt market based strategies rather than internal ones. Despite a post-war trend towards 'internalisation', comparison with the US, Germany and Japan reveals that this has come about only slowly and unevenly, and has not been able to reverse the relative decline in economic performance and national competitiveness.

Cambridge Studies in Management 17

Markets, firms, and the management of labour in modern Britain

Cambridge Studies in Management

Formerly Management and Industrial Relations series

Editors
WILLIAM BROWN, *University of Cambridge*
ANTHONY HOPWOOD, *London School of Economics*
and PAUL WILLMAN, *London Business School*

The series focuses on the human and organisational aspects of management. It covers the areas of organisation theory and behaviour, strategy and business policy, the organisational and social aspects of accounting, personnel and human resource management, industrial relations and industrial sociology.

The series aims for high standards of scholarship and seeks to publish the best among original theoretical and empirical research; innovative contributions to advancing understanding in the area; books which synthesise and/or review the best of current research, and aim to make the work published in specialist journals more widely accessible; and texts for upper-level undergraduates, for graduates and for vocational courses such as MBA programmes. Edited collections may be accepted where they maintain a high and consistent standard and are on a coherent, clearly defined, and relevant theme.

The books are intended for an international audience among specialists in universities and business schools, undergraduate, graduate and MBA students, and also for a wider readership among business practitioners and trade unionists.

Other books in the series
1 John Child and Bruce Partridge, *Lost managers: supervisors in industry and society*
2 Brian Chiplin and Peter Sloane, *Tackling discrimination in the workplace: an analysis of sex discrimination in Britain*
3 Geoffrey Whittington, *Inflation accounting: an introduction to the debate*
4 Keith Thurley and Stephen Wood (eds.), *Industrial relations and management strategy*
5 Larry James, *Power in a trade union: the role of the district committee in the AUEW*
6 Stephen T Parkinson, *New product development in engineering: a comparison of the British and West German machine tool industries*
7 David Tweedale and Geoffrey Whittington (eds.), *The debate on inflation accounting*
8 Paul Willman and Graham Winch, *Innovation and management control: labour relations at BL Cars*
9 Lex Donaldson, *In defence of organisation theory: a reply to the critics*
10 David Cooper and Trevor Hopper (eds.), *Debating coal closures: economic calculation in the coal dispute 1984–85*

Markets, firms, and the management of labour in modern Britain

Howard F. Gospel

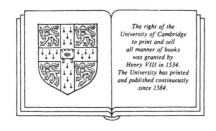

The right of the
University of Cambridge
to print and sell
all manner of books
was granted by
Henry VIII in 1534.
The University has printed
and published continuously
since 1584.

Cambridge University Press
Cambridge New York Port Chester
Melbourne Sydney

Published by the Press Syndicate of the University of Cambridge
The Pitt Building, Trumpington Street, Cambridge CB2 1RP
40 West 20th Street, New York, NY 10011-4211, USA
10 Stamford Road, Oakleigh, Melbourne 3166, Australia

First published 1992

A catalogue record for this book is available from the British Library

Library of Congress cataloguing in publication data
Gospel, Howard F.
    Markets, firms, and the management of labour in modern Britain /
Howard F. Gospel.
    p.   cm. – (Cambridge studies in management; 17)
    Includes bibliographical references and index.
    ISBN 0-521-41527-6
    1. Personnel management – Great Britain – History – 19th century.
2. Personnel management – Great Britain – History – 20th century.
3. Industrial relations – Great Britain – History – 19th century.
4. Industrial relations – Great Britain – History – 20th century.
I. Title. II. Series.
HF5549.2.G7G67   19922
331'.0941 – dc20   91-27288 CIP

ISBN 0 521 41527 6

Transferred to digital printing 2004

AR

To my mother
and to the memory of
my father

Contents

Preface

This book is the outcome of many years' research and writing on the management of labour. Its origins go back to a doctoral dissertation at the London School of Economics on the role of employers' associations in the development of the British system of industrial relations. Subsequently over the years I sustained my interest in the central role of management in industrial relations and carried out further research on wider aspects of labour management in various industries and individual companies. The book provides a synthesis of my work and that of others in the area. I hope also that it makes new contributions in terms of concepts, knowledge, and interpretations.

Inevitably over the years I have accumulated a considerable debt of gratitude to various academic colleagues. B. C. Roberts and H. A. Clegg encouraged my original interest in the role of employers and my belief that they are the prime movers in industrial relations. Colleagues at the University of Kent have commented on various drafts of the manuscript and I would like in particular to thank J. Lovell, S. Glynn, J. Oxborrow, G. Crompton, and G. Rubin. Colleagues at the London School of Economics have also commented over the years and here I am particularly grateful to L. Hannah, T. Gourvish, S. Keeble, D. Baines, E. Hunt, R. Fitzgerald, and J. Tomlinson. Many others have helped with suggestions for improvement on specific themes and chapters. I have received assistance from economic and business historians who have corrected many of my historical errors and misunderstandings - G. Jones, J. Zeitlin, S. Tolliday, J. Melling, A. Reid, N. Whiteside, P. Thane, A. McIvor, R. Coopey, L. Holden, and A. McKinlay. Since this is also a study which comes more or less up to date, I have also benefited from discussions with industrial relations, labour economics, and business colleagues who have provided useful critical comments on more contemporary chapters - K. Sissons, R. Martin, P. Marginson, P. Anthony, A. Pendelton, O. Clarke, F. Bayliss, M. Rawlinson, A. Starkman, and P. Ryan. With such a long series of acknowledgements, it is clear that the usual disclaimers apply. I would also like to thank the various employers' organisations and companies who allowed me access to their records and who provided interviews. These are referred to individually in the notes. In addition, I would like to thank the Economic and Social Research Council and the Nuffield Foundation for financial assistance with some of the research which went into the making of the volume. Finally, I owe a special debt of gratitude to Cathy, without whose support and encouragement this book would not have been possible.

For many years in Britain, perhaps more than in other major industrial countries, labour has been treated primarily as a commodity subject to market forces. At the present time there is much talk about the development of a new approach to the management of human resources. I hope that the conceptual and historical perspective of this book will enable the management of labour to be seen as part of a more complex evolution and will illustrate the constraints and opportunities which we inherit from the past.

1 Introduction: the management of labour

The management of people at work has always been a central problem and challenge for employers. It is a universal problem, but it has been tackled in different ways, at different times, in different countries. As the first industrial nation, Britain occupies a distinctive position with a long legacy of traditions and practices which still influence the way labour is managed in the modern business enterprise. The management, and mismanagement, of labour has had profound consequences for British society and national competitiveness.

This book investigates the development of labour management in Britain. It begins with the inheritance from the nineteenth century and traces continuities and change in the twentieth-century business enterprise. It concentrates mainly on the management of manual workers in industrial enterprises since it was here that the historically predominant pattern of labour management was established. A major theme is that, at an early stage during the process of industrialisation, British employers made certain critical choices about the ways in which labour should be managed. Though at the time these choices had a certain rationality, in the longer term they proved short-sighted and less appropriate. Yet they set a pattern which persisted and profoundly influenced the management of labour in the twentieth-century business enterprise. It is the argument of this book that the outcome of these choices contributed significantly to Britain's relatively poor economic performance from the late nineteenth century onwards.

The book seeks to bridge the gap between traditional business history and labour history. In addition it draws upon contemporary studies of business management, industrial relations, and personnel management. From the Webbs onwards, we have a number of excellent studies of British labour history, which provide valuable insights into labour management, though their main focus has been on trade unions.[1] In recent years there has been a growth of business history, including studies of individual firms and broader surveys. However, these various bodies of literature have not been brought together. What follows draws on earlier historical studies of labour management,[2] but it differs from previous work in several respects. It takes a longer term perspective, beginning in the late nineteenth century and coming more or less up-to-date. It therefore builds a bridge between historical and contemporary studies. It also sets the story in a wider economic and business context, bringing out the importance of market structure and company organisation. In addition, it adopts a broad view of labour decisions and interactions between employers and their workers, by looking beyond narrow aspects of personnel management and management–union relations.

Concepts and definitions

In analysing economic processes economists use the notions of markets and firms. A market exists when there is an exchange of goods or services between sellers and buyers, shaped by the forces of supply and demand and co-ordinated by the price mechanism. Such an exchange is usually a short-term and relatively impersonal transaction. Firms, on the other hand, are economic institutions which operate in markets, but which are distinct from them. Activities within–firms, above a certain size, are co-ordinated and controlled by a hierarchy of managers, and relations within the firm are more likely to be longer term. One way to see the firm is as an administrative mechanism which comes into being and supersedes the market mechanism when it becomes more efficient or more effective to co-ordinate activities and allocate resources internally within the firm rather than externally in the market.[3]

Labour is one of the primary factors of production and represents both a cost and a resource to the firm. Whether the employer sees labour primarily as a cost to be minimised or as a resource to be developed is of considerable importance to the practice of labour management because it shapes the attitudes and practices of employers. In either case, however, it should be stressed from the outset that labour is very different from non-human factors of production, a fact noted by economists of very different persuasions. Thus Marx made the distinction between labour power and labour: what the employer buys in the labour market is labour power or, in other words, the potential and capacity to work; but the employer's continuing problem is how to get actual labour or effort out of the worker in the workplace.[4] From a different standpoint, Marshall made a similar point. For him the uniqueness of labour was that 'human agents of production are not bought or sold as machinery and other material agents of production are. The worker sells his work, but he himself remains his own property.'[5] Similarly, the American institutionalist economist, Commons, placed great emphasis on the provisional and open-ended nature of the transactions surrounding labour. 'The labour contract is not a contract', he wrote, 'it is a continuing implied *renewal* of contracts at every minute and hour, based on the continuance of what is deemed, on the employer's side, to be satisfactory service, and, on the worker's side, what is deemed to be satisfactory conditions and compensation.'[6] Labour is, therefore, more than a commodity which can be bought and sold: employees are a resource which must be controlled and motivated in order to secure productive output.

In this study, labour or human resource management is used as a generic term to cover the set of decisions which employers have long made in order to govern their enterprises. It is taken to cover three main areas – work relations, employment relations, and industrial relations. Work relations covers the way work is organised and the deployment of workers around technologies and production processes. Employment relations deals with the arrangements governing such aspects of employment as recruitment, training, job tenure and promotion, and the reward of workers. Industrial relations is concerned with the representational systems which may exist within an enterprise: in the British context this has often meant management–union relations and the process of collective bargaining. These are obviously rather arbitrary distinctions of convenience and, in practice, there is considerable overlap between them. For the purposes of this book, however, the distinction is used to provide a framework for focusing on and analysing key employer decisions.

The approach adopted sees labour management in a broad context. It places considerable emphasis on the markets within which firms operate, both labour markets and also final product markets. Markets simultaneously represent an opportunity, a constraint, and a threat to employers. In other words, they can provide either an incentive or a disincentive to particular labour strategies. The approach also focuses on the organisational context of the firm, especially its strategy and structure. Strategy is used, in the first place, in the sense now established in the business administration, industrial economics, and business history literature to mean overall market strategies of growth, backward and forward integration, specialisation and diversification. Structure refers to the organisational forms and managerial hierarchies which firms develop to manage their activities. These can either facilitate or impede the choice and development of particular strategies. In this book, however, the terms strategy and structure are further developed and applied to the management of labour. In this context, strategies are defined as the long-term actions and policies used by management to secure a satisfactory labour force, to organise, discipline, and reward workers, and to deal with workers' representational and collective aspirations. Structures are the organisational forms and hierarchical arrangements used to administer such labour policies.

Theoretical framework

The book owes its theoretical ideas and origins to a number of sources. First and foremost, it owes a debt to the institutional tradition in economics. This is an approach which stresses the importance of organisational arrangements and transactions within markets. Writing at the beginning of this century, Commons argued that the basic unit of economic analysis should not be commodities or factors of production, but transactions, in other words, the arrangements through which goods and services are exchanged. He pointed out that there are a variety of institutional forms, such as markets, firms, and cartels, which may coordinate exchanges between individuals or groups. In his writings he developed an argument on the following lines: in a market economy, the scope of the market, its geographical extent, and the degree of competition within the market are key factors which influence transactional arrangements; such arrangements shape the structure or organisation of the firm; different firm structures, he argued, then influence the pattern of labour management and aspects such as union organisation; changes in the market, in particular its 'ever-widening area' and 'increased competitive menace', trigger changes in strategies and organisational forms. For Commons, the analysis of different institutional forms and patterns in various market contexts was central to the study of economic processes in history.[7]

An important contribution to the economist's theory of the firm and one which can be applied to the firm's labour activities is to be found in the classic work by Coase on 'The Nature of the Firm'.[8] In this, Coase discussed why firms come into existence and why they grow. In a sense, he was concerned with the boundaries of the firm, with what the firm itself undertakes and what it leaves to individuals, other firms, and other institutions. Coase suggested that the boundary between the market and the firm, between the external price mechanism and the internal administrative mechanism, is determined by the relative transaction cost of each. Such transaction costs include *inter alia* the costs of dealing with uncertainty, gaining information, and making and enforcing contracts. Where the costs of using the external market mechanism are relatively low, the firm will choose to transact through the market; where the costs of market transactions are too high, the firm will prefer to

internalise activities within its boundaries; the limits to the growth of
the firm will be fixed by the volume of transactions which can be efficiently
internalised. Following Coase, others have identified more complex transactional arrangements than the simple dichotomy between market and
firm. In practice, there exists a spectrum of contractual arrangements,
including markets, firms, and various forms of inter-firm organisation
such as cartels, joint ventures, and subcontracting.[9] Other economists,
such as Williamson, working in the institutional tradition, have tried to
identify different types of structural arrangements *within* firms and to
explain why they exist and with what economic consequences.[10]

Similar ideas have been developed independently in empirical research
by business historians. In the US, Chandler has analysed the growth of
the modern business enterprise in terms of decisions to internalise certain
historically separable business activities.[11] The process of internalisation,
he has argued, began when mass markets and mass-production technologies permitted high volume throughput in production and distribution. Firms grew by increasing the scale of their production or the scope
of their products and by adding new plants. Firms also grew in a
horizontal direction by acquiring other firms in the same industry; they
grew vertically by obtaining related processes involved in earlier or later
stages of production; and they also internalised by developing purchas-
ing, sales, and other functions which they had previously left to others
such as suppliers or merchants. In these ways the small, single-plant,
single-product firm (the S-form firm, to use Williamson's terminology[12])
was transformed into the large, multi-unit, multi-product enterprise.
These strategies of growth then induced a search for new structural forms
of organisation. Over time, firms have moved through various stages. At
an early stage, some developed unified structures, with functionally
specialised departments in large headquarters (the U-form firm). Others,
usually growing by acquisition and merger, remained decentralised federations of relatively autonomous, but legally related, units and adopted
looser holding-company forms of organisation (H-form). Increasingly,
in particular as a result of product and geographical diversification, firms
have moved more towards a multidivisional form of organisation (M-
form), where operations are divided into product or geographical
divisions, but subject to the overall strategic control of headquarters. For
Britain, Chandler, Hannah, and others have used a similar type of analysis
to examine the growth of the modern business corporation. They have
shown, however, that the process of internalisation and organisational
development occurred later in Britain. Smaller firms survived for longer,
and there was less pressure on larger firms to develop new forms of
organisation. Cultural and social factors, such as the strength of family

ownership, may in part explain the differences between the US and Britain. But business historians have tended to emphasise the different nature of factor and final product markets in Britain. More concentrated markets and efficient distribution systems obviated the need, in the case of Britain, to bypass the market and build large centralised firms with extensive managerial hierarchies.[13]

The argument of this book is that these ideas can be developed and used to understand the nature of labour management. At this point it is useful to present certain key propositions. Such a presentation of generalisations risks oversimplifying a set of complex economic and organisational interactions and understating certain factors. However, this framework is set out as a pre-statement of the general thesis to be developed in the course of the book and to help make sense of the detailed historical material which follows.[14]

The initial proposition is simply that, in a market economy, the nature of markets will play a large part in shaping labour decisions. In a sense, to say that markets are important in a capitalist economy is to state the obvious; but the nature of markets, for the various factors of production and for the final product or service, is so fundamental that it can be stated as a proposition. Important features of markets which will be stressed are their size and boundaries, their homogeneity or fragmentation, their stability or instability, and the degree of competition within them. The argument is developed in the book that the nature of product markets in the nineteenth and early twentieth centuries, in particular their heterogeneity and degree of fragmentation, had a profound effect on systems of labour management in Britain. The extension of product markets and the intensification of competitive pressures at various times triggered significant changes in labour management arrangements. Labour markets also shaped employer decisions in various ways. To cite but one: the relative abundance of labour, including craft labour, in nineteenth- and early twentieth-century Britain played an important part in shaping employer policies and practices. In particular, it was a disincentive to the introduction of more sophisticated production techniques and the development of strong internal employment systems.

Of course, markets exist within and are shaped by historical, cultural, and political contexts. To say that markets have been of crucial importance is not to deny the significance of other environmental factors. Employers obviously made their choices in a social and cultural context where historical traditions and attitudes were important. Indeed, in accounting for employers' behaviour, this book places considerable emphasis on the origins and early development of systems of labour management in Britain and the continuities in attitudes and practices.

In addition, the activities of the state shaped events, both by direct government intervention in labour management as through legislation and more indirectly by influencing the market context. Similarly, in the industrial relations sphere, workers and their trade unions have been a significant factor independently influencing relations with employers. However, in a market economy, where some kind of profit maximisation and cost containment are goals, the forces of competition and the nature of markets are of major importance in shaping strategic choices. In other words, markets do not determine behaviour, but are a powerful constraint on choices.

The second proposition is that market forces are mediated through the structure of the firm. In other words, the organisation of the firm itself is of crucial importance in shaping labour decisions. It is significant that the modern business enterprise in Britain developed more slowly than in some other countries. The traditional British enterprise, smaller and often family-owned and -managed, remained the predominant form well into the twentieth century in many industries. Where large firms emerged, they were often loosely organised holding companies in which subsidiaries enjoyed considerable autonomy. The predominance of small firms or loosely co-ordinated larger firms shaped the choices open to British employers for managing labour. Thus choices of strategy and structure at the broader level of the firm both constrain and facilitate the choice of strategy and structure in the area of labour management.

A third proposition is that the nature of the managerial hierarchy is an important variable influencing labour decisions. The managerial hierarchy is made up both of vertical levels (top, middle, and lower managers) and horizontal functions (such as production, finance, sales, and personnel). The effectiveness of managerial hierarchies depends on various characteristics. It depends on the technical training and professional competence of managers. It also depends on the degree of integration or segmentation within the managerial hierarchy between levels and functions. Managers who are better trained and managerial hierarchies which are more integrated are more likely to be better able to manage. It is noted in this book that in Britain family control and management remained stronger and salaried management developed more slowly than in other countries. Also, British management has tended to be relatively less well trained and proficient than in certain other major countries and managerial hierarchies tended to be more segmented. Weak managerial hierarchies, allied with inadequate corporate structures, meant that there was insufficient organisational capability in most British firms to develop and administer strong internal systems of labour management.[15]

A fourth proposition is that the choice of production technology and the division of labour within the firm also shape management labour decisions. Technology is here taken to mean not just machines and technical processes, but also how these are organised and the way workers are deployed around them. The division of labour is in part a function of the extent of the product market and managerial capabilities. Where markets were large and homogeneous and where firms had the organisational capability to organise production in innovative ways, it was more likely that there would be a more extensive and sophisticated division of labour.[16] The organisation of production is also shaped by the availability of labour in the labour market, and here the argument that, up to the Second World War, Britain for the most part had an abundance of labour, including skilled craft labour, is important in that it often acted as a disincentive to change in work organisation. The choices which management makes in this area and its interactions with its labour force are referred to in this book as work relations.

The final proposition is that, in making labour decisions, there are a number of choices open to the employer. However, these choices are not limitless. One way to conceive the choices is as follows: the employer can either externalise activities in the market, internalise them within the boundaries of the firm, or co-ordinate them by various combinations of the two. This concept may be applied to decisions in the three areas of work relations, employment relations, and industrial relations.

In terms of work relations, the concepts of internalising and externalising can be used to analyse a number of important labour decisions. For example, the firm can externalise by relying on different forms of subcontracting to organise production or it can internalise by more directly organising its own workforce. Thus one significant historical change was the movement from putting-out systems of production, to various forms of subcontracting, and to direct production within the firm. Over time, there has been some backward and forward movement between these different ways of organising work. The notion of internalising and externalising can also be used to analyse skill formation and transformation, in other words, training arrangements. Thus the firm can externalise by doing little or no training and poaching or recruiting labour in the market which others have trained. Also, it could be said to externalise by relying on apprenticeship arrangements which are occupationally orientated or by making extensive use of state training facilities which train in externally marketable skills. On the other hand, the firm can internalise by doing its own training and making training more firm-specific.[17] Where and how a worker acquires his skills is of extreme importance: it affects his attitude towards those skills, his control over them, and his attitude to technical change.

In terms of employment relations, the firm can externalise by relying on the external market for labour; by recruiting and laying off as demand changes; by filling higher positions with external as well as internal candidates; and by fixing wages according to external market signals. Alternatively, the firm can internalise the employment relationship by more systematically screening and recruiting workers; by making every effort to make them permanent employees; by developing internal job ladders and using internal promotion wherever possible; by fixing wages more according to internal administrative principles than to market forces; and by developing more extensive fringe benefits, often based on seniority within the firm. In the former situation, where strategies of externalisation are pursued, the employment contract is likely to be of a minimal kind; in the latter it will be more complex and there will be a more highly developed internal labour market.[18] (In this book the term 'internal labour market' is used to describe an elaborate internal employment system relatively insulated from external market forces. In this sense the term is now widely accepted; however, it is something of a misnomer, since what is being described is less of a market and more of an internal administrative system.)

In industrial relations, managements can internalise by seeking to promote their own employee representation system, such as a works council, or by sponsoring a company union. Where management does recognise an outside union, it will seek to bargain domestically within the firm and will handle grievances and disputes internally through its own in-house procedures. By contrast, a firm can be said to externalise its industrial relations when it hands dealings with a trade union over to an association of employers outside the firm. This type of employers' organisation sets wages according to external market criteria and processes grievances through an external disputes procedure. This use of employers' associations is a form of externalisation, though it might perhaps be better termed 'co-ordination by cooperation';[19] certainly it represents a form of delegation to an outside body.

In reality, firms will often use a combination of these strategies. For example, they may use different strategies for different types of labour, showing more of a tendency to internalise in the case of higher level employees who are in short supply or who possess firm-specific skills. They may also move between different types of strategy over time as market conditions change. But such moves occur infrequently and come about slowly. The argument that will be developed in this book is that, in general, British employers in the nineteenth and early twentieth centuries tended to prefer market mechanisms and to externalise their labour activities. This contrasts with tendencies in other countries, especially among large firms in the USA, Germany, and Japan, where there was a stronger tendency to rely more on internal systems of co-ordination. Yet British firms were never monolithic, and it is significant that there were always exceptions to the general pattern. Strategies of externalisation existed where product markets were small, fragmented, and competitive and where labour markets provided an ample supply of workers. They also existed where firms had simple divisions of labour and lacked the organisational capability to develop and administer strong internal systems. In these circumstances, it made more sense for employers to rely on market rather than administrative co-ordination. Strategies of internalisation occurred when administrative co-ordination permitted a more effective and efficient labour management than co-ordination by market mechanisms. Internalisation therefore depended on markets, was related to more sophisticated divisions of labour, and required more advanced managerial hierarchies. The argument is that, through the course of the twentieth century, there has been a growing tendency, on the part of British firms, to internalise labour activities and to develop stronger internal arrangements. However, this development of strategies of internalisation has been slow and uneven.

The contention, then, is that markets, as mediated through firm-level structures, managerial hierarchies, and the division of labour, go a long way to explain the choice of employer strategies in the labour field. Such strategies can be seen in a broad sense as policies of either internalisation or externalisation. Historically, in the British case, limited internalisation represented, for most employers, a rational response to the ease of organising transactions through markets. At the same time, it also represented a failure of employer action, reflecting the weakness of corporate structures and managerial hierarchies. Thus, in Britain, the invisible hand of the market dominated labour management, and the visible handshake of closer and more lasting relations between employers and employees made only slow progress.[20]

As stated so far the argument prompts two questions. First, can it really be said that historically British employers pursued policies in the labour field which added up to anything so grand as strategies? Many might feel that employers merely reacted opportunistically to events and at best muddled through. In the case of British employers, there is indeed much to this contention, and the idea of opportunistic behaviour fits well with the notion that employers pursued short-term, market-orientated policies. However, in considering strategies, a useful distinction may be drawn between *intended* and *enacted* strategies: intended strategies are those which are consciously and purposively developed *ex ante*; enacted strategies are those practices which grow incrementally over time and which, with the benefit of hindsight, reveal a certain pattern of actions *ex post*.[21] In this book, the term strategy is used in both senses. It is argued that historically most British employers did not intentionally develop and implement long-term strategies. Instead they reacted in an *ad hoc* and often opportunistic manner, responding to market conditions. Despite this general pattern, however, there were always some firms which did consciously develop strategies of a more consistent nature, and their number, it is argued, has increased over time. The approach of the book attempts to examine both the general pattern of enacted strategies while at the same time explaining the exceptional espousal of intended strategies.

This leads to a second question. Did employers' labour strategies matter in the sense of their bearing any relationship to the economic performance of firms, industries, and the British economy as a whole? There is, of course, a large literature on the performance of British entrepreneurs and the relative decline of the British economy from the late nineteenth century onwards. Much of this concentrates on factors other than labour; where it deals with labour matters, it has tended to focus on the role of workers and trade unions and has paid less attention to the management, or mismanagement, of labour. The relationship between managerial decisions in this area and economic performance is explored throughout the book. The gist of the argument which will be presented is that the management of labour did matter. In the nineteenth century, British employers pursued labour policies of externalisation which had a certain economic rationality, at least in contemporary circumstances and in the short term. However, as circumstances changed and as foreign firms developed alternative arrangements, these policies became less appropriate for successful business performance. It is hoped that the perspective offered here will provide some insights into the economic performance of British firms and industries.

The book is divided into three chronological parts. The first deals with the inheritance from the nineteenth century, where, it is argued, certain patterns of labour management were set which had a profound influence well into the twentieth century. The second part covers the years from the turn of the century up to the Second World War. This is shown as a period of significant changes, especially in terms of the growth of the modern business enterprise, but also of considerable continuity in terms of labour management. The third part then covers the post-1945 years which are seen as a time of growing challenge to existing patterns of labour management and a period of more rapid adaptation towards more internalised systems. However, significant elements of the older pattern and related attitudes still persisted. The final chapter reverts to the initial propositions and draws some general conclusions. Since the argument places great emphasis on markets, corporate structures and hierarchies, and the division of labour as key variables, each of the historical periods begins with an analysis of this background. This is to be found in the first part of Chapter 2 for the nineteenth century, in Chapter 3 for the first half of the twentieth century, and in Chapter 6 for the post-1945 period. This background is presented rather schematically, but it provides context on markets, firms, and the organisation of production which is essential for the development of the argument. Within each chronological part, work relations, employment relations, and industrial relations are dealt with thematically. It is hoped that this combination of a chronological and thematic approach enables a considerable amount of empirical material to be presented in historical context.

To revert to the basic theme. Where product markets were fragmented and slow growing and where external labour markets were well-stocked and operated reasonably efficiently, this predisposed firms to choose certain labour strategies. Where, in addition, firms were small, or even where they were large but loosely co-ordinated with weak managerial hierarchies, and where traditional technologies and divisions of labour persisted, firms tended to espouse strategies of externalisation and internal systems of labour management remained weak. Where, on the other hand, markets were large and growing, where firms developed the organisational capability to take advantage of this, and where they successfully introduced more sophisticated technologies and forms of work organisation which required more firm-specific labour, employers tended to make certain decisions about labour which led to more internalised systems. In Britain, the former type of strategic choices predominated from the nineteenth century onwards and created a set of institutional arrangements and attitudes which persisted well into the twentieth century. Change towards more internalised systems of human resource management has come only slowly and unevenly. International comparisons suggest that British employers relied on externalisation more than their counterparts in other advanced economies such as the US, Germany, and Japan; these strategies have had adverse consequences for economic performance and national competitiveness.

Part 1

The inheritance

2 Markets, firms, and the management of labour in the nineteenth century

A central argument of this book is that market and firm structures and the organisation of production had a major impact on the management of labour. Market conditions provided either an incentive or a disincentive to particular labour strategies; corporate structures and managerial hierarchies either facilitated or obstructed the implementation of particular policies. The organisation of production, in part shaped by market and firm structures, but also chosen by employers, in turn promoted or constrained labour policies. In this chapter the nineteenth-century background of market conditions, corporate structure, and the organisation of production is examined. Within this context, the chapter then examines managerial decisions in the areas of work relations, employment relations, and industrial relations and shows how, for the most part, British employers pursued strategies of externalisation.

Markets and firms

During the course of the nineteenth century, markets grew in geographical scope, largely as a result of improvements in transportation and cost reductions. At the end of the century, some markets remained predominantly local in nature, for example, in building, in consumer durables such as clothing and furniture making, and in non-durables such as brewing and baking. Other markets were already national in scope, especially those in packaged consumer goods such as soap, biscuits, sugar confectionery, and cigarettes. Still other markets in which British firms operated, such as cotton, iron and steel, and shipbuilding, were more international in scope. In the late nineteenth century in most markets there was an increase in competition, and in particular manufacturers involved in international trade became aware of an intensification in foreign competition, especially from the US and Germany. However, despite calls for protection, Britain remained, up to the First World War, an open economy committed to free trade.[1]

There were other features of British markets which need to be stressed. Most British firms produced a broad range of goods and, with a few exceptions, there was only a slow trend towards standardised mass markets. Firms chose to specialise, produced on a 'bespoke' basis, and were content to differentiate their production. Within Britain, substantial differences existed in markets with a broad spread from high quality and luxury to low quality goods. In overseas markets, British firms exported to a large number of countries, in some of which they had established particular market niches and, in Empire markets, they usually enjoyed favoured positions. This meant that the markets for British manufacturers were extremely diverse, and there was less progress towards standardisation than was developing at this time in the US or Germany.

Though most British markets were subject to strong competitive pressures, there also existed in Britain a long tradition of market sharing and price fixing.[2] In the late nineteenth century, confronted by new competitive pressures and a squeeze on profits, there was a growth in such collusive practices and in the number and stability of cartel associations. This was not hindered by legal sanctions in Britain, unlike in the US where from 1890 onwards so-called trusts became illegal. It will be argued below that these practices had important implications for labour management: where successful they reduced competitive pressures on firms to innovate in labour matters, and trade association activity encouraged the reliance on employers' organisations in the labour market.[3]

In most industries the typical late nineteenth-century firm was a small or medium-sized, single-plant operation, employing tens of workers and with limited capital assets. Most were private companies, usually both family-owned and -managed and rarely adopting limited liability status.[4] There were, of course, exceptions to this. The railway companies were amongst the largest enterprises in Victorian Britain, with massive capital assets, professional managers, and tens of thousands of employees. By 1900 a number of other large firms had emerged in manufacturing industry. These included firms in certain sectors of textiles, such as textile finishing and sewing cotton (J. & P. Coats, Bleachers' Association, and Calico Printers); in armaments, shipbuilding, and iron and steel (Vickers, Armstrong Whitworth, John Brown, Cammell Laird, Dorman Long, and Stewart & Lloyds); in chemicals and related industries (Brunner Mond, Nobels, the Gas Light & Coke Company, and the South Metropolitan Gas Company); and in consumer goods industries (Lever Bros., Imperial Tobacco, Huntley & Palmers, and the large breweries).[5] The majority of these, however, were relatively new creations at the turn of the century and, at first, had a limited effect on the pattern of labour management in Britain.

Two further points must be made about the few large firms which had emerged in manufacturing by the end of the century. First, while some of them were large by international standards, many were smaller in terms of capital and output than their American and German counterparts, particularly in iron and steel and engineering. In part, the reasons for this related to market size and structure. By the late nineteenth century, the British economy was already smaller than that of the US and was growing at a slower rate than either the US or Germany. Furthermore, within Britain, markets were geographically concentrated and relatively efficient with good commodity exchanges and distribution networks which, to some extent, obviated the need to build larger firms.[6] Second, many of the larger British enterprises, especially those created by merger, operated as holding companies which were loosely organised as federations of firms, with small central headquarters, little co-ordination or integration, and with operating decisions left to the constituent companies. In most cases owners and their families continued to control and manage both at holding company and subsidiary level. Herein was another contrast with the US (and, though to a lesser extent, with Germany) where larger enterprises had emerged which were more integrated and co-ordinated by more extensive managerial hierarchies.[7] However, again there were exceptions in Britain, with some medium and large firms developing more centralised forms of control and more extensive managerial hierarchies. These exceptions included the large railway companies as well as manufacturing enterprises such as the gas companies, some large chemical companies (Nobels, Brunner Mond, United Alkali), some consumer goods manufacturers (J. & P. Coats and Lever Bros. at Port Sunlight), and some of the American-owned firms located in Britain (Singer Sewing Machine Company and British Westinghouse). On the whole, however, even in larger firms, organisational and managerial structures remained rudimentary.[8]

Managerial hierarchies with special reference to the management of labour

The cadre of managerial employees grew only slowly in nineteenth-century Britain. Even by 1907 the proportion of managerial, technical, and clerical staff to production workers in manufacturing industry was only 8.6 per cent, smaller than in the US and Germany.[9] As significant was the fact that a smaller proportion of British managers had been educated to college or university level than their counterparts in the US, Germany, or even in the embryonic Japanese large firm.[10] Broadly speaking, owners and managers who had received any formal training beyond school level were most likely only to have served an apprenticeship and only a small proportion had attended any sort of technical college.[11] Lower level managers and foremen had at best served an apprenticeship and were usually promoted from the shopfloor.[12] However, among the sons of owners and senior managers in large firms, a growing proportion went to private schools or the older universities where they tended to study liberal and classical subjects.[13] In this way, by the late nineteenth century, a divide was emerging in some larger firms between those at the top, who received an education fit for a 'gentleman', and lower management, who prided themselves on 'practical' experience rather than formal education or training.[14]

Early British industrialisation had not depended greatly on formally educated scientists and engineers. Even by the late nineteenth century, engineers and scientists, with university or college education, were rare in British industry. For the most part technical staff acquired their competence through an apprenticeship or pupillage of some kind. Engineers, for example, were likely to have combined an apprenticeship, on the shopfloor or in the drawing office, with some part-time college education, perhaps leading to membership of a professional association.[15] From the final quarter of the nineteenth century onwards, there was a growing criticism of British deficiences in technical and scientific training, especially when compared to Germany and the USA. There are a number of possible explanations why British firms may have been less receptive to university- or college-trained manpower. First, since few entrepreneurs and senior managers themselves had benefited from a technical education, it is likely that they failed to see its importance in others and provide good career opportunities for such staff. Second, where firms needed expertise, they could look to the market and buy it in, from other firms, from abroad, and from consulting engineers and chemists.[16] Third, many British firms, relying on well-tried techniques and with access to a relatively abundant supply of skilled manual labour, felt little need to develop their managerial and technical hierarchies where graduates would be appropriate.[17] These deficiencies were extensively (though inconclusively) investigated and debated at the time. In practice, it is likely that, in the more scientifically based industries, such as chemical dyestuffs and electrical engineering, where Britain had initially been a pioneer in terms of inventions, the paucity of technical manpower retarded innovation and impeded performance.[18]

In terms of labour management, hierarchies remained particularly rudimentary and traditional. In smaller firms the owner himself was directly involved in the management and supervision of workers, though in all but the smallest this function was shared with others. In practice, this often meant the delegation of responsibilities to internal subcontractors or senior skilled workers. Under internal subcontracting systems, the functions of recruiting a labour force, monitoring production, and paying workers were handed over to a subcontractor or gang master. Such arrangements were widespread in nineteenth-century industries such as coal mining and iron making. So also were systems where skilled men hired, supervised, and paid their own helpers or underhands as was the custom in cotton spinning, shipbuilding, and pottery.[19] Such practices seem to have persisted longer in Britain than in other countries. By the late nineteenth century, however, internal subcontracting had been considerably reduced as competitive and technological changes pressured employers to cut out these middle-men and replace them with their own foremen. Nevertheless, the foremen who took their place still often ran their departments with considerable autonomy in matters of hiring, work allocation, and labour management. Only a few larger firms developed more elaborate supervisory systems more directly under the control of a hierarchy of middle and senior managers.[20]

Continuities and change in the organisation of work

In considering work organisation it is useful, by way of introduction, to go back to the classical economists for they paid considerable attention to the division of labour and the organisation of work. In *The Wealth of Nations*, Adam Smith argued that the subdivision of work into more specialised activities provided real efficiency advantages: it increased proficiency, reduced time-wasting, and stimulated mechanisation. The resultant increase in prosperity offset any disadvantages in terms of narrow tasks and worker alienation. For Smith, the division of labour was dependent on the market and the extent of the division was limited only by the extent of the market.[21] A further advantage of the division of labour was pointed out by Babbage, namely that it allowed employers to allocate jobs to workers according to their specialist skills and to deploy skilled workers exclusively on skilled work, paying them accordingly. For him, also, the main force driving the division of labour was competition in the market.[22] By contrast, Marx analysed the division of labour within the firm more in terms of production than market relations. It was the capitalist's need to control production and extract more surplus value from workers which, in his view, created the division of labour. With the availability of more advanced technologies and the application of scientific principles, control could increasingly be built into machinery with the result that workers were reduced to unskilled machine minders.[23] Later Marxists have stated a more general deskilling thesis: according to Braverman, under capitalism employers seek to reduce the skill content of work so as to make labour more substitutable, to reduce training costs, and to minimise worker control over the production process. Put another way, the capitalist uses deskilling to transfer knowledge of the work process from the worker to himself, thereby increasing his own control.[24]

In practice, the causes of the division of labour, the intentions of employers, and the actual working-out of technical and organisational changes were extremely complex. Overall, in the nineteenth century, there were considerable continuities in Britain in terms of work organisation. In cotton textiles, for example, traditional methods of working remained widespread. Though towards the end of the century there was some introduction of new ring spindles and automatic looms to replace mule spinning and traditional looms, change was limited. Faced with competitive pressures, cotton employers sought to intensify work within existing technologies, but their success in this respect was in turn limited by resistance, in particular from skilled workers.[25] In most sectors of engineering too, though new machines were available and introduced and though the employers won two notable victories (in 1852 and 1897–8) against the trade unions over the right to introduce new methods of working on such machines, in practice most firms persisted with traditional work methods and did not push through major technological reorganisation. As Zeitlin has shown, they preferred to resort to cost cutting and work intensification rather than to introduce new methods of mass production.[26] In iron and steel British employers continued to rely on traditional skills and used labour-intensive processes at a time when American and German producers were developing newer techniques, using more capital equipment, and relying less on skilled labour.[27] In coal mining, change also came slowly and traditional methods of working prevailed throughout the British coalfields, with only limited use of coal-cutting and other machinery.[28]

Various reasons have been put forward as to why there was so much continuity. For example, it is sometimes argued that British craft unions imposed high costs on technological and organisational change thus rendering innovation unattractive. This may be true in part, but it is easy to exaggerate the strength of trade unionism at this time and to argue from particular instances to a general proposition. Even in the case of shipbuilding, where craft unions were particularly strong, most recent studies have questioned the negative effect of trade union organisation and practices.[29] It is also sometimes suggested that British entrepreneurs were conservative and deficient in technical knowledge and a willingness to apply new science-based methods.[30] Again there may be some truth in this, though the existence of exceptions casts doubt on a general explanation on these lines. A more powerful explanation of continuity, it is argued here, focuses on the nature of markets and firms. On the labour market side, in Britain in most trades there was an adequate supply of workers, including skilled labour; there was, therefore, no great incentive to substitute capital for labour as was the case in American and to some extent German industry. On the product market side, as already suggested, many British firms produced a wide range of goods for diverse markets, which meant there was less incentive to standardise products and introduce mass-production methods. Small- and medium-sized firms and loosely administered larger firms, which predominated in many British industries, did not pursue long-term investment or production policies which would have led to new techniques and patterns of work organisation.[31]

However, there were areas of British industry where in the late nineteenth century employers introduced considerable changes in production technologies which substantially altered the organisation of work. These changes occurred in industries where new technical processes became available, where markets were created for standardised products, and where large firms grew up to co-ordinate mass production. This was the case in particular in process type industries such as chemicals and some areas of food processing. In the alkali sector of the chemical industry, in the final quarter of the nineteenth century, the firm Brunner Mond replaced the traditional Leblanc method of batch production with the new Solvay process of continuous production.[32] In the manufacture of gunpowder and soap, semi-continuous processes replaced hand-production methods and the two industries came to be dominated respectively by Nobel and Lever Bros.[33] In certain consumer-goods industries, new processes were adopted to serve growing mass markets and these in turn came to be dominated by a few large firms. From the 1880s onwards, in the flour-milling industry, the traditional stone-grinding method of milling in wind- and water-mills was replaced by automatic roller milling. One result was that, relatively quickly, two firms, J. Rank & Co. and Spillers & Co., came to dominate the industry.[34] In sugar refining H. Tate & Co. and A. Lyle & Co. transformed sugar boiling into a modern industry with the introduction of superheated steam and centrifugal processing machines.[35] The production of standardised flour and sugar, together with growing mass markets, encouraged technological change in biscuit baking and chocolate confectionery. These traditional trades were transformed by the introduction of new machines and the beginnings of flow line production. Soon a small number of large firms came to dominate – Huntley & Palmers, Peak Frean, McVitie & Price, Carrs, Jacobs, Cadburys, Frys, and Rowntrees.[36] In the manufacture of cigarettes and matches new American continuous process machines and pneumatic transfer systems also transformed traditional work methods and again the industries came to be dominated by leading firms, Imperial Tobacco and Bryant & May.[37] In all these cases, there were substantial changes in the organisation of work. Some of this involved deskilling, the creation of more semi-skilled and unskilled jobs, and greater employer control over production. However, old skills often survived and new skills were also created, especially in maintenance areas.

In those industries, with craft origins, but where the market was large enough, there were also changes in work organisation. Thus, in engineering, in the bicycle industry, a few manufacturers recognised the demand for more standardised products and introduced new machine tools and interchangeability in assembly.[38] Likewise, the American Singer Sewing Machine company equipped its Clydeside factory with new automatic machine tools in the 1880s, thus considerably expanding its semi-skilled labour force and earning the firm a reputation among the Scottish business community as the epitome of 'the fine art of production'.[39] In the armaments sector of the engineering industry, where demand was for larger runs and often more stable than in other sectors, a few large firms such as Vickers, Armstrong Whitworth, and the Birmingham Small Arms Company were large investors in new machine tools and leaders in production techniques involving interchangeable parts, large batch production, and the use of special 'feed and speed' men to monitor machine operations.[40]

The main motivation behind most of these changes was to take advantage of the opportunities offered by new technologies and expanding markets and to gain economies of scale. In some cases, such as the gas industry, the desire to eliminate more skilled labour from crucial stages in the production process may have been crucial.[41] But it was usually not the case that labour considerations were of central importance, and the evidence is against a simple deskilling thesis. This is not to deny that changes were taking place in the late nineteenth century in the deployment of skill: some traditional manual skills disappeared or were reduced in industries such as iron and steel, printing, and areas of engineering; however, many old skills survived and new skills were also created in areas such as maintenance and electrical work. In industries where change was considerable such as parts of the chemical and food-processing industries, labour had never been particularly skilled and does not seem to have constituted a problem for employers. Here technical change often meant less heavy manual work and different responsibilities for workers. In industries where skilled labour was crucial, one of the most striking points is that it often continued to be central and workers maintained considerable control. A final point on the organisation of work is that, even by the end of the nineteenth century, there was in Britain little in the way of a 'scientific' approach to the management of production. It is true that some new ideas and practices, both indigenous and imported from the US, were beginning to emerge concerning production organisation, cost accounting, and new methods of wage payment. However, these had made little progress in Britain before the turn of the century and had no effect on the majority of firms.[42]

Employment relations

We turn now to employment relations and look at the recruitment and training of workers, the nature of jobs, and the type of pay and benefit systems. The recruitment of labour in the nineteenth-century enterprise was usually *ad hoc*, casual, and often based on family contacts. Where subcontracting existed it was left to the subcontractor to take on the number of workers required. Where labour was directly employed, recruitment was delegated to the foreman who made his own selection at the factory gates.[43] Discharge was also the responsibility of the foreman who often acted instantly and arbitrarily. As one engineering employer put it, 'The workman may be told by the foreman at a moment's notice that he is no longer wanted.'[44] Once recruited, training of the labour force took a number of different forms. In the first place, employers' initial reaction was to poach labour and to benefit from skills acquired elsewhere. In a period of high labour mobility, as during most of the nineteenth century, this was a reasonable expectation. For most work where little skill was involved, training was minimal and consisted of casually acquiring experience on the job. For work of a more skilled nature, opportunities were provided to pick up the trade on the job. The single most important formal method of training in the nineteenth century was the craft apprenticeship served over a five- or seven-year period.[45] Various aspects of the apprenticeship system need to be stressed. First, outside small workshops, employers did not themselves provide or control the training. Rather they delegated it to the foreman who in turn handed it over to a skilled journeyman. It was up to him then to find the time to train the apprentice. Second, in this way the apprenticeship constituted a low-cost method of training, and apprentices were a source of cheap labour. Third, though the apprenticeship was usually served within one firm, the expectation was that the apprentice should acquire all-round, externally marketable skills. The standards varied from firm to firm, but there is reason to believe that much training had a high general content. In large part this suited employers who, where product ranges were broad, required a versatile workforce; it suited the apprentice who wished to be mobile; equally it suited the trade union because adherence to standards of all-round training simultaneously limited the supply of entrants into the trade and increased workers' chances of mobility.

The amount and type of training was one factor which affected the structure of jobs and the security, or otherwise, of employment within the firm. Job tenure varied considerably. At one extreme, there were those jobs where employment was by the day as in dockwork; in other instances, the worker was hired on a 'job and finish' basis as in building and shipbuilding; other jobs were for a season as in some agricultural and food-processing work and unskilled jobs in gas works. In addition outworking was still widespread in parts of textiles, clothing, and footwear and here workers were employed and paid by the piece.[46] In other areas of factory employment, where plant and equipment needed to be run more intensively, there was in the late nineteenth century a downward trend in the proportion of labour hired on a casual basis and an increase in the proportion of workers more or less permanently employed by the firm.[47] However, almost all industries were subject to cyclical fluctuations and periodic layoffs. Within the firm there were differences in security of employment between classes of labour. Foremen and those in principal clerical positions had more security than manual workers. The core of skilled men had more chance of regular employment than less skilled men and women for most of whom job tenure was precarious.

Pay and benefit systems were for the most part commensurate with this pattern of employment and were rudimentary in nature. Most nineteenth-century workers were paid by time rates with levels fixed according to customary notions. In the case of skilled men, craft unions tried to insist on the standard rate, the union rate for the external labour market; and, in relation to this, the rates of other workers were set. Adjustments up or down were then made on the basis of changes in the cost of living or the selling price of the product and in some cases this was accomplished by automatic sliding-scale arrangements.[48] There was some increase in the use of piece work in the late nineteenth century. Depending on the type, piecework can represent an essentially short-term commodity view of the employment relationship between the employer and employee. Certainly, simple proportional piece-work systems, where the worker was paid exclusively for the number of items produced, with no guaranteed fall-back wage, represented a minimal relationship. Such systems were used in outworking employment and in clothing, footwear, and the light metal trades. In the late nineteenth century there was a growth in more elaborate piece-work systems of the bonus kind which had an advantage for the worker in that a minimum time rate was usually assured.

However, these were often regressive and the bonus was usually fixed so that it increased at a diminishing rate.[49] Commensurate with these pay systems, the formal provision of benefits such as paid holidays, sickness schemes, and pensions was relatively rare.

Thus the majority of nineteenth-century employers provided limited benefits and used simple pay systems. They preferred to link pay either to customary notions or to short-term measures of output and to adjust wages according to changes in the cost of living in the locality or to the selling price of the product in the external market. Internal wage structures were unplanned and rudimentary. However, the cash nexus was not the only bond between employers and workers, for there was, in nineteenth-century Britain, a long tradition of industrial paternalism.

Paternalism: traditional and bureaucratic

Paternalism provided an ideological dimension to the employment relationship, based on notions of protection, reciprocal obligations, and harmony. As such, it was a method of self-justification for the paternalist and a means of persuading employees to accept their position in the employment relationship. In addition, paternalism provided economic arrangements which denoted a more comprehensive approach to the employment relationship. The paternalist employer offered, if not higher wages, then at least more regular employment and earnings, plus a broader array of benefits, and in return expected greater attachment and loyalty from his workers.

Early and mid-nineteenth-century paternalism, with antecedents reaching back to agricultural origins,[50] covered a wide spectrum. The most prominent examples were some of the great northern mill owners. By comparison with other firms, they offered more regular earnings, provided company housing, and in some cases built model villages with schools, churches, and recreational facilities.[51] In some cases religious sentiment undoubtedly played a part. Pollard, however, has argued that such employers were motivated less by a definite religious or moral outlook and more by a pragmatic assessment of their circumstances.[52] Many had built new factories, away from the main industrial centres, often to take advantage of better sources of water power, and, in large part, their paternalist provision was intended to attract and retain a labour force and to ensure efficient and dependable use of new plant and equipment. It is notable also that the main paternalist firms were large and successful, sometimes with dominant market positions which enabled them to finance the costs of paternalism. Though paternalistic provision of this kind existed in smaller firms, it was always on a lesser scale and more tentative and precarious.[53]

The essence of traditional paternalism was as follows. First, it was of a personal nature, in that there was a significant degree of personal knowledge and mutual interaction between the employer and his workers. Second, it was locally based and relied on a strong link between family, company, and community.[54] Third, the provision of benefits was a gift from the employer, thus it was both *ad hoc* and *ad hominem* (the term is used advisedly since it was less likely to cover women) and there was no contractual right to benefits. Essentially, traditional paternalism was commensurate with the owner-controlled single-factory or at least single-locality enterprise where an ideology of personal attachment and community could be fostered. It was difficult to sustain this in larger, multi-unit, national companies, thus creating the need for new approaches and systems in such enterprises. On these lines Joyce has suggested that paternalism declined in the late nineteenth century and gave way to a more instrumental attitude to labour. For him the main factors causing this decline were the loosening of the influence of religious ideas, the growing impact of more independent, class-based political ideas, and increasing urbanisation and suburbanisation which physically distanced both workers and owners from the place of work and eroded the notion of a factory community. Joyce also stresses changes on the employers' side, especially the spread of the limited liability company and the decline of family involvement.[55]

However, a small number of large firms did start to develop employment systems different from both traditional paternalism and the dominant employment pattern which it has been suggested was one of minimal attachment and externalisation. It is important to examine some of these more bureaucratic employment systems, since they represented attempts at internalisation of the employment relationship and had features akin to what economists now term internal labour markets, defined as more complicated internal employment systems relatively insulated from external market forces.[56]

The best place to start is with the railway companies which were the largest and most capital-intensive enterprises in Victorian Britain. As already stated, they were pioneers in using joint-stock organisation and in developing managerial techniques. Their employment policies were also distinctive. In the first place, they recruited labour rather more systematically, often requiring references and proof of ability to read and write.[57] Once recruited, if the worker wished to stay in employment and did not infringe company rules, the practice of most companies was to keep workers until retirement age, offering the possibility of promotion through an elaborate hierarchy of grades and classifications with different levels of pay and benefits. Promotion through the grades might sometimes be affected by favouritism, but it depended most on seniority and loyalty. The wages of those at the bottom were low, but at the top were good and in some cases were supplemented by bonuses for long service. Some of the benefits provided by the railway companies, such as housing, were traditional in nature.[58] More novel was the provision by some companies of sick pay and pension schemes based on length of service.[59] Overall, these systems were less personal, more bureaucratic, and covered a larger number of dispersed operating units than in the traditional paternalist firm.[60]

Some of the large gas companies provide other examples. The two largest firms were the main London companies, the Gas Light & Coke Co. and the South Metropolitan Gas Co., both of which were more systematic and selective than other companies in their recruitment.[61] They provided internal training systems for their key workers and offered reasonable security of employment to core process workers and fitters, with progression up an albeit short hierarchy.[62] Along with this core, they also employed a large number of labourers who were treated less favourably and laid off when demand fell.[63] Key workers were obliged to be mobile within the firm and to move to care and maintenance jobs, for example, in the summer months when demand for gas fell. Both firms paid good wages and offered extensive benefits. Thus the Gas Light & Coke Co. introduced sick pay and pension arrangements. The South Metropolitan also provided an extensive range of benefits such as paid holidays, sickness, accident, and insurance schemes, and pension arrangements. It constituted what Melling has called 'virtually an insular welfare state'.[64] In the case of the South Metropolitan its employment provisions were aimed at preventing the incursions of trade unionism. After the famous strike of 1889-90, the company extended its arrangements: it converted an earlier profit-sharing system into a so-called co-partnership or share ownership scheme; it transformed its pension arrangements from an optional to a compulsory basis; and it established, as a rival to the Gas Workers Union, an internal representation plan which gave employees a say, albeit limited, in the administration of the system.[65]

A number of other large manufacturing firms developed similar arrangements. In chemicals, Brunner Mond provided good internal training, offered relatively secure jobs, and in the final decades of the nineteenth century began to provide paid holidays, sick benefits, and a pension scheme.[66] In the rapidly expanding consumer goods industries, a few large firms such as Lever Bros. and Cadburys also developed new and more systematic arrangements. Both were well-known for the provision of housing in their model villages at Port Sunlight and Bournville. Both also introduced new employment techniques. Lever Bros. provided internal education and training, paid holidays, sick pay and a pension scheme. The firm also introduced a copartnership scheme under which certificates were issued entitling holders to an annual dividend. According to Lord Lever, 'the wages system had broken down as the sole or only solution to the labour problem'.[67] Likewise Cadburys provided continuation schooling and technical education and extensive fringe benefits.[68] Recently Fitzgerald has pointed to similar examples in other large consumer-goods, food, and brewing companies.[69] It has also been argued that similar systems existed in some large firms in craft-type industries, for example in engineering and shipbuilding. Firms such as Vickers, Armstrong Whitworth, and Beardmores have been cited.[70] While it is true that these firms did provide good internal training, job security for key workers, and various welfare benefits, they were exceptions and most firms in less favourable market positions in such industries provided only minimal employment systems and conformed to the predominant pattern of externalisation.

Employment pattern explained

There are two main questions which this description of employer policies and employment patterns pose. Why was the predominant pattern one of minimal attachment between employers and their workers, rudimentary pay and benefit systems, and externalisation? Why, in a minority of firms, did there emerge a more innovative pattern with more regular employment, more complex pay and benefit systems, and more internalisation? A satisfactory explanation needs to comprehend both of these patterns.

There are a number of possible ideological and cultural explanations. It might be argued that the pattern of employment relations in Britain was set in the nineteenth-century age of *laissez-faire*, when the dominant belief was that the employer should be free to hire and fire and the worker equally free to quit and move. The employer should pay the market price of the labour he bought, but the worker should remain independent and responsible for his own welfare. Thus, Maine argued that social relations and law in England had over time evolved from being based on 'status' and had come to be based on 'contract'.[71] The pre-industrial notion of a fixed rights and obligations in society had been replaced by a contractual notion of work and an acceptance of the free mobility of labour.[72] Dicey, writing about law and public opinion in

England, also stressed the development of the notion of free contractual agreements as a hallmark of the British system.[73] Thus it could be argued that the ideology of *laissez-faire* influenced the practice of employers and workers. A problem with this explanation, however, is that it is difficult to demonstrate empirically the connection between ideas, law, and practice. Nor does it explain why there were exceptions, unless these are seen as the idiosyncratic policies of individual paternalists influenced by personal morality or religious values. Though it might be possible to argue this in some cases, it certainly does not explain all. It also leaves unexplained why employers developed such policies at particular times.

There is another possible ideological and cultural explanation which relates more to workers and their trade unions. The argument here is that workers also accepted *laissez-faire* principles and valued their independence and mobility. In the case of craft unions, their ideology was based on a set of interrelated ideas: personal ownership of skills and freedom to transfer these; common treatment for all workers of equal skill; payment of a wage based on the rate for the job; and beyond this the independence of the worker in determining his own welfare either individually or through trade union collective self-help. Thus workers, or at least those who had power through their trade unions, preferred a *laissez-faire* system of employment.[74] This explanation is consistent with the fact that many of the examples of extensive internal provision cited above were situations where trade unions were weak or non-existent. Indeed, some were also situations, as on the railways and in the gas industry, where employers were determined to exclude trade unions. Similarly, this explanation might also explain the relative absence of such arrangements in engineering, shipbuilding, building, and printing where craft unions were strong. However, some reservation must be registered. The absence of trade unionism certainly did not imply the existence of comprehensive welfare provision. In addition, one must be careful not to exaggerate the power of trade unions, whose membership was small before the twentieth century, and by itself craft unionism is insufficient explanation of the weakness of internal labour market-type arrangements in nineteenth-century Britain.

A more fruitful approach is to place nineteenth-century firms in their market context. The labour market conditioned employers' thinking and practices. Throughout most of the nineteenth century, there was always an elastic supply of labour in Britain, especially unskilled but also skilled craft labour.[75] From the employers' viewpoint, external labour markets might not be perfect, but they were sufficiently good for there to be no strong inducement to bypass them by creating internal markets. In a buyers' market for labour, there was no strong incentive, except in the case of a few key workers, to retain labour and offer high wages and benefits.

One problem with this labour-market explanation by itself is that it does not at first sight explain the existence of exceptional firms. In part, this objection may be met by the argument that these firms faced exceptional labour-market problems both in recruiting and retaining labour. The large internalising firms cited above were capital intensive and some had technologies which were industry- or even firm-specific. In these cases special aspects of their employment relations may have been developed for two reasons. In the first place, there was a strong pressure on such firms to operate their plant and equipment as intensively as possible in order to secure an adequate return on investment and for this worker co-operation was essential. They also needed to be more selective in recruitment and to devote more attention to training when expensive equipment was involved and where this might also be unique to the firm. The costs of turnover were therefore higher for them. Secondly, it could be argued that the workers who entered these firms, acquiring skills and experience which could not be used elsewhere, had an incentive to stay. Also because they were less easily replaced, they were able to secure more favourable treatment from their employers. Though this argument has some real force, there are still problems. By no means all the workers in these firms were skilled: indeed the majority were semi-skilled or unskilled. Moreover, there were other industries, for example shipbuilding and footwear, where technology and techniques were industry-specific but where extensive internal provision did not emerge. Thus, though industry- or firm-specific skills might be an important factor, this is not in itself a sufficient explanation.

It is therefore necessary, for a full explanation, to include the firm's product market and the related effect of this on the firm's organisation and division of labour. Most of the firms which started to develop something like structured internal labour markets were companies usually operating in large and homogeneous markets and using continuous process-type technologies or ones where continuity of operations was important. Either because of a quasi-monopoly position or other market advantages, they were less subject to violent shifts in product demand. They were therefore better able to provide more regular employment and more elaborate benefits. Moreover, to exploit their market situation and to co-ordinate their various activities, these firms developed extensive managerial hierarchies and effective co-ordination. They therefore had the organisational resources and capability to develop and administer more comprehensive employment policies than smaller employers or less well co-ordinated firms. The majority of firms in the British economy in the late nineteenth century enjoyed less favourable product markets and were smaller and less well co-ordinated. When faced with a downturn in demand, it was easier for them to lay off workers and it made less sense for them to develop comprehensive internal employment systems.

Coming to terms with trade unions

Sooner or later most employers have to deal with the representational aspirations and collective tendencies of their workers. In nineteenth-century Britain this meant learning to cope with trade unions. Recognition of unions developed slowly and unevenly in the Victorian period. Many employers in craft industries such as engineering, shipbuilding, and printing and in industries such as cotton and coal mining had recognised trade unions, though grudgingly, by the final quarter of the nineteenth century. By 1888 there were some three-quarters of a million trade unionists, about 10 per cent of adult male workers. Between 1889 and 1892 union membership increased to around 1.5 million, some of it associated with so-called 'New Unionism' as organisation spread to less skilled workers and hitherto unorganised industries such as the docks and gas. Thereafter membership fell, but picked up again from the mid-1890s onwards, so that, by the turn of the century, it stood at about two million or approximately 15 per cent of the adult male labour force. This represented a higher level of membership and employer recognition than in any other industrial country.[76]

In many industries, therefore, trade unions were recognised by employers by the turn of the century. The main groups of employers who stood out against recognition were in predominantly semi- and unskilled industries such as the railways, gas, and shipping where companies used traditional tactics of blacklisting and the importation of replacement labour in their attempts to exclude unions.[77] In 1909 the Chairman of the South Eastern Railway Company strongly expressed the right to manage philosophy: 'The Company has refused, and would continue to refuse, to permit a third party to come to their board room to discuss with them how they were to carry on their business.'[78] However, in their recognition of trade unions other British employers had shown a pragmatic acceptance of the fact that, though they might be able to defeat trade unions in set-piece confrontations, they could not ignore or exclude them entirely from their businesses. For these employers, the costs of excluding them were becoming increasingly high, and in addition some saw that there could be advantages in recognising trade unions given certain conditions. As Phelps Brown pointed out, 'the trade unions of the Victorian era commended themselves, at least negatively'.[79] Unorganised workers could be more unpredictable than trade unionists and refusal to recognise unions threatened periodic disruption. Recognition, on the other hand, held out the prospect of encouraging responsible action and enforcing labour discipline. Where there was collusion between employers in wage fixing, it also offered the potential of reducing competition and increasing market control.

As already indicated, recognition was mainly of trade unions for skilled male workers. Craft unionism had deep roots in many British industries and, as has already been suggested, craft workers had considerable discretion and control at work. This craft control was in large part developed out of workers' independent actions. In part, however, it arose because of the nature of British employers: small and loosely co-ordinated larger firms, with weak managerial hierarchies, dependent on flexible production systems, had to accept much of the independence and job control of their skilled workers.

A very significant feature of employer recognition of trade unions in Britain was that it was often conceded and became formalised through the medium of an employers' organisation. Such associations had a long history in Britain,[80] but from the final quarter of the nineteenth century there was an increase in their number and stability. At this time national federations were established in most major British industries. Thus the National Association of Master Builders was formed in 1877, the Federation of Master Cotton Spinners in 1891, and the Engineering Employers' Federation in 1896.[81] The predecessors of some of these associations had earlier sought to break trade unions when market conditions provided the oppportunity. However, once union power had grown to such an extent that the costs of trying to exclude it had become too high, there seemed to be advantages in recognition through an employers' organisation. Employers thus hoped to deal with unions from a position of collective strength and acted in the knowledge that their competitors were in the same position. Such a medium of recognition was also convenient, especially for small and medium-sized firms, which did not have the managerial resources to deal directly with trade unions.

Recognition by an employers' organisation probably helped unions recruit and maintain membership for it was more likely to convince reluctant employers and spread union coverage wider. Turner in his study of the cotton unions, for example, concluded that recognition through an association assured higher levels and stability of membership than would otherwise have been the case in that industry.[82] However, this method of dealing with trade unions through an association also tended to confirm and extend multi-unionism in British industry. In other words, when national recognition was conceded to different unions, it became incumbent on all member firms to accept such unions if they obtained a presence in their workplace. In engineering, for example, from 1898 onwards federated firms were obliged to accept the unions which had been recognised at national level and failure to do so could lead to expulsion from the Federation.[83] Thus employer policies, though they did not create the potential for multi-unionism, did much to sustain it. As we will see later, in the longer term multi-unionism created problems for British employers.

Employers and collective bargaining

During the years of prosperity of the mid-Victorian period, craft workers and their unions developed and enforced trade practices on employers, covering matters such as apprenticeship, deployment of workers, overtime working, and the use of piece work. Along with this, they sought to impose wage increases unilaterally throughout a district. Beginning in the 1860s and increasingly in the 1870s, as trade turned down and concern about foreign competition grew, employers in some industries tried to establish more regular and formal collective bargaining arrangements. This was done through employers' associations and involved the creation of so-called conciliation boards for fixing wages and conditions and handling disputes. There were many examples, but the best known were in hosiery, building, and certain coalfields and iron-making districts.[84]

Such arrangements were usually locally based, covering a town or district which suited a situation where labour and product markets were still often local in scope. At first the codes of wages and conditions which were created were minimal in nature. Wages were based on the rate for the job in the local labour market and adjusted automatically according to a sliding scale based on external fluctuations in the selling price of the product. This usually entailed only additions to or subtractions from key rates. In other words, the agreements did not create detailed wage structures and it was left to the individual firms to fill the gaps. The main initiative for these schemes seems to have come from the employers. It is true that the unions and their members gained certain advantages, especially formal recognition and a floor of basic wages and conditions. On the other hand, the unions were expected to abide by the formal agreements and assert discipline over their members. The employers used these collective bargaining arrangements in the 1870s and 1880s to assert greater control and contain restrictive craft practices. By taking disputed issues to joint boards, where employers could mobilise their collective strength, they hoped to check such practices and enforce precedents favourable to themselves. In some cases local wage agreements served to reduce competition between firms and long-term sliding scale arrangements gave the employers some wage predictability.[85]

A further stage in the development of collective bargaining occurred in the 1890s and 1900s when a combination of circumstances provided a new stimulus. By that time, some of the older arrangements had broken down and in the 1890s workers used the improved economic circumstances to re-impose restrictive job controls. This coincided with a renewed concern about foreign competition and a period of accelerated technological change in industries such as engineering, shipbuilding, and footwear. Again, when the opportunity occurred, employers took the initiative, increasingly acting at an industry-wide level through their associations. In coal mining, for example, a Wages Board covering the Miners' Federation was established in 1893 and by stages slowly extended throughout the British coalfields. In the same year, in cotton spinning, after a major employers' lock-out, a national disputes' procedure was established under the so-called Brooklands Agreement. In the footwear industry, again after a lock-out asserting managements' rights, a national procedural agreement was established in 1895. The most famous procedure, however, was that created in engineering after the historic 1897–8 lock-out.[86] This created arrangements which were emulated by other employers and which were to last in engineering into the 1970s. The agreement contained a formal statement of management's right to manage; a procedure was established under which disputes could be taken from the factory to regional and national employers' panels; while disputes were going through the procedure management had the right to introduce changes and the union was obliged to refrain from strike action. The procedure thus provided a mechanism for settling disputes and making agreements. It was also intended to contain workforce trade union activity and to enable the full power of the organised employers to be mobilised in defence of points of principle.[87]

Following on the creation of these procedures, there was also from the 1890s a slow growth of national agreements on wages and conditions. In cotton weaving the first national wage agreement was established in 1892 and in cotton spinning the number of local piecework price lists was reduced to two, which from 1906 were adjusted simultaneously. A 1904 agreement in coal mining introduced the practice of national percentage changes to district base rates. In the following year the first national wages agreement was concluded in iron and steel and in 1907 national wage bargaining was introduced in shipbuilding.[88] Thus, by 1910 a Report on Collective Agreements could conclude that, 'There is manifested a tendency to supersede narrow wage scales by lists having a wider application, shop lists being absorbed in local lists, and local lists in uniform lists whose operation is coterminous with that of organisations by employers.'[89]

Again, trade unions and their members gained certain advantages from the development of national wage agreements, extending a floor of basic wages and conditions over a broader geographical area. Simultaneously, however, these arrangements also restricted unions, especially under long-term agreements and during prosperous periods. For the employers they also imposed basic obligations of recognition and collective bargaining. However, in the employers' case, these were outweighed by considerable advantages: they prevented attempts by trade unions unilaterally to impose wages and to leapfrog claims between firms, and, in some industries, they also served to reduce or control competition by removing wages from contention between firms.[90]

Thus, by the turn of the century, collective bargaining arrangements had been created in a number of major British industries. These were based on organisation among employers which slowly developed from local to regional and finally to national level. However, it should be added that this externalised system provided only a minimal framework of wages and conditions and did not altogether displace craft control and workshop bargaining. Such practices persisted and re-emerged periodically, when market conditions were favourable, to challenge the stability of formal collective agreements. As will be shown later, this was to be a distinctive feature of British industrial relations in the twentieth century. The state played a part in the creation of these systems in that it encouraged machinery designed to promote voluntary conciliation practices.[91] The unions played a more important role in the creation of these systems, both through direct initiation and indirectly through the pressure they put on employers. However, the main initiative came from the employers who, through their associations, laid the foundations for the fuller development of industry-wide collective bargaining in the twentieth century.

Conclusions

The legacy from the nineteenth century was to have a profound effect on the development of labour management in twentieth-century Britain. The context was a structure of small and medium-sized firms, operating in highly diversified product markets. Britain's fledgling large firms were mainly loose holding companies, slow to develop tighter structures and extensive managerial hierarchies. In the final quarter of the nineteenth century, competitive pressures increased both at home and abroad, but simultaneously there was a rise in collusive market behaviour. In many sectors of the economy traditional work methods persisted or changed only slowly, reflecting the structure of markets, the nature of firms, and a failure to invest. In a few industries in the late nineteenth century there were the beginnings of a change towards new methods of mass production, though this was not to be fully realised until the twentieth century. In this context, and in a situation of relatively elastic labour supply, the predominant pattern of employment relations in British industry was one characterised by minimal commitment on the part of both employers and workers to one another, and only a few exceptional firms had developed more extensive internal labour market type arrangements. In industrial relations, many British employers had recognised trade unions and were beginning to create collective bargaining systems based on membership of employers' organisations and industry-wide agreements outside the firm. The predominant pattern of labour management was, therefore, one of reliance on external market methods of coordination rather than the development of strong internal systems.

Part 2

Continuities and change in the first half of
the twentieth century

3 Markets, firms, and the organisation of production

This chapter surveys the economic and business context within which British employers managed their labour force from the turn of the century to the Second World War. It stresses the major market fluctuations which resulted in dramatic shifts in the balance of power between employers and their employees. The chapter considers changes in market structure, in particular the growth of restrictive and protectionist practices which contributed to the maintenance of the traditional pattern of labour management. The period also saw a significant growth of large firms, especially in the newer sectors of industry; however, changes in corporate structure and managerial hierarchy came only very slowly and this inhibited the development of labour management. Finally the chapter deals with the management of production. Though there were important changes in production methods, there was also considerable continuity in work organisation and traditional patterns of work relations remained strong in many industries.

Economic conditions of war and depression

The early years of the twentieth century saw a continuation of the relatively poor economic performance of the British economy which had first become evident in the late nineteenth century. In the Edwardian period up to the First World War, there was a sharp deceleration of growth in output, industrial productivity, and incomes. Investment overseas yielded higher returns than capital invested in British industry and Britain's share of world manufacturing output and trade fell.[1] It is not surprising that in these circumstances concern about foreign competition grew and anxieties about Britain's ability to meet the challenge mounted.[2] The First World War hastened some trends and retarded others. It stimulated growth in newer industries, such as chemicals and electrical engineering, but it also brought new growth in the older staple industries such as coal, iron and steel, and shipbuilding. One major result of the war was that Britain ceased to be the centre of the world's trading network and many of Britain's export markets contracted as countries formerly dependent on its goods either sought alternative sources of supply or began to replace imports. This highlighted a problem, the early signs of which were discernible in the late nineteenth century, namely the declining competitiveness and vulnerability of British manufacturers in world markets.[3]

The economic history of the interwar years saw some of the most severe fluctuations ever in British industrial history. Britain emerged from the First World War into a short boom and the continuation of wartime full employment. However, in 1920, the boom broke, leading to one of the worst depressions in British history. Industrial production fell by nearly 20 per cent and exports by 30 per cent and by spring 1921 unemployment in the insured trades had reached 15 per cent, with much higher levels in the staple industries.[4] Between 1922 and 1929, there was an unsteady upswing. However, the recovery of the 1920s was not as strong as in other countries, and unemployment stuck at around 10 per cent of the insured workforce. The return to gold at the high pre-war parity in 1925 placed British manufacturing industry at a cost disadvantage in world markets.[5] In the collapse of the world economy following the American slump in 1929, Britain moved into a second severe depression. In the years up to 1932 industrial production fell by one tenth; private sector investment dropped by a quarter; and exports fell by one third. In 1932 the number of insured unemployed rose to 23 per cent of the insured workforce. However, as the downturn was from a lower level in relation to productive capacity than in other countries, the British depression of the 1930s was less severe and destabilising. Though there were some cuts in money wages, these were not as great as in 1920-21 and, largely because of an improvement in the terms of trade and falling prices, the real wages of those in work actually rose.[6]

After the financial and political crisis of 1931, and with the advent of a serious balance of payments deficit, Britain came off the gold standard and introduced tariff protection. Along with cheaper money, rising real incomes, and a boom in housebuilding, these measures helped to promote the upswing which took place between 1932 and 1937. Over these years, industrial production and gross investment each rose by around 45 per cent.[7] In absolute terms, economic activity in 1937 reached a higher level than in the previous peaks of 1913 and 1929. Exports slowly picked up, though much of the recovery was due to rising domestic demand. At the peak of the recovery in the third quarter of 1937 unemployment fell to just under 10 per cent of the insured workforce. To put this in perspective, growth rates in the 1920s were better than in the decade immediately before the war, though relative to many other major industrial countries, they were still poor. However, during the recovery of the 1930s the situation was reversed and Britain's productivity performance improved markedly. Rates of growth in that decade were probably higher than at any period since the middle decades of the nineteenth century and were better than in most other countries. During these years and indeed up until 1950, Britain began to catch up after years of falling behind.[8]

It has already been stressed in the previous chapter that historically the British labour market was characterised by a relatively elastic supply of labour, both unskilled and skilled. This continued throughout the period of the interwar years. Unemployment rarely fell below 10 per cent of the insured labour force and, even in the best years, there remained a hardcore of about one million insured workers without jobs, concentrated mainly in the staple industries of shipbuilding, cotton textiles, iron and steel, and mechanical engineering and in the coalfield areas of England, Scotland and Wales. Because of deficiencies in data and widespread underemployment in earlier periods, it is difficult to make comparisons. However, over the period 1870–1914, the level of unemployment probably averaged over 5 per cent; even during the best years of the interwar period, 1929 and 1937, it was double that figure; by contrast, in the first twenty years after the Second World War unemployment averaged only 1.5 per cent.[9] In these circumstances, British employers found themselves in a buyer's market for labour, and this had profound consequences for the employment policies which they adopted.

Behind these macroeconomic movements were important changes in the structure and organisation of British industry – the rise of newer industries, the increase in product market collusion, the advent of protectionism, and the growth of concentration. All had important implications for the management of labour and will be considered below.

Changes in market structure

The interwar years witnessed important changes but also significant continuities in the structure of British industry. Before the First World War, Britain had been less successful than the US and Germany in establishing itself in some of the newer industries such as electrical engineering, motor vehicles, and chemicals. The war itself stimulated production in these areas and in the 1920s and 1930s motor vehicles, electrical products, the newer branches of chemicals, artificial fibres, and food processing expanded rapidly. On the other hand, the older staple industries – coal, textiles, shipbuilding, iron and steel, and the traditional branches of engineering – declined during the interwar years, being badly hit by growing self-sufficiency elsewhere and tariffs and by the emergence of more efficient competitors. Yet, still up to the Second World War, Britain remained heavily committed to these older industries which continued to account for a substantial proportion of output and employment.[10]

In Chapter 1 it was suggested that the level of demand, the degree of competition and collusion, and the boundaries of the market were important factors influencing the labour activities of the firm. Before the First World War Britain was an open economy subject to increasing competition from American and continental manufacturers. After the war, with the advent of depression in 1920, there was a scramble for orders and an increase in competitive pressures both at home and overseas. In many sectors American goods were highly competitive; continental producers re-emerged more quickly than had been foreseen; and in the Far East Japanese competition became apparent for the first time.[11] However, one of the striking features of the interwar years was an increase in collusive practices of various kinds. Both in terms of formal trade associations and informal restrictive practices, collusion increased during the First World War, encouraged by the rationing of raw materials and government controls.[12] As the 1918 Report of the Committee on Trusts stated, 'there is at the present time in every branch of industry in the UK an increasing tendency to the formation of trade associations and combinations, having for their purpose the restriction of competition and the control of prices'.[13] As demand fell with the onset of depression, some trade associations collapsed and others loosened their restrictive practices. However, this was often only an initial reaction to the appearance of excess capacity, and mutual adversity soon led to renewed collusion.[14] Thus, in 1929, another government committee remarked on 'the tendency for separate productive undertakings to associate themselves with other enterprises with a view to regulating output, prices, and other matters'.[15] From the 1930s onwards, there were additional factors which made collusion more effective. The merger wave and increase in concentration which occurred in the 1920s made it possible in some industries for a few bigger firms to collude. The adoption of protection in the early 1930s reduced the threat of import competition and thus strengthened cartel arrangements in the home market. The state, which had since the late nineteenth century tolerated restrictive agreements, took a more positive attitude towards them and was more prepared to give support to attempts to control capacity and fix output quotas. This trend continued through the Second World War.[16]

Throughout most of the nineteenth century, the boundaries of product markets had been extending, largely as a result of better communications and lower transportation costs. Working against these broadening tendencies, however, were countervailing political factors leading to trade restrictions. During the interwar years there was a rapid growth in protectionism throughout the world. The erection of tariff barriers overseas not only raised the competitive hurdle for British manufacturers and increased rivalry in third-country markets but also threatened to increase competition in Britain's home market, since, throughout the 1920s, while some individual industries and products were given tariff support, Britain remained one of the most open markets in the world. However, this openness slowly changed. The First World War had seen the introduction of duties on motor cars, cycles, and other 'luxury' goods. Protection for certain chemicals and other 'key industries' was also introduced during and after the war. For other products, protection was introduced under 'safeguarding' legislation in 1921 and 1925. Pressure for protection mounted from businessmen, especially in iron and steel, shipbuilding, and engineering. However, it was not until the crisis of 1931 and the emergence of a large balance of payments deficit that Britain introduced a general system of tariffs which was later elaborated into a complex system of imperial preferences aimed at expanding trade within the Empire.[17]

Protection had various effects. On the one hand, it created a more assured home market, helped business confidence, and stimulated domestic production. On the other hand, it limited exports and redirected trade towards imperial markets. By the Second World War Britain had reduced her trade with Europe and the US and had increased her reliance on Empire and Dominion markets. On the whole, these markets were smaller, less sophisticated, and constituted a fragmented total market. They were also growing more slowly than the markets of the US and Europe and in the case of the Dominions and India were in the longer term to industrialise in precisely those areas where Britain supplied them with products.[18] Together protection and collusion created softer markets and allowed inefficiencies of various kinds, including labour inefficiencies. One report in 1944 concluded that the growth of collusion was 'one of the most significant economic developments of the last quarter of a century' and added that 'the proliferation of trade associations is one of the major reasons why the efficiency of British industry lags behind that of the United States'.[19] It will also be argued in Chapter Five that protection and collusion also encouraged the growth and stability of multi-employer, industry collective bargaining in Britain.

Corporate structure and organisation

In the previous chapter it was stressed that the typical Victorian firm was small or medium sized, usually had one single factory, and was owner controlled. A combination of internal growth and the turn of the century merger wave saw the emergence of a large firm sector in British manufacturing before the First World War. However, these firms were often created for defensive, market-control reasons rather than in the interests of greater efficiency and the firms tended to remain loosely coordinated federations with little development of professional management.

Concentration in industry increased rapidly in the 1920s both as measured by concentration in particular industries and by the share of the largest 100 industrial companies in total output and market valuation. Before the First World War the largest manufacturing firm in Britain in terms of assets was the sewing-thread maker J. & P. Coats with a market value of £45 million; by 1930 five more companies – Unilever, Imperial Tobacco, ICI, Courtaulds, and Distillers – exceeded that value, and in the case of the first three by a very substantial margin. In terms of employment there was also a marked shift towards larger firms. Before the war the largest manufacturing employer was Fine Cotton Spinners and Doublers with around 30,000 employees. By the 1930s there were at least ten manufacturing firms employing this number or more and the largest of them, Unilever, ICI, and GKN, employed 50,000 or more; in total nearly 1.7 million worked in the 135 largest industrial firms employing 5,000 or more workers.[20]

Growth in firm size came in part from internal expansion of firms. However, a significant proportion of the increase in the size of British firms in the decade after the First World War came from mergers. It has been calculated that, for manufacturing industries, three quarters of the increase in concentration was due to mergers. In the 1920s nearly two thousand firms were absorbed in mergers and acquisitions and these mergers accounted for about one third of total investment expenditure in manufacturing industry.[21]

The reasons for mergers and the growth in concentration were complex. The end of the war encouraged some firms such as Vickers and Nobels to diversify out of armaments and acquire firms in other sectors. In the 1920s there was a shift in opinion away from a belief in the merits of small-firm competition towards a belief in so-called 'rationalisation' and the advantages of larger-scale enterprise. The continued conversion of many private firms into joint stock companies and the growth of the stock exchange also provided the opportunity and financial means for growth and merger.[22] Most important, however, were the market threats and opportunities of the period. On the one hand shrinking markets in the 1920s and the presence of growing foreign competition posed a threat to British manufacturers which led to defensive mergers. On the other, there was after the war more recognition of the opportunities offered by product and technical innovation and by economies of scale and marketing.

Though the growth in concentration affected most industries, it was most pronounced in the newer expanding sectors. Thus ICI, formed in 1926 from the four largest firms in the chemical industry, controlled more than one third of UK chemical output. Between them GEC, English Electric, and Associated Electrical Industries dominated the electrical engineering industry. Areas of food, drink, and tobacco became highly concentrated and dominated by a few large companies – Unilever, Ranks and Spillers, Cadbury-Fry and Rowntrees, Reckitts & Colman, Distillers, Imperial Tobacco. By contrast, concentration ratios in many of the older staple industries remained much lower. In coal, textiles, mechanical engineering, and printing the typical firm remained small. Though there were mergers in iron and steel and shipbuilding, these industries were mainly characterised by medium-sized firms, and in the case of iron and steel, British companies still remained much smaller than their American and German counterparts.[23]

After 1930, the number of mergers fell in the wake of depression and the growth in restrictive and protectionist tendencies. However, one important feature of the 1930s and 1940s was the growth in plant size. In manufacturing industry the proportion of total employment in big plants employing more than 1,500 workers rose from 15 per cent in 1935 to 24 per cent in 1951. The percentage in smaller plants (those employing less than 200) fell proportionately from 44 to 35 per cent. Again the trend towards larger plants was particularly noticeable in newer sectors such as motor vehicles, chemicals, and electrical products. Thus, many of the big firms created in the 1920s began in the 1930s to make larger scale investment in newer and bigger plants. Yet, as postwar studies were to show, for the most part, British plants remained smaller than those in the US and Germany.[24]

The slowness of organisational change

The growth of the large firm in the interwar years occasioned a mixed response in terms of corporate structures. In Chapter 2 it was shown that the turn of the century mergers resulted, for the most part, in loose, holding-company type arrangements. In other words, the merged companies failed to develop strong main boards and head offices with extensive staffs; subsidiary companies remained relatively autonomous and continued to be managed by their previous owners; and there was only a limited development of managerial hierarchies and control systems.[25] Merger, followed by organisation on these lines, had the advantage of reducing competition, helping control markets, and providing some economies of scale, while also economising on the costs of organisation building and of recruiting and training managers. On the other hand, loose structures prevented the full realisation of organisational economies of integration and of production economies of scale. This situation contrasted with the USA and Germany, where larger firms had started to build new centralised, functionally controlled enterprises and to develop more extensive managerial hierarchies.[26]

In Britain, after the merger wave of the 1920s most firms continued to be organised on holding company lines. The autonomy of constituent enterprises was retained and as a consequence little rationalisation took place. Competition between subsidiaries continued and, though merged firms might be under the banner of a larger firm, in practice they retained considerable autonomy. However, there were some notable exceptions and some developments in corporate structure in Britain, especially from the mid-1920s onwards. Some of the largest companies did develop head-office capability and started to define functional responsibilities and to develop managerial specialisms.[27] A few even began to experiment with multidivisional structures, where strategic decisions and the oversight of the firm were the responsibility of the main board and senior headquarters staff, while production and more routine matters were decentralised to product or geographical divisions. For example, after its creation in 1926, ICI moved in this direction. Initially it centralised its organisational structure; directors were given functional responsibilities; a number of central strategic committees were created; and an enlarged central office of service departments was established. At the same time it rationalised its production capacity, closing down old chemical works and concentrating production on more efficient plants. In the late 1920s and early 1930s, ICI moved deliberately towards a more decentralised system of product divisions, each with its own delegate board responsible for production matters, but subject to the overall financial and strategic control of head office.[28] A few other companies such as Unilever, Dunlop, Spillers, and Turner & Newall moved in the same direction.[29]

A number of factors help to explain this embryonic innovation in corporate structures in the interwar years as contrasted with the turn of the century merger wave. There was after the war a greater awareness among businessmen of the problems and opportunities involved in larger size. This was reflected in the 'rationalisation' movement, a burgeoning management literature, and the increased interchange of information and

experience between firms.[30] Some stimulus may have been provided by
the American firms which expanded their activities in Britain during the
interwar years and which brought with them new management techniques.[31] Also important was the change in the pattern of mergers, for
in the interwar years there was an increase in merger by diversification
into related areas and this created a need for new, more complex structures.

Overall, however, organisational innovation came slowly in Britain.
In 1939 the majority of Britain's largest firms were organised on traditional holding-company lines. Though a growing number were developing
some form of centralised organisation with functionally specialised
departments at headquarters level, often these firms contained elements
of holding-company arrangements. Even as late as 1950 only about a
dozen firms had adopted a multidivisional form of organisation and the
majority of these were subsidiaries of American or other foreign companies.[32] In some industries firms were particularly slow in moving
beyond the holding-company form of organisation. Prominent among
these were firms in the engineering sector. For example, the largest
engineering firm at the end of the First World War was Vickers, with its
origins in iron and steel, armaments, and shipbuilding. In 1901 it had
diversified into motor cars with the acquisition of Wolseley and after the
war it acquired British Westinghouse & Carriage Co. which had itself
acquired British Westinghouse Electrical & Manufacturing Co. However,
it attempted to run its extensive and diverse operations on holding-
company lines. In part as a result of this it ran into difficulties and in
the late 1920s sold off its motor car, electrical engineering, and special
metals interests.[33] Other examples of engineering firms which failed to
develop beyond the holding-company form were Armstrong Whitworth,
John Brown, Associated Electrical Industries, Birmingham Small Arms,
Tube Investments, Hawker Siddeley, and GKN.[34] The leading British-
owned motor-car companies, Morris, Austin, and Rootes, remained under
one-man control and similarly failed to develop fully integrated, well-
organised structures.

Chandler has contrasted the speed with which American and British
firms developed new organisational forms and has explained this in large
part in terms of the persistence of conservative family management in
Britain.[35] Certainly the boardrooms of many British companies remained
dominated by family members. Merger with other companies might bring
representatives of other families on to the new main board, while at the
subsidiary level allowing the old family to retain a substantial degree of
control. Such vested interest inhibited the rationalisation of capacity and
of company structure and retarded the introduction of professional

management into the higher reaches of many firms.[36] Other factors, however, were more important in encouraging the holding-company form. Even the largest British companies were smaller than their American counterparts and perhaps had less need for the more formalised and bureaucratic structures that American firms were developing. Domestic British markets were smaller than those in the US and as a result more efficient in terms of distribution. It was therefore less pressing to develop structures and hierarchies to handle marketing and distribution. In addition, the less standardised nature of British markets and the strength of brand loyalties often encouraged the maintenance of a range of competing products within a company. Protection and collusion probably also played a part in reducing the pressure for better forms of organisation. In the longer term, failure to create efficient administrative structures and managerial hierarchies meant an inability to take full advantage of coordination and of production economies of scale and had important implications for the management of labour.

Managerial hierarchies

During the first half of the twentieth century there was an increase in the number of managerial and related staff in British industry. In 1907 the proportion of administrative, technical, and clerical employees in manufacturing industry constituted 8 per cent of the workforce. By the mid-1930s this had risen to 15 per cent and by 1948 to 20 per cent. Most of this increase came in the 1930s and 1940s and brought Britain closer to American and German levels.[37] Along with an increase in the number of managers and support staff went an increase in functional specialisation. Older established functions such as works engineering and accounting grew as did newer ones such as design, sales and marketing, distribution, time study, and personnel.[38] In this respect, there was a growing sophistication in managerial hierarchies in Britain, especially in bigger firms in newer industries. However, a number of important qualifications need to be added. First, as has already been suggested, family control and management remained stronger in Britain than in either the US or Germany. Key managerial positions were usually reserved for family members and firms paid less attention to recruiting and developing their salaried managers. Second, at a time when a growing proportion of American, German, and Japanese managers were receiving a training, often at university level, in applied technical and business subjects, only a small minority of senior British managers were similarly qualified. At the higher reaches of management in large firms the 'gentleman amateur' was a common type, while at middle and lower levels the 'practical man', who possessed little in the way of formal qualifications, remained dominant.[39] A third weakness was that British managerial hierarchies were often not particularly well integrated. The growth of functional specialisms and the increasing divide between top (often family) management and lower level line management led to an increased stratification and segmentation of managerial hierarchies.[40] In the large firm, directors and top management, with their liberal education, constituted an elite of 'general' management, distanced from lower level line management with their more 'practical' training and 'shop' approach. Likewise, the small, though growing number of scientists and technologists were often cut off from line management and both top management and specialists alike were often divorced from the manufacturing process proper. In production areas management was particularly weak: it was here that 'practical' managers predominated and traditional foremen, largely untrained in management, continued to enjoy considerable discretion and represented a traditional pattern of authority and control at workplace level.[41]

In the area of labour management there was an elaboration of hierarchy. The First World War had encouraged the growth of 'welfare work' within British industry to deal with recruitment, record keeping, and canteens and recreational facilities. The number of full-time welfare specialists grew from under 100 before the war to over 1,000 in 1918. After the war there was some reduction in numbers, as firms were relieved of wartime regulations and, with the onset of depression, began to cut back on staff. However, through the 1930s the numbers increased again and by 1939 there were around 2,000 managers engaged full-time on labour matters. This number increased during the Second World War to around 5,000.[42] What had been called 'welfare work', often carried out by female staff of relatively low status in the management hierarchy, increasingly came to be called 'labour management' or 'employment management' or 'personnel management' and the work came to be carried out by male managers of higher status. Probably the first department actually called an 'Employment Department' was established by the large progressive Manchester engineering firm of Renold Chains in 1909.[43] Other companies, including Brunner Mond, followed suit during the First World War. In larger firms the work was often divided into welfare, covering recruitment, record keeping, health and safety, and recreational activities, and industrial relations, covering trade unions and wage bargaining matters.[44]

There was no obvious source of recruitment for these new personnel managers and very few firms had management training programmes to develop them. Companies therefore often relied on recruiting from else-where. Some of the early personnel managers came from government service: R.L. Roberts who established ICI's Labour Department, for example, had worked for the Post Office and had helped to run labour exchanges.[45] Others came from academic or consultancy backgrounds and a few had worked in America: thus C.H. Northcott, the labour manager at Rowntrees from the mid-1920s onwards, had worked as a consultant in the US and A. Shaw, who joined Metropolitan Vickers in the early 1930s, had also worked in the US in the time-study area.[46] The increasing specialisation in personnel management was reflected in the establishment of professional associations and a burgeoning literature. The first Welfare Workers Association was established in 1913 and had developed by 1931 into the Institute of Labour Management and by 1946 the Institute of Personnel Management. In related areas the Institute of Cost and Works Accountants was founded in 1919 and the Institute of Industrial Administration in 1920. These were followed in the 1930s by the Works Managers Association and the Office Managers Association.[47]

However, it is important not to exaggerate the sophistication of labour management in Britain at this time. Even by the end of the Second World War, most big firms did not have central personnel or industrial relations departments. Most personnel managers continued to be promoted up through the pay or records office or were recruited from among line managers and supervisors. At the level of subsidiary companies and individual plants, labour matters were left to incumbent managers who in turn often delegated to middle-level line managers and foremen. Of course it was natural that a large part of labour matters should be left to line managers. But, in effect, given the loose corporate structures and the continuation of traditional patterns of command, this often meant a lack of planning and coordination of labour management.

Work relations and the organisation of production

It was argued in Chapter 2 that change in work organisation came slowly in late-nineteenth-century Britain and, in many sectors of industry, tradi-tional, unskilled-labour and craft-intensive methods remained strong. This was not least because the majority of British firms, small and medium in size, lacked the financial and organisational resources to push through a thorough transformation of their production systems. It also made sense for them to use the plentiful and versatile skills of the labour force in the production of a wide range of goods for the many varied markets which British industry served. As the official history of the wartime munitions industry during the war put it, 'It would probably be true to say that no country in the world could show such a high level of workmanship, or so much out-of-date machinery.'[48] It is true that, in the late nineteenth and early twentieth centuries, there had been significant changes in some industries with the introduction of new methods and processes which made possible a greater subdivision of work and the gradual replacement of skilled men by less skilled workers. Along with this, in the early years of the twentieth century, there had been some development of indigenous thinking on the theory and practice of management and a growing interest in new American ideas of 'scientific management'.[49]

The First World War, with the large demand for munitions and general supplies, had an important effect, especially on the metal-working industries. New factories were built, existing factories extended, and new machinery and processes were introduced. In the engineering industry, for example, there was an increased installation of machine tools such as turret lathes, capstan lathes, and universal milling machines, many imported from the US. As demand grew and skill shortages increased, the tendency was to install automatic machine tools which could be used by semi- and unskilled workers and more extensive use was also made of gauges and jigs of various kinds which enabled such workers to perform more complicated jobs. In addition, there were improvements in factory layout, planning and costing, and the Government encouraged the standardisation of components and products.[50] Also, during the war the consumption of electricity doubled and this offered employers the opportunity to redesign factory lay-out and to control more closely the pace of operations.[51] In addition, wartime agreements between union leaders and the government, later backed up by legislation, permitted the employment of semi-skilled workers on work hitherto the preserve of skilled men. The legislation made it illegal to obstruct methods aimed at increasing war production or to maintain practices which might adversely affect output.[52] In these circumstances, new methods were introduced and a greater subdivision of labour occurred; dilution, or the substitution of skilled craftsmen by unskilled and semi-skilled workers, gradually increased.[53]

However, in practice, changes in production were less thoroughgoing than is sometimes suggested. In 1917 the President of the Institute of Mechanical Engineers argued that, 'Except in a few cases, workshop organisation here has not received the attention given it in America or Germany. There are still shops without definite planning of the progress of the work, without adequate equipment of jigs and gauges, and without standard shapes of tools or a toolroom; where men drift about in search of tools or tackle, or wait in idleness for drawings and material; where machinery is obsolete and light so bad that good work could not be done if the machinery were up to date.'[54] The exceptional circumstances mainly affected the munitions industries and the production of large quantities of standardised goods such as armaments. The wartime legislation did not apply to private work and, when dilution was attempted, it met with shopfloor resistance.[55] Moreover, dilution was not as extensive as is sometimes suggested. Women were rarely substituted for skilled men and were usually put onto already subdivided jobs. In heavy engineering and shipbuilding, they were little used. Even the upgrading of semi-skilled men to skilled status seems to have been quite rare, amounting to only about 4 per cent of all changes in working practices.[56] For the most part, skilled craftsmen possessed real skills which, in many jobs, could not be replaced by diluted labour. Also it should be remembered that the whole point of replacing skilled men by dilution was usually to upgrade them to the more skilled jobs of tool-setting and supervision.

During the war trade unions enjoyed an extremely strong position in a very tight labour market and, in these circumstances, they could and did resist management changes. The legislation which employers could have used to force changes in production was in fact seldom employed. Moreover, it could be a double-edged weapon for employers since it obliged them to consult with unions and guaranteed that wartime changes in the organisation of work would be of a temporary nature.[57] This increased the hesitancy of employers and strengthened the resolve of workers. As Reid has suggested, British employers did not enthusiastically embrace dilution or work reorganisation. 'With a few exceptions, British employers stubbornly maintained conservative attitudes and had little faith in the proposals to rationalise labour-intensive methods of production. Indeed, it was frequently managements which put up the strongest opposition to dilution, because each firm wanted to retain as much skilled labour as possible.'[58]

At the end of the war, a Board of Trade report, while suggesting that some British firms were as good as any in the world, concluded more generally: 'There can be no doubt that many of our older works are manufacturing at costs which could be greatly reduced if their works as a whole were on a larger scale, better planned and equipped with plant and therefore capable of being worked in the most efficient and economical manner.'[59] In drawing the contrast with the US and Germany, it attributed much of this to the conservatism of the British manufacturer and the existence of a large number of medium and small firms, 'each with a separate organisation, separate establishment charges, separate buying and selling arrangements, and each producing a multiplicity of articles. Some of them seem to take a special pride in the number of things they turn out.'[60] In the circumstances of the postwar boom, most employers, wishing to take advantage of market opportunities and preferring to avoid trouble with their unions, chose to retain traditional methods.[61] According to the Webbs, after the war, 'British employers did not set themselves to apply mass production to the making of engines and motor cars, agricultural implements and machinery generally, nor make any dramatic advances in its application to the production of sewing machines, bicycles and electrical apparatus.'[62]

With the onset of depression from 1920 onwards, employers were confronted by the threat of greater competition and the opportunity of reduced union power. Their first reaction was to dismiss workers, reduce manning levels, and cut wages. A subsequent reaction was to re-assert manageiial prerogatives against the trade unions. In part these offensives attempted to facilitate changes in production techniques and work organisation; to a greater extent, however, they were aimed at increasing management control and intensifying work within existing technologies. One of the most dramatic was in engineering, where in 1922 the Engineering Employers Federation (EEF) locked out all the unions in the industry over the question of management's right to organise production.[63] The employers were determined to show that in areas of work organisation there could be no 'dual control or veto on management'.[64] The lock-out lasted three months and ended with the unions returning to work on the employers' terms. In coal mining, confronted by declining international competitiveness, the employers sought to restore their position by a more extensive use of labour and, after their victory in 1926, forced longer hours on the coal miners. In the early 1930s, in another major confrontation over work organisation, the cotton employers sought to increase the number of looms worked by each weaver from four to eight. In this case the dispute ended in a compromise and weavers agreed to work six looms but to do less cleaning.[65]

Overall, during the depressed years of the 1920s and 1930s, there was a tightening of managerial controls and an intensification of work. This involved a broader reduction of union restrictive practices. One commentator, writing in 1935, could say, 'Restrictive practices imposed by trade unions are actually fewer than they were, and of less importance. Employers in a number of industries have referred to conditions in their fathers' or grandfathers' time, and have admitted that, comparatively, their own grounds for complaint are small.'[66] However, such a tightening of managerial control and an intensification of work had limitations. During the upswing in the 1930s, traditional practices began to creep back and spread to new sectors such as motor cars and electrical engineering.[67] The EEF certainly believed this. As early as 1934, for example, when a shortage of skilled labour was becoming apparent in the Midlands and the South, the Federation told its members that, 'The situation calls for the greatest discretion on the part of managements and makes it most desirable that firms, before making any serious changes in working conditions obtaining in their works should give their Local Association an opportunity of seeing that the change is in such order that no justifiable objection can be taken to it by the trade unions.'[68]

Littler has suggested that, during the interwar years, 'scientific management' played a significant part in restructuring work organisation in Britain.[69] Before the First World War, there was some knowledge of scientific management techniques, and new techniques were introduced such as rate fixing, premium bonus systems, and more specialised forms of supervision. However, this indigenous British development was largely *ad hoc* and piecemeal. If 'scientific management' is taken to mean Taylorism,[70] then, as has already been stated, it had little impact on British industry before the First World War. True, during the war there was increased interest in work organisation and factory administration, with some notions being drawn from scientific management.[71] Again, during the so-called rationalisation movement of the 1920s, interest grew. In part drawing inspiration from German industrial organisations and from American mass production methods, rationalisation meant both technological reorganisation within the factory and structural reorganisation of firms and industries as a means to greater efficiency. In the mid-1920s it was advocated by leading industrialists and management thinkers and accorded some support by trade union leaders. Insofar as rationalisation dealt with the reorganisation of work, it did have an affinity with ideas akin to 'scientific management'. However, in Britain in the mid-1920s the rationalisation movement was more concerned with structural and financial reorganisation and it was in this respect that it had its main impact. By contrast, the movement had little direct effect on management techniques or on patterns of work organisation in most firms.[72]

It was only in the late 1920s and especially in the 1930s that scientific management really began to affect the practice of British industry. Elements such as time-studied incentive schemes were easily adapted since, as J.A. Hobson said, for an employer, these made 'sound commonsense'.[73] Other aspects were clearly allied to an interest in fatigue, welfare, and psychological aspects of work.[74] A number of prominent individuals played a part in promoting the ideas and practice of scientific management. A. Shaw, for example, had worked with the Gilbreths, the pioneers of motion study in the US. She introduced motion study into Metropolitan Vickers' Manchester factory in the early 1930s and subsequently extended it throughout the AEI company.[75] Bedaux and his consultancy firm, established in Britain in 1926, was an important channel. The Bedaux company offered a package of work measurement, job reorganisation, and incentive wages. In particular, the Bedaux form of scientific management was adopted in new light industries such as electrical products, motor components, mass produced clothing, and food processing and was used by firms such as Lucas, Wolsey Hosiery, J. Lyons, Huntley & Palmers, Peak Frean, Unilever, and Kodak.[76]

However, the actual impact of scientific management should not be exaggerated. Formal scientific management ideas and practices were introduced by relatively few firms. Though Bedaux was an important influence, when the TUC conducted a survey in the early 1930s it found that 91 out of 104 unions contacted had no experience of Bedaux and 5 of those which had encountered the system claimed to have successfully resisted its introduction.[77] Littler estimates that approximately 250 firms employed Bedaux consultants during the interwar years.[78] Yet, even in these firms, Bedaux methods were often introduced into one particular plant or department and not throughout the whole company. Even then, resistance by workers to the speed-up, de-skilling, and job loss which they feared, often led to it being suspended or modified. As important in slowing down the introduction of scientific management was hesitancy on the part of management: top management was often not prepared to invest in new production systems and line managers and foremen were often less than enthusiastic about systems which they felt threatened their traditional position.[79] During the Second World War, there was a greater extension of time and motion study, but on the whole its introduction in the interwar years was slow and piecemeal and its effect on British industry was limited.

Technical innovation, work organisation, and productivity

One major technical change in the early twentieth century, affecting almost the whole of manufacturing industry, was the spread of electricity as the main source of motive power. Electrification removed some of the constraints on factory organisation, permitting the use of machines with their own power source, the more efficient arrangement of machinery, and a faster and more regular organisation of production.[80] Other technical changes and resultant changes in work organisation were greatest in the newer industries. In motor vehicles and electrical products, for example, there was an increased use of special purpose machine tools which could be operated at faster speeds and by semi- and unskilled labour. In assembly areas, changes were most dramatic because it was here that the main advances were made in assembly-line methods. The elements of flow-line production (standardised parts, the arrangement of machines and work operations sequentially rather than by type or function, and the transfer of materials and parts by conveyors) had existed earlier,[81] but in the interwar years these were used on a larger scale and became a more established feature of work organisation. In turn, the introduction of assembly lines made management rethink the division of labour and replan the manner in which work was done. In particular they offered management greater control over the speed of operations, curtailed the mobility of workers by tying them down to individual work stations, and encouraged a greater subdivision of work.[82]

In the chemical and related industries, there were also significant technological innovations and changes in work organisation. Most important were the scaling-up of operations, the development of flow processes, and the introduction of more sophisticated instrumentation to monitor and control production. This reflected a move towards more synthetic reactions and catalytic conversions and a shift from batch production to semi-continuous and continuous processes. ICI, with its size and growing corporate capability, was a leader and was able to undertake investment on a massive scale, including the expansion of the Billingham complex where nitrogen fertiliser was produced using high-pressure chemical technology.[83] The implications of these changes for work were that much heavy manual labour was reduced and more accurate control methods replaced rule of thumb and worker control over the production process. However, it should be remembered that much of the work in the chemical industry was already semi- or unskilled and that new processes created new skills and put some workers into strategic positions.

In the new consumer goods industries there was also technological innovation. In food processing, automation and instrumentation increased in flour milling, biscuit baking, jam making, and canning, with the introduction, especially in the 1930s, of semi-continuous processes, conveyor belts, and new packaging machines.[84] In the new synthetic fibres industry the use by Courtaulds and British Celanese of continuous process systems and automatic methods of mass production led to an expansion of semi-skilled work and an increase in female employment.[85] In parts of the clothing industry, as a mass market developed, there was also rapid technological change. Sewing machines, conveyor belts, and flow production became common, especially in the 1930s in the clothing factories of Leeds and London.[86]

However, in these newer industries changes in production organisation were often limited. In the motor-car industry, for example, British firms tended to introduce new machinery in an *ad hoc* manner and were less thoroughgoing than their American counterparts in linking production together by assembly-line methods. As a result they established less direct control over the production process and less machine pacing of work. In part this may have been because of worker resistance, though from 1920 to the mid-1930s trade unions were not an important factor. Rather more important, choice of work organisation was determined by the fragmented nature of British markets, by policies of product differentiation, and by the weakness of managerial hierarchies. British firms relied more than their American counterparts on labour-intensive methods, and craft workers maintained an important position in the production process. As will be argued in the next chapter, British motor manufacturers (with the exception of Ford) sought to increase productivity by the more extensive use of piecework systems.[87]

In the 'old' industries, though there was also technological change, this was less extensive. In the heavy mechanical sectors of engineering, such as marine, locomotive, and textile machinery, jobs were often one-off or small batch and traditional methods remained strong.[88] In shipbuilding, the main development was the gradual supersession of hand riveting by pneumatic riveting and the introduction of electric welding. However, though welding had been pioneered in Britain, the technique spread only slowly in comparison with overseas yards. In other respects also the British shipbuilding industry lagged behind. There was less investment in power machinery, mechanical handling devices, and prefabrication and sub-assembly facilities.[89] In iron and steel, during the First World War, there was a long overdue expansion of basic hearth production and, during the interwar years, investment in new integrated mills. However, in Britain investment was often of a patchy nature, extending the life of existing plant. Much of the British industry remained poorly equipped, with inadequate furnaces, poor lay-out, and insufficient mechanical handling devices.[90] In cotton textiles, there was an expansion of automatic weaving and ring-spinning, both of which were faster and cheaper than traditional methods. However, even in the late 1930s, only one-third of Lancashire spindles were of the more modern ring type and only one-tenth of looms were automatic.[91] In coal mining, mechanical coal cutters and conveyors were introduced on a larger scale, especially by a few large firms and in a number of newer pits. Yet, on the eve of the Second World War, only 60 per cent of coal was cut by machines in Britain whereas in the US and Germany it was virtually 100 per cent, and the use of mechanised conveyors was even more limited in Britain.[92]

This description of technical innovation and changes in work organisation poses three final questions. First, why was change more limited in some British firms and industries than in others and why was it so often less than in other major industrial countries such as the US and Germany? Second, what effect did changes have on control over the labour process? Third, what effect did the management of work organisation have on productivity?

Change occurred where there was a certain combination of market and organisational factors. It occurred in industries which had large and growing markets, some sheltered from foreign competition either by protection (cars) or international agreements (chemicals) or being buoyed up by a growing home consumer demand (processed foodstuffs and electrical products). These were also industries where a few large firms had developed which had the organisational and managerial capability successfully to plan and implement new investment and forms of work organisation. By comparison with the US and, to some extent, Germany, there were fewer such firms in Britain. In these industries trade unions were weak and played little part in obstructing the course of work innovation. In other industries, such as shipbuilding, cotton, and coal, trade unions were stronger and their activities may have slowed down change. However, during most of the interwar years, union power was greatly reduced. Of much more importance in explaining the slow nature of change in work organisation was the fact that these were industries where markets were either very competitive or depressed or fragmented and where small and medium-sized firms had insufficient capital or organisational resources successfully to implement major changes. In these circumstances, firms chose to continue to use the adequate supplies of labour, which could always be laid off when necessary, and preferred to pursue a more intensive working of existing technologies. However, in these industries there were always some exceptions. For example, some of the larger coal companies which developed new mines in the eastward extension of the Yorkshire, Nottinghamshire, and Scottish coalfields also introduced newer methods and ways of working.[93] Some of the larger steel companies, such as United Steel and Stewart & Lloyds, opened new integrated mills and reorganised their production processes.[94]

Braverman argued that employers have pursued strategies of deskilling aimed at cutting costs and reducing worker control over the production process. Undoubtedly, over this period, an increased subdivision of work took place in many industries. At the same time, however, such subdivision also meant an increase in the complexity of knowledge and techniques, and work became more specialised. One cannot therefore conclude that overall skill levels declined. In some cases there may have been a deskilling and loss of independence such as when new technologies were introduced in cotton, steel, and coal mining. Often, however, there was the creation of whole new types of semi-skilled work as in the newer industries such as motor vehicles and electrical products. The concept of 'tacit' skills has been used to describe the informal and uncodified abilities which even unskilled workers often possessed.[95] In other areas there was undoubtedly an upskilling as in maintenance work. Moreover, technical changes often maintained or even enhanced the potential for worker control over the production process. Nor can one conclude that it was the employers' intention to deskill work in order to reduce worker control and to maximise profits. In reality employers were concerned with reducing costs and improving efficiency in many different ways. This included labour strategies such as wage reductions and the intensification of work. Change was introduced above all because the new machines and processes were more efficient and effective. In so far as labour considerations were important, it was often less the recalcitrance of labour and more the supply and price of labour which weighed with employers. It would seem that employers were not driven by a simple desire to deskill labour, but that technology, markets, and organisational factors were the paramount influences shaping the organisation of work.

Productivity growth in manufacturing industry slowed before the First World War and lagged behind other major industrial countries; during the shake-out of labour in the early 1920s it rose rapidly; the 1930s was a period when productivity growth again increased and British growth rates were as high or higher than in other countries. Rising trade union power may have played some part in lower productivity growth in the Edwardian period, but a failure of investment, especially in potentially high-growth sectors such as chemicals, motor vehicles, and electrical products, was more important.[96] The weakness of unions thereafter may have been a factor in the higher productivity growth of the interwar years. In addition, investment in new plant and equipment were important especially in the newer industries in the 1930s. However, taking the economy as a whole, through the interwar years, investment was relatively low and capital output ratios were falling. This would suggest that a significant part of the increase in productivity must have come from either a more extensive or more intensive use of labour. Since hours were reduced after the First World War and since little overtime was worked during the interwar period,[97] productivity growth cannot have been due to a more extensive use of labour. It must therefore have been due to an intensification of work often within largely unchanged technologies. The demanning of the early 1920s and early 1930s was undoubtedly an important factor,[98] as were continued fears of unemployment and tighter management control. Though there were improvements in British productivity performance, by the late 1930s Britain lagged behind the US and, in some sectors, Germany.[99] In large part, differences can be explained by the fact that there were in Britain more old plants using out-of-date machinery and incorporating traditional working practices. This, in turn, is to be explained by a combination of factors. Where labour was relatively expensive, as it was in the USA, the rate of obsolescence of capital was higher, and firms adjusted more rapidly to newer methods which required less labour.[100] Where, as again in the USA, markets were larger, the incentive to introduce large-scale mass production was greater. And where firms were larger and more centrally coordinated, as they were in many sectors in the USA and Germany, they were better able to plan their investment and production strategies.

Conclusion

This chapter has outlined the economic and business background necessary to understand the labour policies and practices of British firms from the turn of the century to the Second World War. It has stressed the movement towards larger enterprises, the development of new forms of organisation, and elaboration of management hierarchies. However, it has also stressed the slow speed of change and the persistence of older forms of organisation. There were significant process innovations and changes in work organisation in this period, and productivity growth, after falling off before the First World War, rose in the interwar years. However, the rate of change varied considerably between and within sectors. Overall, the gradual and patchy nature of change must be stressed. This is not surprising given the exceptional fluctuations of demand during these years and the reluctance of the many small and medium-sized firms in the British economy to risk the heavy investment and overheads implied by large-scale modernisation and reorganisation of their production processes. Even larger firms often lacked the strategy and coordination to push through changes in production. In addition, the labour supply situation encouraged the maintenance of unskilled-labour and craft-intensive methods of production rather than more physical- and human-capital intensive methods.[101] Where British employers did try to deal with the problems of productivity, they often resorted to an intensification of work within the existing technology and relied on other employment policies to control and motivate labour. In this market and organisational context most British firms continued to pursue labour policies based on strategies of externalisation, and it is to these that we turn in the next chapter.

4   The evolving employment relationship

In Chapter 2 it was argued that in terms of the employment relationship nineteenth-century employers pursued strategies of externalisation and did not develop strong internal labour systems. The predominant pattern of employment in British industry was one of loose association of employers with their labour force and of employees with the firms for which they worked.[1] Firms relied on the external labour market for hiring and firing, they took labour on and laid it off as market conditions dictated, and most paid minimal attention to the training of employees. Wages were largely fixed according to external market signals and non-wage benefits were rudimentary. At the same time, however, a small number of firms pursued different strategies and developed something more like internal labour markets, with more complex and elaborate employment systems. During the first half of the twentieth century, this basic pattern did not change greatly. With the exception of wartime, labour market circumstances did not encourage major change and weak organisational structures and managerial hierarchies were a constraint on the development of more elaborate employment systems. However, there were some important developments during this period and this chapter investigates a number of diverse aspects of employment – the tenure of jobs, patterns of recruitment and training, the payment of wages, and the increasing importance of non-wage benefits.

The market context

The interwar years were characterised by large-scale unemployment sandwiched between periods of wartime full employment. The extremely tight labour market which developed during both wars produced some similar consequences. Firms found it difficult to attract and retain labour; workers were quick to realise that they could more easily find alternative employment; and government direction of labour into munitions work increased mobility. In order to reduce excessive labour turnover, both governments and employers introduced a range of measures seeking to regulate the market. In the First World War the government initiated a system of leaving certificates which workers in war industries had to obtain before they could leave their jobs.[2] In the Second World War, under the Essential Work Order, workers could neither leave their jobs nor be dismissed without official permission. In return for this loss of job freedom, workers were guaranteed job security and a weekly wage even when work was not available.[3] In both wars government prompting also encouraged the appointment of welfare and personnel officers, improved medical, health, and safety provision, and the establishment of canteens and other amenities.[4] Thus, during the wars many workers obtained greater security and formality of employment; employers, in turn, saw a reduction in their ability to employ labour on a casual hire-and-fire basis and had to provide better conditions and facilities. Wartime union strength and pressure gave this tendency added momentum.[5] At the end of the First World War, government regulations were rapidly dismantled, and many firms cut back the amenities and welfare provision introduced during the special circumstances of wartime. However, various aspects continued such as canteen and recreational facilities and in this way there was a lasting impact.[6] The effects of the Second World War were more lasting. At its end, though security of employment and the guaranteed wage were discontinued, employer initiatives proved more durable, not least because of the full employment which followed in the 1940s and 1950s.

It is necessary to stress the effect during the interwar years of high and fluctuating levels of unemployment.[7] From 1921 until 1940 there were never less than one million insured workers unemployed, equivalent to around 10 per cent of the insured labour force. The bulk of unemployment was structural and concentrated in the older staple industries and in the north and west of the country. At certain times, especially 1921–22 and 1929–33, there were superimposed on top of this high levels of cyclical unemployment. In these circumstances, it was unlikely that most firms would change their employment policies from the pattern of externalisation described in Chapter 2, since it was easy for them to take on and lay off labour at will. Hence traditional employment patterns continued. Casual work persisted – among day workers in the docks, building workers, and casuals who took up marginal employment when it became available. In shipbuilding, employers met the adverse economic situation after 1920 by laying off labour for long periods of time and, when trade picked up, continued to call in workers in squads for a particular stage of construction, only to lay them off again when that stage was completed.[8] In coal and cotton, those who had jobs were subject to short-time working, with reduced hours per day or days per week. In iron and steel and other industries, where it was uneconomic to work fewer hours or to shut down for short periods, lay-offs were for longer periods of weeks and months.[9] Even in formerly secure employment, such as the railways and gas, structural change and increased competition led to temporary layoffs and redundancy.[10]

Though the older staple industries were the worst affected by unemployment, both short-time and periodic lay-offs also took place in the newer industries. Thus in the motor-car industry there were short-time working and lay-offs, once sufficient cars had been produced for the peak sales season in the spring and summer.[11] In this way there were months of full employment, with overtime and high wages. But, once order books were filled, and given the reluctance of firms to carry high stocks, men were laid off.[12] In such circumstances, some skilled men would be kept on, but less skilled men and women were 'given their cards' and told to wait until they were 'called for'. In the electrical industry, the production of radios and other household appliances was also subject to seasonal demand with short-time and lay-offs in slack periods. In industries employing large numbers of female workers, such as electrical goods, motor components, and food processing, extensive use was made of part-time and temporary work, short-time and seasonal lay-offs, followed by compulsory overtime in busy periods.[13]

In this way the general economic circumstances of abundant labour and scarce jobs encouraged the maintenance of traditional employment practices. There was little incentive to change the predominant pattern of externalisation of the employment relationship or to develop stronger internal labour market-type arrangements. However, certain important changes did occur, and these are considered below.

Job tenure and training

It has been suggested in Chapter 2 that even before the First World War there was some reduction in casualism and a slow increase in the proportion of workers more or less permanently attached to an employer.[14] Internal subcontracting and indirect employment had all but disappeared from most areas of British industry apart from building. In other situations, as in the 'butty' system in some coalfields, or in shipbuilding where platers employed their own helpers, or in cotton where spinners employed their own piecers, the subcontractor was more akin to a foreman or principal worker.[15] Most labour had come to be directly employed and paid by the firm.

In other ways also during the interwar period the labour market became less fluid and workers in jobs became more permanently attached to firms. Despite the absence of official statistics, one can draw some conclusions about labour turnover (the ratio of employees who voluntarily left a firm in a given year to the average number of employees during that same period) and labour retention (the ratio of employees who remained with the firm over the year to the number employed at the beginning of the year). It would seem that pre-First World War labour mobility was high. We know, for example, that geographical mobility was high in the late nineteenth and early twentieth centuries, and, though not all geographical mobility involved labour turnover, there was much overlap.[16] In the case of some skilled workers up to the late nineteenth century, there was a tradition of 'tramping' in search of employment and this was supported by their trade unions and not disapproved of by employers. For their part unskilled workers were even less likely to develop attachment or be given permanence. It is well known that they suffered from higher unemployment and later studies show clearly that turnover tends to be higher among the unskilled.[17] As has already been stressed in Chapter 2, employers considered it natural to adjust to cyclical and seasonal fluctuations in demand by discharging workers.

During the First World War, turnover at first increased because of the greater availability of jobs, the influx of new labour into factories, and the tendency for newcomers to turn over more rapidly than longer-term employees. The concern with turnover (at the time called 'labour wastage' or 'labour maintenance') was reflected in a number of contemporary studies stressing the costs involved in turnover. Attention was drawn to the costs of recruiting and training labour, the higher costs of supervising a rapidly changing labour force, the lower productivity of new staff, and the lost output of experienced leavers.[18] For its part the Government during the war sought to increase labour stability and prevent the bidding up of wages by implementing the system of leaving certificates. Employers reacted by introducing the various welfare measures referred to above. Together these measures seem to have had some effect and, after rising in the initial stages of the war, turnover later fell. It rose again with the end of the war, only to fall dramatically from 1920 onwards and to fall again between 1929 and 1933. It was only from the mid-1930s onwards that it began to rise again. Concern about turnover re-emerged and continued through the Second World War, leading to government and employer counter-measures described above.[19]

This pattern of turnover and retention would support the view that unemployment was the key factor: in times of high unemployment workers were reluctant to quit their jobs and, as employed workers stayed longer, the employment relationship became more stable. However, other factors were also at work. Compared to the pre-war period geographical mobility was probably less in the interwar years – partly owing to growing rigidities in the housing market, partly to the distance in location between declining and expanding industries, and partly because of improved unemployment benefit.[20] In addition, the flow of labour as a result of immigration and emigration was lower in the interwar years than it had been before the First World War.[21] These macro factors were also mediated through the changing employment practices of firms – or at least of some firms.

Thus, there were some changes, albeit uneven, in methods of recruitment and discharge. In the years before the First World War a few firms had started to hire labour in a more systematic way through an employment office.[22] During the war more firms established such offices staffed by so-called welfare or employment managers. Their function was to recruit workers where previously engagement had been left to foremen or line managers.[23] During and after the war, an increased emphasis was placed, by some firms, on more systematic selection. As one employment manager wrote in reference to the traditional *ad hoc* system of hiring by the foreman at the factory gates: 'the engagement of personnel is now increasingly a specialised function and not incidental to supervision'.[24] Another commentator noted, 'the selection of the most suitable individuals is of the utmost importance in order to avoid loss of time, trouble and money in training unsuitable material'.[25] Most of the books and manuals published at the time stressed the need for two stages of selection: firstly, some kind of job analysis to determine the characteristics of the job; secondly, an interview, possibly involving basic tests, to determine the suitability of the applicant.[26] There was also greater discussion and more formal use of internal transfers as a way of matching workers to jobs.[27] In turn, lay-offs came more and more to be handled by the employment office or by managers rather than the foreman. Disciplinary dismissals increasingly had to be sanctioned by higher management, thus removing the foreman's right to sack workers on his own initiative.[28] However, at this point an important qualification must be added. More formal systems of hiring and firing spread only slowly; most firms used no criteria beyond the obvious ones such as past experience and availability for work; most workers were still engaged only after a perfunctory interview, leaving the 'weeding out' of unsuitable workers to a process of trial and error on the job; and lay-offs and dismissals were still often arbitrary.[29]

There was some shift of emphasis in the area of training. In Chapter 2 it was pointed out that, other than just picking up a trade, apprenticeship was the main formal method of training in Britain. It was also argued that the traditional apprenticeship was a form of delegation with strong external elements – the apprentice was handed over to the foreman or skilled man and training was supposed to be in all-round and therefore transferable skills. During the First World War and the depression years, the apprenticeship system was disrupted and the ratio of apprentices to journeymen declined.[30] The growth of new semi-skilled work, not learned through apprenticeship, also reduced the importance of this traditional method of training and both wars gave an impetus to factory-based training programmes.[31] During the interwar years there was a growing feeling that special programmes were the most efficient and cost-effective method of training within the firm.[32] A number of companies instituted such arrangements: these were usually leading firms within their sectors, such as Armstrong Whitworth, G. & J. Weir, Mather & Platt, Metropolitan-Vickers, British Westinghouse, Richard Thomas & Baldwin, Stewart & Lloyds, Cadburys, ICI, Lever Bros., Dunlop.[33] In addition, night school training in technical colleges began to be more widely used, as did, particularly from the 1930s onwards, day release schemes. This implied an increased emphasis on training to standards and on formal credentials, especially City and Guilds and Ordinary and Higher National Certificates.[34] Despite this, however, for most manual workers who received training, this consisted almost entirely of practical work on the shopfloor which was less costly to the employer and which produced an immediate pay-off in terms of cheap but productive labour.[35]

In practice, there were still relatively few special training departments or training officers within British firms. Out of 1,573 engineering firms surveyed in an official enquiry in 1925, only 26 had separate 'apprentice masters' whose duty was to organise the training of apprentices, and the existence of such company officers did not necessarily imply that the training was done in a special training department.[36] For the most part, the evidence suggests that throughout the interwar years the majority of employers did nothing to develop the apprenticeship system and a growing number valued it more as a source of cheap labour than as a way of providing the skilled human resources of the future.[37] This was perhaps not surprising given fluctuations in demand, low profits, and abundant labour supply. In the longer term, however, it was short-sighted and marked a significant failure in the development of human resource capability in Britain.

The maintenance of employment and redundancy payments

There were other developments in this period which entailed a greater acceptance of responsibility on the part of employers for maintaining and stabilising the labour force. Short-time working, for example, had been used before the First World War to meet fluctuations in labour demand, especially in the cotton and coal industries.[38] In the interwar period short-time working increased, especially in the early and mid-1920s and again in the early 1930s, and spread beyond traditional areas. There are two ways of viewing short-time. On the one hand, it can be seen as a continuation of casualism, based on a commodity view of labour with hours fluctuating according to the demand for the product.[39] On the other hand, it was better for the worker to have working hours reduced or to be temporarily laid-off rather than to be permanently discharged. A reduction in normal working hours implied the maintenance of the employment relationship and secured some income. Temporary lay-off was based on an implicit and sometimes explicit commitment to re-employ when times got better. A distinctive feature of short-time working during the interwar period was indeed that it was more organised and systematic, a feature encouraged by the operation of the state unemployment benefit system which during the interwar years allowed employees to draw benefit when working alternate days.[40] Though state subvention supported and reinforced short-time working, it does not detract from the fact that employers had an interest in retaining their employees, especially their skilled workers, and organised such schemes themselves.[41]

Another development in the interwar years was the provision by a few large firms of supplementary unemployment pay in addition to the flat rate national unemployment benefit. For example, the large gas companies, including the South Metropolitan and the Gas Light & Coke, established special funds from which additional benefits could be paid to workers who were laid off.[42] At various times, other employers, in industries as diverse as flour milling and banking and insurance, contemplated contracting out of the state system and establishing their own schemes.[43] Outside the provisions of the legislation, a number of large firms established their own schemes to supplement the state system. The number was not large, but included Lever Bros., Boots, ICI, Rowntrees, Cadburys, Frys, and a handful of others operating in relatively stable markets and requiring labour with firm-specific skills.[44] Rowntrees, for example, introduced its scheme in 1921 as part of a set of measures to stabilise employment. When the firm had to lay off workers, it paid an additional benefit on top of the state benefit. This was intended to bring single workers up to 50 per cent of their normal weekly earnings and married men up to 60 per cent, plus an extra allowance of 5 per cent for each dependent child, subject to a maximum of 75 per cent of normal earnings. The fund paid benefit for one week for each two months of employment for the first two and a half years of employment and one week for each subsequent three months. The scheme, which was funded entirely by the firm, covered 90 per cent of the firm's employees at its York and other factories. Boots introduced a similar scheme in 1921 which paid a benefit equivalent to the difference between the unemployed worker's income from all other sources and 75 per cent of his normal average wage. Boots also tried to stabilise employment by manpower planning, more systematic selection, and transfer of workers.[45] Though it might be argued these schemes made it easier to lay off workers, they did provide some commitment to the continuation of the employment relationship and were an incentive to the firm to stabilise its employment. They were also an incentive to employees to secure regular full-time jobs and to maintain continuity of employment since, in most cases, there was usually a qualifying period in terms of length of service and the level and period of benefit was based on length of employment.[46]

The late 1920s and early 1930s also saw the beginnings of compensation or redundancy payments for those who were laid off permanently. Provision for such payments was made by a number of large gas and electricity companies, by some food companies, especially in the flour-milling and confectionery industries, and by ICI and Lever Bros.[47] For example, during the late 1920s and early 1930s, the flour-milling firms, under the leadership of Ranks and Spillers, operated a scheme under which those workers made redundant as a result of rationalisation were paid from an employers' fund in the form of annuities, periodic benefits, or lump-sum payments. Though there may have been a humanitarian element in this scheme, the big firms in the industry undoubtedly saw such payments as a way of getting worker and union cooperation over rationalisation and closure.[48] Another firm which established a redundancy compensation scheme in the late 1920s was the large stationery and paper-products manufacturing firm of John Dickinson & Co.[49] In the early 1930s the London, Midland & Scottish Railway Co. closed its steel works at Crewe which at that time employed 600 workers. Since the closure was not a direct result of amalgamation, the workers were not eligible for statutory compensation under the 1921 Railway Act. The firm, after absorbing some of the workers by transfer within the company, paid the remainder each a lump sum based on length of service.[50]

The companies which devised such schemes were uncertain as to the precise principle underlying their arrangements – whether they provided a relief for hardship, compensation for lost job rights, or a means of securing cooperation with rationalisation. They were also unclear about the best form of provision – special pensions and annuities for older workers, periodic benefits, or lump-sum payments.[51] Though limited in number and in the amount paid, these compensation schemes were a beginning and a nascent recognition of job property rights. As one

American commentator said of the schemes, they 'encouraged budgeting labour requirements, hiring more scientifically, improving dismissal procedures, training workers more widely to enable transfers, letting normal labour turnover deplete the working force to actual needs, introducing labour displacing machinery more gradually and intelligently'.[52] A British commentator noted, 'The schemes also have the advantage that they offer some inducement to the firms as far as practicable to stabilise their employment by reducing the amount of short-time and the number of dismissals.'[53] Of course, it must be stressed that the schemes were exceptional. The Mond-Turner conference had recommended in 1929 that 'all firms... should set up a reserve fund, to be set aside from profits, for the purpose of assisting displaced workers'.[54] The TUC had subsequently asked the main employers' organisation, the National Confederation of Employers' Organisations (NCEO), to discuss this in the context of other methods of stabilising employment. However the NCEO, representing the majority of employers, rejected the idea and indeed favoured the reduction of state unemployment provision.[55]

Wage systems

On wage matters, British employers thought in terms of money rather than efficiency wages. In other words, they thought in terms of the money level of wages and the external relationship which wages bore to those paid by other employers rather than in terms of the relationship between wages and output within the firm. Before the First World War there were some who had argued for a high-wage, high-output approach to labour management.[56] But this was not a view which commended itself to most British employers. In the interwar years there continued to be those who put this case. In their book *The Secret of High Wages*, B. Austin and W.F. Lloyd drew the contrast between the American employers' better understanding of the concept of high-efficiency wages and British employers who sought to minimise money wages and relied on piecework as the main incentive device to higher output.[57] Piecework, they noted, led to uncertainty for employers and employees alike and to restriction of output by workers, especially where management resorted to cutting rates when earnings got too high. In the interwar years the coal owners were the most important and prominent, though certainly not the only, case of a group of employers who looked to lower wages and longer hours as a solution to their economic problems.[58]

The system of district and national collective bargaining which had developed in many industries by the First World War may have encouraged this approach to wages in that through such arrangements employers hoped to set wages as low as possible. There were very few firms which explicitly pursued a high-wage, high-output policy. For a time one was the Ford Motor Company. It followed the practice of its American parent, did not join its industry employers' association, and eschewed the use of piecework. It paid a high wage but expected in return high productivity and tight discipline. In this it was considered a dangerous deviant, and the Engineering Employers' Federation (EEF) tried hard to dissuade other engineering firms from following its example. In the 1930s depression Ford abandoned its high-wage policy, though not its adherence to time rates.[59]

The criteria used in wage fixing continued to have a large external element. Comparability and relativities between groups of workers were the most important factors underlying the wage structure. For adjusting wages, the 'state of trade' remained the most important criterion. In some industries, notably iron and steel, this continued to be done automatically for some grades by the use of sliding scales based on the selling price of the product. In coal mining from 1921 an elaborate scheme existed for making adjustments on the basis of the proceeds or profits of each mining district.[60] Such schemes had real shortcomings. They concentrated on only one factor and, where they were industry-wide, they could not take account of firm-level differences in productivity and profitability. One development during the First World War was the emergence of the cost of living as an explicit criterion in wage fixing. During the war, in the absence of a free market within which the value of the product could be set and hence the value of labour determined, the government encouraged the use of the cost of living index for adjusting wages. By the end of 1922, about three million workers were covered by automatic sliding-scale arrangements. When, from the recession onwards, the cost of living fell and wages were automatically reduced, these arrangements began to fall out of favour with trade unions, and the number covered declined to about one and a half million by 1939. During the Second World War, however, the number covered again increased to about two and a half million.[61]

Thus, in terms of wage fixing, great emphasis was placed on external criteria such as the state of trade and the cost of living. Less emphasis was placed on internal criteria such as productivity and profitability. One, though minority, exception to this was the tradition of profit-sharing in British industry. This took various forms: in a few cases ordinary shares were distributed; more usually cash bonuses were paid on top of the normal wages. There were three periods when profit-sharing obtained some popularity: in the late 1880s and early 1890s, just before the First World War, and in the years after the First World War.[62] A few leading firms were involved – including the South Metropolitan Gas Company which established a scheme in 1889, Lever Bros. in 1909, Boots in 1912, and ICI in 1928. Over time, the emphasis of such schemes shifted. Some of the earlier schemes were primarily and openly anti-trade union, while later schemes were more orientated towards encouraging performance. Profit-sharing was seen increasingly as a direct incentive and also as a way of reducing labour turnover and increasing worker commitment.[63] However, it always remained an exceptional practice: before the First World War there were 125 firms with profit-sharing schemes; by the outbreak of the Second World War there were still only 266 schemes covering about 223,000 workers.[64]

There were various reasons why profit-sharing did not become more prominent in British industry. Some have suggested that trade union opposition was a significant factor, and it is true that unions were strongly opposed to some of the earlier schemes which were openly anti-union. They were also suspicious of any scheme which aimed at increasing worker loyalty to the firm at the expense of trade unionism. Unions preferred a standard wage rate throughout a craft or industry, whereas under profit-sharing workers' incomes varied between firms and, within firms, varied between workers. Moreover, unions found it difficult to reconcile individually based profit-sharing with collective bargaining.[65] However, the evidence suggests that the opposition from rank-and-file members was never very strong and unions could not block the introduction of profit-sharing schemes where management wished it. The main reason for their rarity was that most British employers, especially in the staple industries, were not interested. They preferred to rely on national collective bargaining, plus piecework within the firm.[66]

Indeed the growth of payment by results or piecework was a much more important development in the first half of the twentieth century. Some industries, notably textiles, had long made extensive use of piecework, while others, such as building and printing, remained predominantly time work. But in a significant number of industries, such as engineering, iron and steel, and food and drink, there was a substantial shift towards piecework systems. In 1886, in engineering, for example, only 6 per cent of turners and 11 per cent of machinemen were on piecework. After the lock-out of 1897–8, the employers asserted their right, over trade union opposition, to introduce piecework, and the number of such schemes gradually increased. By 1906, 24 per cent of fitters, 32 per cent of turners, and 42 per cent of machinemen were paid by results of some kind.[67] The First World War saw a further increase in piecework, stimulated by the introduction of automatic machines operated by less skilled labour, longer production runs, and the need to boost war output. By early 1917, at least one-third of engineering firms were working on a piecework basis.[68] By 1926 the proportion of fitters on piecework was 51 per cent and by 1938 this had risen to 62 per cent, with as many as 81 per cent of turners and machinemen paid by results of some kind.[69] The increase in payment-by-results continued during the Second World War, stimulated by similar factors as during the First War.[70] Engineering saw the most dramatic changes once again, but other sectors were also affected. Thus, taking all industries, the number of wage earners covered by payment-by-results rose from 25 per cent in 1938 to 32 per cent by 1951.[71]

To understand the implications of the spread of piecework, it is necessary to distinguish the different types of payment-by-results systems. The oldest and simplest was straight piecework. Under such a system, the worker was paid a fixed money price for each unit of output. Wages then varied simply according to the units of output produced and the relationship between wage and output was linear. This form of piecework constituted a simple market transaction between the employer and the pieceworker. There were no safeguards for the worker and the basis of the system was 'no work, no pay'. Where work was interrupted because of shortages of materials or parts, the worker bore the risk. On the other hand, when demand was high and the flow of materials uninterrupted, the worker could, theoretically at least, push earnings up to the physical limit. From the workers' point of view, such a system had a major disadvantage because of its insecurity and fluctuations. Of course, this might also work to the employers' disadvantage and lead to resentment and labour turnover. But, from the employers' point of view, there were more serious disadvantages. Unit labour costs tended to remain constant at all levels of output, and the employer could not benefit from any increased worker productivity, without cutting rates, which in turn made workers restrict output.

The payment-by-results systems which firms increasingly used from the early twentieth century onwards tried to overcome these various problems. For example, it became more common to include a minimum fall-back time rate in payment-by-results systems which provided some basic income guarantee to the worker.[72] In engineering the EEF and the Amalgamated Society of Engineers (ASE) agreed the principle of guaranteeing minimum time rates.[73] The practice of paying 'waiting time' also spread in certain industries, so that when a worker was unable to work for reasons beyond his control, he was paid something, either a basic time rate or a proportion of average piecework earnings.[74] Not all firms made these provisions and in some industries such as clothing, and in outworking employment, pure piecework continued.[75]

Most of the payment-by-results systems which spread from the beginning of the twentieth century were of the so-called premium bonus type. Under these systems, the worker was guaranteed a basic rate. On all output above the basic level expected for the guaranteed rate, the worker earned a bonus or premium per piece. Increasingly in the interwar years, as methods of work measurement spread, the bonus was calculated not in terms of physical output *per se*, but in terms of time or time saved. Usually a so-called standard time was set for a job and a bonus was paid in relation to the time saved in carrying out the job or for the extra output in the time allowed. The bonus could be set in various ways, and in the interwar years there was a growing literature on the subject. It was possible, for example, to fix the bonus in such a way that it was very similar to straight proportional piecework, with earnings rising in the same proportion as output. This, however, did not have strong incentive advantages from the employer's point of view. Alternatively it was possible to fix the bonus so that as output increased, the money price paid for each unit effectively increased. Such so-called 'progressive' systems were intended to encourage above average performance and were thought to be particularly useful when direct labour costs were only a small proportion of total costs. In such circumstances it was considered an advantage for the firm to pay more for labour if the total output could be increased and overhead costs spread over a larger output.[76] Significantly such schemes were less common in Britain than in the US where labour costs were high, but small in relation to capital. In Britain the opposite was true and most systems were of the so-called 'regressive' type, in the sense that the more units a worker turned out, the more money he would be paid in aggregate, but the less he got per unit. In this way labour costs automatically declined as output increased.[77]

In various ways during this period piecework systems became more formalised and more subject to safeguards for workers. In engineering, for example, around the First World War a number of rules grew up governing piecework. In the first place, as has already been noted, basic time rates came to be guaranteed. Secondly, the idea also became established of a 'minimum piecework standard', or the amount which a pieceworker *should* be able to earn.[78] Thirdly, as a safeguard against rate-cutting, it was agreed in 1919 that piecework prices and bonus times could not be altered unless the materials, means, or methods of production were changed. Finally, it was agreed that piecework prices and bonus times should be fixed by mutual agreement, with disagreements being subject to review under the industry's disputes procedure. The engineering employers were prepared to make these concessions because they saw piecework as a crucial part of their strategy. In the longer term, however, in the post-Second World War period, the spread of piecework was to create problems for employers.

In contrast with the growth of piecework and inventiveness in terms of new bonus systems, much less attention was paid to time-based systems of payment. In fact, the majority of workers in Britain still continued to be paid by time, although most of the systems were of a rudimentary nature. In traditional areas, such as the building and woodworking trades, the time rate was usually fixed on the basis of customary differentials and was adjusted in line with the state of trade and changes in the cost of living. In only a few industries, as on the railways, in banking and insurance, and in the public sector, were there more complex systems of job grades, classifications, and hierarchies.[79] It was only in the late 1930s that there were new developments in terms of time-based systems, with the beginnings of job analysis and job-grading, the forerunner of modern job evaluation and merit rating. These involved the use of explicit criteria, such as length of training, dexterity and skill, and level of responsibility, to compare jobs within a firm in order to work out internal wage structures. Before the Second World War interest in job evaluation was confined to a few firms such as ICI, Unilever, Courtaulds, Pilkingtons, and Cadburys.[80]

Non-wage benefits

For most manual workers, non-wage benefits remained rudimentary or non-existent. In those cases where provision was made by the employer for sickness and old age, this was usually informal and *ex gratia* and directed at certain types of employees, especially supervisory and clerical staff. Most manual workers continued to have minimal non-wage benefits, reflecting the loose and short-term nature of the attachment between the employer and his employees. However, there was change during this period and an extension of more formally constituted benefit schemes.

In the area of pensions, before the First World War, there were various types of provision. Some workers, usually skilled men, provided for themselves through trade unions, friendly societies, and insurance companies. The years 1908–9 saw the beginnings of the state system, though until 1926 this was very limited, means-tested, and confined to those over 70 years of age. In the late nineteenth and early twentieth centuries, employer provision at first took the form of company-sponsored savings clubs, provident funds, and friendly societies, intended to help with unemployment and sickness, but which were also used in an *ad hoc* way to provide pensions for old age. However, as we saw in Chapter 2, a number of large employers had started to promote more formally constituted schemes, though at first these were restricted to white-collar employees. Prominent among such employers were the railway companies, the gas companies, and such large firms as J. & P. Coats, Fine Cotton Spinners & Doublers, J. & J. Colmans, W. D. & H. O. Wills, and Siemens and, in white-collar employment, the banks and insurance companies. By the mid-1920s an increasing number of large firms were providing pensions as a contractual employment right to their employees, both white and blue collar, and the number of formally constituted and funded schemes continued to grow through the 1930s, when the large insurance companies first offered pension packages to industrial firms. By the late 1930s about a tenth of British workers were in employer-based pension schemes and manual workers constituted a significant proportion of those covered.[81] Historians who have examined the origins of company pension schemes in Britain have stressed that employers were the main initiating force.[82] It was employer policies which encouraged the growth of firm-based schemes and which determined their shape – this rather than any prompting from the state or from workers or their unions. In some cases benevolence and traditional paternalism may have been significant employer motives. But most employers realised that there could be real benefits from providing pension schemes. They saw them as a way of attracting and retaining labour of the right sort and as a means of increasing worker loyalty and attachment to the firm. The actual rules of the pension schemes which emerged in the first half of the twentieth century lend support to this interpretation: there was usually a qualifying period; benefits were related to length of service; and early leavers lost all or most of their entitlement. The concentration of the early pension schemes in large firms suggests that they were an attempt to develop a more extensive, bureaucratically based employment relationship internal to the firm.[83]

There was also an extension of sick-pay schemes. In the late nineteenth century a minority of employers made *ex gratia* payments to workers off sick or requiring medical attention.[84] Such payments were regarded as benevolences to be given or withheld by the employer without question from the recipient. From the 1880s onwards a growing number of firms started to sponsor works' sick clubs, benevolent funds, and savings schemes into which workers contributed and from which they received benefits. Where firms insisted on membership as a condition of employment, the club had to be registered as a friendly society. The clubs were subsidised by the employers either by means of an annual fixed sum or on a *per capita* basis or by paying a proportion of the benefits.[85] During the interwar years there was a slow growth of employer-based schemes. In some cases this involved greater employer support for contributory sick clubs which continued to exist throughout the period. In other cases, especially in larger firms and for supervisory and white-collar workers, employers established schemes financed from their own funds. In the case of white-collar staff these usually entitled those off sick to full wages for a period during their absence.[86] The rules of sick schemes bore certain similarities to those of pension arrangements in that there was usually a minimum period of service required in order to qualify and the length of payment was tied to the duration of service with the firm. By the late 1940s, about a half of the claimants for state national-insurance benefit were also covered by employers' sick-pay schemes, though this varied greatly between classes of workers – the proportion ranging from about one third among manual workers to 90 per cent for white-collar staff.[87] As with pensions, the main initiative behind sick-pay schemes seems to have come not from trade union or state prompting,[88] but from employers, and mainly from a few large firms, whose intention was to retain labour and elicit cooperation.[89]

One significant development in terms of fringe benefits at the end of the interwar period was an increase in holidays with pay for manual workers. Paid holidays may be seen as a fringe benefit in the sense that they are an addition to the simple cash relationship and are an indication of a more permanent employment relationship based on continuous service. After the First World War the provision of paid holidays spread gradually, but then increased substantially from the mid-1930s onwards. In part this was due to a desire of employers to forestall statutory imposition and in part it was prompted by the 1938 Holidays With Pay Act. Thus the number of manual workers entitled to paid holidays grew from about one and a half million in 1936 to four million by 1939, out of a total workforce of about 18.5 million manual and clerical workers.[90] There was at first some resistance from the employers' associations, especially in coal, cotton, and parts of engineering, but the bigger firms, especially in the newer sectors, went ahead and introduced paid holidays.[91] An analysis of the provision of schemes and rules again shows a certain pattern: most required a qualifying length of service; they were restricted to regular employees and excluded part-time and temporary workers; under many schemes the number of days entitlement and the level of pay were tied to length of service; and leavers did not usually get their holiday days as pay.[92]

Thus, in the interwar years there was an extension of fringe benefits over and above the cash nexus and, increasingly, formally constituted benefits came to replace more informal arrangements. This was a sign of an increasing internalisation of the employment relationship, especially in larger firms. However, fringe benefits were still limited both in extent and in the numbers covered. Moreover, given industry-level collective bargaining, weak firm-level trade unionism, and employers' insistence on managerial prerogatives, these fringe benefits were not usually subject to formal collective bargaining. An important final point must be made. The provision of such fringe benefits, together with others such as canteens and washing facilities, was usually different for different groups of workers – managerial, supervisory, white collar, and manual. In part this reflected the deep-rooted class distinctions in British society, especially between the 'works' or 'hourly' or 'weekly' employees on the one hand and 'staff' or 'salaried' employees on the other, with the latter not only enjoying better pay and shorter hours, but also more secure jobs, better sick pay, and superior pensions. Such status distinctions in part also reflected conscious employer policies, designed to reinforce divisions at work as well as to secure the loyalty of more strategically placed employees.[93] Whatever the reasons for them, they were to remain deeply entrenched in firms' employment policies.

Conclusions

The period from the early twentieth century through to the Second World War saw a continuation by most British employers of what might be termed externalisation of the employment relationship. Firms relied on the external market for hiring and firing, they took labour on and laid it off as required, paid minimal attention to the training and development of employees, and fixed wages largely according to external market signals. These policies were shaped by inherited attitudes as well as by economic and organisational circumstances. Most employers preferred to provide minimal wages and benefits and to hire and fire in a traditional manner, marginally adjusting to shifts in demand. They saw labour as a commodity to be purchased at the going rate in the market place, but with only minimal rights and benefits within the workplace. These attitudes accorded well with market structures and company organisation in the interwar years: they suited product markets subject to uncertainty and fluctuations; they corresponded with labour markets where there was an abundant supply of labour; and they suited both small and medium-sized firms as well as large, but loosely coordinated, enterprises. In these circumstances a pattern of externalisation and market-based relations prevailed.

The period, however, also saw some significant changes. It saw a further decline of traditional paternalism, based on *ex gratia* informal provision by the employer and on close links between firm, family, and locality. The reasons for this decline included the growth, during two world wars, of trade unionism and collective bargaining and the development of state welfare provision. As important, however, was the growth of larger, multi-plant and managerially controlled enterprises, signifying a decline of local ownership by an identifiable group of individuals or families and the passing of close personal and local links. Of course, elements of an older-style paternalism continued and were to be found in both large and small firms. Such paternalism could even be created anew, as, for example, in the case of some of the colliery villages in the new Nottinghamshire coalfield.[94] On the whole, however, it became increasingly difficult to maintain. More significant for the future was the slow development of a more complex and extensive employment relationship. This was the result of a gradual set of changes which reinforced each other over time, including macro-economic changes, the spread of collectively negotiated agreements, and the development within firms of more modern personnel policies. The changes involved a closer attachment of workers to firms, more elaborate internal labour market systems, and more extensive wage and benefit provisions. This more stable and complex employment relationship was to be found most clearly in a number of large firms, especially in the newer sectors of industry, where market and technological factors both permitted and required new patterns of employment.

5   Employers, unions, and collective bargaining

In the late nineteenth century an embryonic system of industrial relations had developed in Britain based primarily on employer recognition of trade unions through employers' associations, which negotiated and administered agreements covering procedures and wages and conditions. The procedural arrangements for handling disputes and negotiating agreements had become national in scope, while agreements on wages and conditions were less well developed and primarily covered only a district or region. This system of multi-employer bargaining was another aspect of the externalisation of labour management by British employers. The system suited employers in that it allowed them to maximise their collective strength through their associations, to counter the pressure for job control from skilled workers, and to reduce some of the uncertainty surrounding the fixing of wages and conditions. It also economised on the costs of investing in strong internal structures and hierarchies. It was argued in Chapter 2 that the main initiative for these arrangements came from the employers. However, the trade unions also obtained some real benefits – in particular formal recognition and a growing standardisation of pay and conditions. Union members also gained some benefits, but they often felt constrained by the system as the events of the years before the First World War showed. This chapter argues that in the first half of the twentieth century employers maintained and extended this exter-nalised system of industrial relations, though towards the end of the period it was beginning to exhibit contradictions and weaknesses. For the most part, British employers failed to develop domestic arrangements internally within their firms.

The pre-First World War period

Had British employers wished to get rid of trade unions and collective bargaining, the depressed conditions of the first years of the twentieth century and the legal reversal for trade unionism in the Taff Vale decision of 1901, gave them something of an opportunity. However, as Clegg,

Fox, and Thompson pointed out, 'There were relatively few instances of organized employers taking advantage of it to attempt to weaken or destroy the unions.'[1] In part this may be taken as evidence that British employers saw some advantages in working with trade unions. In larger part it indicated that employers lacked the organisation and determination at both national and firm levels to pursue a costly strategy of union exclusion. However, some major employers, such as the shipping and railway companies, did remain anti-union, and others used the opportunity more vigorously to diminish union influence and to impose restrictive, long-term wage agreements on the unions. With the return of fuller employment from 1906 onwards, union membership rose from 2.6 million members in 1910 to 4.1 million, or about a quarter of the working population, in 1913, and the number of strikes rose over the same period from 521 to 1,459 per year.[2] For some workers, such as the railwaymen and many unskilled workers, strikes represented an attempt to gain recognition and introduce collective bargaining. In areas where collective bargaining already existed, the unrest of these prewar years was often a reaction to procedural and wages agreements which had been created over the two previous decades. Many of the strikes in building, engineering, and cotton attempted to shake off the restrictions of the new systems and to reassert trade practices held in check since the mid-1890s. In addition, long-term agreements on wage rates were seen by some union members as a cause of stagnant or falling real wages. In these circumstances, because of the involvement of union leaders in the official procedures, the action tended to be local and led by shop stewards, who began to emerge as important work group leaders.[3]

A number of agreements were challenged and rejected by the unions and their members during the years before the war. Thus, in 1913, the cotton spinners' union gave notice to terminate the Brooklands Agreement; in shipbuilding the boilermakers' society abrogated the main national agreement; in the London building trades the employers locked out union members who, on three separate occasions, rejected agreed settlements; and in engineering the Amalgamated Society of Engineers (ASE) terminated the national procedure in 1914. On the eve of the First World War, then, there was uncertainty as to the continuity of some of these agreements. On the other hand, there were clear signs that the employers were determined to maintain the arrangements. The EEF, for example, refused to negotiate on wages and conditions until the ASE agreed to the reintroduction of the procedure. The outcome was a revision on terms more favourable to the union.[4] A similar mixture of strength and shrewd concessions on the part of the employers reestablished the systems in cotton and building. Meanwhile during these years, the two main groups of employers of manual labour who had stood out most strongly against unions, the railway companies and the shipping employers, finally conceded recognition. In 1911 the railway companies, under union and government pressure, accorded recognition, albeit in an arm's-length manner through a system of conciliation boards.[5] Similarly, the shipowners, after more than a quarter century of fierce hostility to trade unionism, also recognised in 1911, but in a reluctant and indirect manner without any permanent machinery being established.[6] Overall the total number of conciliation and collective bargaining arrangements in Britain grew from 64 in 1894, to 162 in 1905, and 325 in 1913.[7] Thus, though fragile, the collective bargaining institutions created in the late nineteenth century remained in place and were even extended on the eve of the First World War.

The war and its aftermath

The First World War was important in terms of consolidating and extending this system of industrial relations. The wartime history of industrial relations has been told many times – often with an emphasis on the more dramatic but less enduring aspects.[8] Here it is necessary to emphasise a number of points. Trade union membership increased substantially, rising to 6.5 million in 1918 and continuing to increase to 8.3 million in 1920, by which time union membership represented about 45 per cent of the working population.[9] In the period up to 1920, for the first time, trade unionism achieved a presence in most areas of British industry. Simultaneously, employer organisation increased and solidified, in part in response to rising union membership and militancy, in part in response to the prompting of government.[10] In a report in 1917, G. R. Askwith, the Chief Industrial Commissioner, stated,

As regards the extent to which various employers' associations cover the ground, it may be said that all the more important industries of the country are adequately represented by one or other of the associations and that, on the whole, the associations include in their membership the majority of the firms engaged in their respective trades.[11]

In 1914 there were 1,487 employers' organisations; by the early 1920s this had risen to 2,403 and membership coverage was greatly increased.[12] Along with enhanced organisation on both sides, there went a greater recognition by employers of trade unions. Those employers who had already recognised unions for skilled men now formally acknowledged unions for semi-skilled and unskilled workers. Recognition was also extended further in previously poorly organised industries such as chemicals and food-processing and, in addition, there was some limited recognition of unions for white collar and supervisory staff.[13]

During the war, collective bargaining developed in two main directions. In the first place, wartime conditions extended the scope and depth of workplace bargaining. The industrial truce which trade union leaders entered into with the government at the beginning of the war prevented them leading official strike action. Yet wartime conditions increased the need for consultation and bargaining at the workplace. Alterations in production techniques, the introduction of new types of work, and changes in wage rates at shopfloor level, all required frequent adjustments. Also, full employment, rising inflation, and the extension of payment-by-results systems created further pressures and opportunities for workplace bargaining which came increasingly to be conducted by shop stewards.[14] In engineering, shipbuilding, mining, printing, and building, workplace representatives had existed before the war and had already begun to play a part in informal bargaining.[15] For the most part, however, their prewar function had been to act as intermediaries between the union and the membership and to serve as guardians of district standards. As such, employers gave them little recognition. However, in the special circumstances of the war, they assumed a real bargaining function and came more and more to negotiate on wages and workplace conditions. As shop steward activity increased, employers reluctantly accepted the necessity of recognising them and the value of dealing with works committees which they sometimes formed. 'Often', said an official report, 'the institution of a works committee is due to the initiative of an employer or manager ... who finds that his task is greatly eased if he can deal with an accredited representative of the workmen.'[16]

These factors can be seen clearly in the case of the engineering industry where the most formal recognition of shop stewards was accorded. Limited recognition was first conceded by Coventry engineering employers after a strike in 1917 and then, later in the same year, by the Engineering Employers nationally. At the end of the war, though shop steward power was declining, the Engineering Employers pushed for an agreement with all the main engineering unions on shop steward recognition. Signed in 1919, this agreement was an attempt by the employers to bring shop stewards within the existing 'constitutional' framework of the industry.[17] The agreement allowed workers to elect shop stewards; names of stewards, their constituencies, and the unions to which they belonged were to be passed by the union concerned to management; provision was also made for joint works committees which were to serve as an official stage in the industry disputes procedure; and stewards on works committees were given the right to visit parts of the plant outside their constituency. By linking shop stewards and works committees with the industry's Provisions for Avoiding Disputes, the employers intended to take controversial questions away from the stewards and pass them over to district and national union and association officials. In its general provisions, the agreement stated, 'shop stewards shall be subject to the control of the trade unions and shall act in accordance with the rules and regulations of the trade unions and agreements with employers... Employers and shop stewards and works committees shall not be entitled to enter into any agreement inconsistent with agreements between the Federation or local association and the trade unions.'[18] This clearly represented an attempt by the employers to circumscribe and contain the independent activity of stewards at the workplace.[19]

During the First World War collective bargaining also developed at the industry level. In an attempt to contain the upsurge in workplace activity, both procedural and wage systems at national level were recast, extended, or introduced for the first time. Here government intervention played a part, and the compulsory arbitration arrangements which the government established for the period of the war were of particular significance. In response to rapid increases in the cost of living, the arbitration authorities came to treat each industry as a whole and awarded national across-the-board increases. These narrowed differentials between firms and areas and familiarised the two sides of industry with the notion of national arrangements.[20] The reports of the official Whitley Committee between 1917 and 1918 were also important in recommending the extension of voluntary collective bargaining. The Committee chose as its format joint industrial councils, made up of representatives of trade unions and employers' organisations at national and district level, with joint works committees at plant level, and with bargaining over wages and conditions concentrated at industry and district level. In its essentials, this format was drawn from already existing arrangements and its effect was mainly to extend collective bargaining to previously unorganised and partially organised industries.[21]

However, even in the absence of government intervention and prompting, it is likely that industry-wide bargaining would have developed further. Multi-employer bargaining was, after all, the tried and tested response of employers to union pressure and shopfloor assertiveness. The establishment of interlocking procedural and wage systems at district and industry level was seen by employers as a way of checking union leapfrogging and controlling independent worker action at the level of the workplace. Recognising the strength of the trade unions, employers felt that there were real advantages in dealing with them collectively. Moreover, as a Ministry of Labour report put it, 'Many employers prefer not to deal with trade unions in the works but with the outside trade union organisation.'[22] Thus, by 1920, in most British industries firms had come to rely heavily for industrial relations purposes on agreements negotiated by employers' associations. Such agreements were pre-dominantly negotiated by the central headquarters of the employers' federation and the trade unions concerned, as national bargaining super-seded district and regional bargaining. *Prima facie*, these arrangements constituted a well-ordered system, providing a framework of wages and conditions and a means whereby issues not settled within the firm could be taken outside the company and through an external procedure. By 1920 there were in Britain over 2,500 multi-employer agreements, of growing formality and detail, covering either particular districts, regions, or whole industries, and directly or indirectly covering more than half the working population.[23]

Collective bargaining through the depression years

The advent of depression in autumn 1920, and the shift in the balance of power, put severe strains on this system and presented employers with an opportunity to reshape it if they so desired. Overall they did not, though the story is mixed. The rapid deflation and rising unemployment certainly presented an opportunity for employers to cut wages, and reductions were massive between 1921 and 1923, with many of the rèductions being made relatively automatically through the national machinery, especially where sliding-scale arrangements existed.[24] Trade union membership fell by about one-third, or 2.7 million, in the two years 1921 and 1922 and thereafter continued to decline, though less steeply and with some temporary increases. Yet, even at its lowest interwar point in 1933, the total membership of 4.4 million was higher than it had been before the war.[25] In practice, actual union strength held up much better than the membership figures would suggest, since sympathy towards trade unionism remained on the part of many workers and state unemployment benefit provided a floor under union activity.[26] Despite, or perhaps because of, the dramatic disputes in the early 1920s, employers realised that an out-and-out attack on trade unions would be extremely costly. Instead they were prepared to continue formal recognition through their associations, in the knowledge that other firms were in the same position.

In the circumstances of the early 1920s, workplace bargaining was undermined and shop steward activity considerably reduced. Many works committees which had been established in earlier years ceased to operate, while others were much diminished in activity and scope. Some employers refused to deal with workplace representatives and used the opportunity to get rid of union activists. However, the experience was uneven, and shopfloor collective strength often persisted, especially among skilled men in industries such as engineering where, also, national recognition of shop stewards provided a floor of formal rights and helped maintain steward existence.[27] At national level some of the collective bargaining arrangements collapsed, especially in those industries where Whitley-inspired machinery had not had time to take deep root. The number of Whitley-style councils and committees, for example, fell from over 100 in 1920 to 47 by 1926, and many district councils ceased to function.[28] However, it must be stressed that overall most multi-employer arrangements survived and employers were willing to sustain them, as some of the main confrontations of the post-1920 period demonstrate.

In engineering, for example, the employers were determined to use the recession to reaffirm the industry's procedural framework and to reassert the rights which they believed it enshrined. Since the ASE had withdrawn in 1913 from the 1898 Terms of Settlement, there was no formally agreed statement of managerial functions. During the war, workers had been able to claim a greater say in decision-making and impose restrictions on management. When the post-war boom broke and unemployment rose, the engineering unions became more defensive and restrictive, in particular on overtime working, the introduction of payment by results, and machine manning. The Engineering Employers, for their part, were determined not to see their prerogatives further undermined and wished to reduce costs by curtailing union practices. From early 1921 the Federation took a harder line with the Amalgamated Engineering Union (AEU – formed in 1920 by a merger of the ASE and a number of smaller unions) and threatened to lock out its members over a number of different issues: a union embargo on overtime, restrictions on the working of payment by results, and refusal to allow firms to operate certain machines except on conditions laid down by the union.[29] At length, in late 1921 the Federation forced the AEU executive to sign a memorandum accepting a new managerial functions clause and abandoning the claim to block managerial changes in disputed situations. When the AEU membership rejected this, in March 1922, the Engineering Employers locked them out and later extended the lock-out to 50 other unions in the industry.

This lock-out, lasting over three months, was the largest dispute in the interwar years outside coal mining and ended with the unions returning to work on the Employers' terms. The EEF made it clear that the dispute was about their formal rights and managerial functions. They were determined to stress one important principle, namely that there were certain areas where management had authority and where there could be no 'dual control or veto on management'.[30] The so-called 'status quo' question (that is, what happened, under the procedure, when the union objected to proposed managerial changes) had been fudged in 1914 when the procedure alone had been confirmed. But it was an inevitable issue, given management's claim to be able to introduce changes, the workers' right to object under the procedure, and the delay subsequently involved in hearing a case. The employers strongly denied the need to obtain trade union consent before changing working practices and held that a settlement of this issue was a necessary requirement for the efficient operation of their businesses and for the integrity of the industry's collective bargaining framework. The agreement which ended the lock-out reaffirmed the procedural system and extended it to all unions in the industry. It stated that 'the employers have the right to manage their establishments and the trade unions have the right to exercise their functions.'[31] The unions were forced to recognise the employers' right to make changes and henceforward, while cases were going through procedure, work was to be carried out 'under the conditions following the act of management'. In the course of their victory the employers dealt a severe blow to the substance of workplace bargaining and increased the discretion of employers locally to press conditions on the unions. Bargaining was increasingly focussed at national level or made subject to national constraints. When, from time to time during the interwar years, the unions showed any restiveness with these arrangements, the EEF used a combination of promises and threats to put them off.[32] On wages and conditions, also, the aim of the employers was to maintain the national system of bargaining. Thus, at various times, they threatened to lock out unions which tried to pursue claims for a particular class of workers, such as foundrymen and toolmakers and checked the re-emergence of district wage movements and pattern-setting by high-wage areas.[33] Later, they refused to accept sectional bargaining on behalf of separate parts of the industry such as motor cars and aircraft which from the mid 1930s onwards enjoyed greater prosperity than the rest of the industry.[34] Along with this, they always prohibited plant or workshop claims while national negotiations were in progress – though, on this issue, as will be seen, they were less successful.[35]

In coal mining, the events of the 1920s dealt a more serious blow to the substance and practice of collective bargaining. However, again, the system of multi-employer bargaining survived. In fact, the disputes of these years were very much concerned with the structure of bargaining. The coal owners were one group of employers who had never really favoured national bargaining, preferring instead that wages and conditions be negotiated at district level according to district circumstances and with bargaining about details taking place at pit level. It was the Miners' Federation which favoured national bargaining and the government which during the war had helped bring it about. From the early 1920s the employers, faced with falling prices, low productivity and profitability, and fierce competition in foreign markets, concentrated their attention on the wage-bargaining system and on reducing wages costs.[36] In 1921, after decontrol of the industry and a four months' lock-out, the employers forced wage reductions on a district by district basis, thus weakening the substance of industry bargaining, though a national board and minimum wage remained. The return to the gold standard in 1925, and its impact on the profitability of coal exports, further exacerbated the situation and brought about a climax. After the bitter seven months' lock-out of 1926, following the collapse of the General Strike in sympathy with the miners, the coal owners insisted on the complete abolition of the national bargaining system and demanded district agreements, incorporating wage reductions and increases in hours. They followed up their victory with a vigorous reassertion of managerial prerogatives and, in Nottinghamshire, Derbyshire, and South Wales, with support for the breakaway so-called Spencer union.[37] Yet, it needs to be stressed that most coal owners and most district employers' associations did not abrogate recognition nor support the Spencer union, and it is significant that the owners who did support the breakaway union looked not to complete non-unionism, but to this alternative union as a bargaining partner.[38] Moreover, in dismantling national bargaining, the owners still preferred multi-employer bargaining, though at the district level where the union was weaker and where bargaining could be more closely related to prices and profits.

A few points may be made here about the General Strike of 1926. For the most part, employers did not use the defeat to abrogate agreements. Many were indignant at what they saw as the breach of procedures and, in some cases, they demanded trade union assurances and a stricter wording of procedural agreements. Yet outside of the coalfields, no major group of employers withdrew recognition at national or district level. At shop-floor level there was some individual victimisation and further undermining of workplace organisation; but, in terms of the balance of bargaining arrangements, this served only to strengthen national as against workplace bargaining.[39] Moreover, employers did not push for further reductions in wages and conditions and in this respect the coal owners were exceptional. Even during the depression years of 1929–33 wage cuts were nowhere near as large as in the early 1920s, and the index of national wage rates fell by only 4.5 per cent between 1929 and 1933.[40]

Since prices were falling, this meant that real wages rose. The coal dispute and the General Strike had demonstrated the high cost of set-piece confrontation, and employers did not use the aftermath of the General Strike to reshape the British system of industrial relations. Some, it is true, did seek the removal of legal immunities for strikes and considered the legal enforceability of agreements. However, employer pressure for legal changes was neither universal nor particularly insistent.[41] After the General Strike, the episode of the so-called Mond–Turner Talks between leading businessmen and senior trade unionists also showed that British employers were reluctant to introduce major changes.[42] Clegg has concluded that 'on this occasion Britain missed an opportunity to reconstruct its system of industrial relations to meet the requirements of the future'.[43] Despite some novel ideas and much strong rhetoric, the Mond–Turner proposals were essentially posited on the existing system of collective bargaining, and the whole episode of the Talks suggests that most British employers were unwilling to develop new initiatives in industrial relations.[44]

In the economic crisis of 1929–32 there were some further challenges to the system of multi-employer bargaining. Whereas coal and engineering had provided the main test cases of collective bargaining in the 1920s, cotton textiles became the major area of dispute in the 1930s. In that industry the long-established national system of collective bargaining collapsed — at least for a time. In order to force a wage reduction in 1929, the cotton employers locked out their workers for three months. Then, in 1931, as competitive pressures intensified, the weaving employers again used the lock-out in order to force their workers to accept a larger complement of looms per weaver. This was not a new idea, but at the time it was seen as more pressing and as a key aspect of managerial prerogatives. However, the employers, confronted by strong worker opposition, were not completely successful in introducing new methods of working. Frustration over their limited success, and union resistance to industry-wide wage cuts and hours increases, led individual employers to try to make their own arrangements. In 1932 both the weaving and spinning employers' organisations decided to suspend all collective agreements and to leave their member firms free to wring whatever concessions they could out of their workforces at mill level. After several months of conflict, the Ministry of Labour intervened, industry collective bargaining was re-established, and a new price list was agreed which accommodated more loom working. However, a more indirect threat continued in the form of furtive undercutting of the collectively agreed rates, especially by small and non-federated firms. This led the employers and unions to look again to government and, in 1934, the Cotton Manufacturing

Industry (Temporary Provisions) Act was passed, enabling national wage agreements to be legally enforced throughout the industry. Thus, after initial reverses, industry-wide multi-employer bargaining was restored in the cotton industry in the mid-1930s.[45]

Engineering, coal, and cotton were the three most important industries subjected to severe pressures on their collective bargaining systems. On the other hand, there were industries where there was an extension of multi-employer arrangements. In building, for example, the collective bargaining system became more elaborate and grew in pace with the extension of labour and product markets. Before the First World War, bargaining took place at town or district level with wages adjusted in response to local economic forces. During and immediately after the war, in an attempt to control leapfrogging between districts, the employers' associations extended the bargaining area to cover whole regions. In 1920 it was again the employers' initiative which led to the introduction of national wage regulation. Under this system, towns and districts were graded nationally to enable wages to vary with differences in the local cost of living, while, within each district, standard rates were fixed for all building workers. Regional agreements on working rules remained, but these had to be ratified by the national employers and trade unions. The machinery did not always work smoothly in the first decade of its existence. In 1924 the trade unions, feeling that wages were being held back and dissatisfied with the constraints of the procedure, threatened to secede. The employers responded with a national lock-out to maintain the system. On other occasions, plasterers and bricklayers tried to pursue sectional claims. In all cases, however, the employers strongly supported and sought to extend the system. As the employers' organisation stated: 'The National Federation of Building Trades Employers will resist to the utmost of its power any action having for its object the substitution of sectional methods of regulation, either nationally, regionally or locally for the national industrial method of negotiation at present in force.'[46] The arrangements in building and related trades were underpinned by various local commercial arrangements, price fixing, and collusive tendering.[47] In the steel industry the national system of collective bargaining was elaborated and extended to cover most workers in the industry. Here, wages continued to be fixed according to a sliding scale based on variations in steel prices.[48] In shipping, there developed a particularly close relationship between the large shipping companies and the seamen's union, and an increasingly comprehensive and uniform system of wages and conditions. In this instance, the system of route sharing and rate fixing through the so-called shipping conferences helped.[49] On the whole, the industries where national agreements were most comprehensive and effective were those which were either sheltered from foreign competition or where there were collusive arrangements between firms. As an official report pointed out, 'Trade competition by employers is a powerful factor in determining to what extent the members of an association will adhere to a common policy, and the action of non-associated firms in securing orders, or even the fear of such action, must necessarily influence the associated firms.'[50]

The theory and practice of industry bargaining

Why did British employers choose to externalise their industrial relations in the manner described above? What was the rationale on which this system of multi-employer bargaining was constructed? These arrangements had procedural, managerial, and wage advantages for employers. Management conceded recognition to trade unions and, in return, the unions agreed to work within the procedural arrangements and negotiating machinery.[51] Collective bargaining could take place at various levels, but there was usually a mechanism to transfer issues to national level. When a dispute arose at workplace level, it could be processed up through the procedure and, very importantly from the employer's point of view, while a case passed through the various stages, the union was obliged to keep the peace and refrain from strike action. Overall, the aim of the employers was to concentrate bargaining at national level where, if necessary, they could deploy their full collective strength. It was also the intention to restrict bargaining to a narrow range of issues and to retain other matters as managerial prerogatives. In some agreements this was explicitly stated in a 'management functions' or 'managerial prerogatives' clause. The presumption was that, by concentrating bargaining at a level external to the firm, management was more likely to prevent a successful challenge to prerogatives within the firm. On matters of wages and conditions, the employers' intention was that national agreements would preclude lower-level claims and, by increasing standardisation, would go some way to taking wages out of competition between firms. Thus, to use Flanders's terminology, the arrangements offered employers both *managerial* control advantages within the workplace and *market* control advantages over wages in the marketplace.[52] All this is not to deny that trade unions and their members got something out of these arrangements: along with recognition, they acquired some check on employers and a growing standardisation of wages and conditions, which were real benefits in the period after 1920 when the unions were in no position to dictate terms.

Such, then, was the theory and rationale on which the system was based. In practice, however, there was a wide gap between the theory and the reality. This discrepancy varied between industries, between firms within an industry, and over time according to changing economic circumstances. It existed in terms both of procedural matters and wages and conditions, as will be discussed below.

Though, in theory, machinery existed at three levels – workplace, district, and national – with interlocking procedures, in practice most firms had only rudimentary collective bargaining machinery at plant level. During the war, some employers had set up joint works machinery and, in engineering, the 1919 agreement formally made provision for plant-level works committees, though in practice these were rarely established. In Whitley industries the national joint industrial councils encouraged works councils as part of the comprehensive system envisaged in the report.[53] However, relatively few works committees and councils were established and many of these did not survive the onset of depression.[54] The survivors limped on as weak consultative bodies or as the first stage of industry disputes machinery, usually upstaged by the authority of the external procedure. The fact is that neither employers nor national union executives were favourably inclined to plant-level machinery. At company level, in the growing number of multi-plant companies, there was hardly ever machinery which covered the whole company and, in industry disputes procedures, there was rarely provision for a company stage. Indeed it could be argued that the existence of external machinery inhibited the growth of internal plant and company arrangements. For the employers this had one apparent advantage in that it discouraged the presence of union full-time officers in the workplace. In engineering, for example, the disputes procedure laid down that deputations of workpeople might be accompanied by their union organiser, but in such cases a representative of the local employers' association was to be present.[55] In other industries, firms were explicitly disallowed by their employers' organisation from negotiating directly with union officials or indeed even from communicating with them.[56]

The disputes procedures based on this machinery performed a valuable function for employers who liked to stress the conciliation or peacekeeping function of procedure. The unions, who raised the vast majority of cases, were obliged to take each case through the various stages of procedure and, while a case was going through, were obliged to keep the peace. Most disputes were settled in the early stages and the further a case went the less likely it was to be settled in the employees' favour.[57] However, again, the use of the procedure was very much subject to economic circumstances. In periods of economic upswing the number of cases tended to rise, but so also did the number of disputes occurring outside the procedure. Thus, as economic activity rose from the mid-1930s, workers started to take action independently of their unions. It has been estimated that by 1936 half of the strikes in the engineering industry were in breach of procedure.[58] Such unconstitutional action was inevitable given the fact that the aspirations and activities of shopfloor workers could not always be expected to coincide with the terms of national agreements and given the often exasperating amount of time taken to go through procedure. But, even when unconstitutional action took place, the procedure was still of some use to the employer: the trade union was placed in an 'unenviable position' and was under pressure to discipline its members.[59]

The national systems were intended to uphold the rights of management and to prevent trade union interference in the internal workings of the firm. However, in practice, economic circumstances and production requirements served to undermine formal rights. In engineering, for example, the employers fought the 1922 lockout to reestablish their prerogatives after the encroachments during the period from 1910 onwards. Their victory was overwhelming and certainly reduced shop-floor power. But, despite the victory and the depression, there is evidence that, in the more traditional sectors of the industry and the more skilled departments within firms, craft unions maintained many of their traditional practices.[60] The employers' reluctance to invest in new production systems, their dependence on craft work, and the weakness of managerial control systems sustained these practices. During periods of economic upswing management had to tread carefully. As early as 1934, for example, when a shortage of skilled labour had become apparent in the Midlands and the South, the EEF told its members:

The situation calls for the greatest discretion on the part of the management and makes it most desirable that federated firms, before making any serious changes in working conditions obtaining in their works (even though the change may come within the category of a managerial act) should give the Local Association an opportunity of seeing that the change, and the method in which it is proposed to introduce the change, are in such order that no justifiable objection can be taken to it by the trade unions whose members may be affected.[61]

Even in periods of low economic activity, management often knew that the effective implementation of change depended on the cooperation of the workforce. Lower level management realised this even more and were prepared to waive formal rights when these contradicted local custom or threatened established practices.[62] From the mid-1930s, as unionisation increased and as shopfloor organisation spread to less skilled employees, worker confidence and assertiveness grew. Some of the practices which had traditionally been the preserve of the skilled craftsman spread to new areas of the expanding motor vehicle, aircraft, and electrical engineering sectors.[63] Though these were usually less restrictive than traditional craft demarcations and were often linked to bargaining under piecework schemes, in time they came to constitute a real check on managerial prerogatives. There is evidence of similar experience, especially from the mid-1930s, in other industries, such as mining, building, steel, and shipbuilding.[64]

In the case of wages and conditions, there was also a gap between the theory and the reality of the system. Again the actual form and extent of this gap varied between industries and according to economic circumstances. In periods of downswing and depression the movement of rates and earnings kept in step. However, at such times, the tendency was for employers to offer less than the nationally agreed rates. In periods of upswing and boom, the tendency was towards the payment of wages and conditions above national rates. Thus, during the period from 1910 to 1920, and again from the mid-1930s through the Second World War, there was a strong tendency for the increase in earnings to be faster than the increase in nationally agreed rates.[65] Some of this greater increase in earnings took the form of overtime, upgradings, and genuine productivity increases during rising economic activity. Much, however, took the form of straight additions, fictitious extras, and 'easy' piecework rates, reflecting both the employers' desire to attract and retain labour and the enhanced bargaining power of work groups on the shopfloor. This tendency also reflected the decentralised and weak managerial control systems in British firms and the multitude of informal shopfloor understandings which this allowed.

This gap in wages was more or less of a problem according to the intentions of the parties. Not all employers and unions intended that national agreements should be tight and sufficient in themselves. An important prerequisite for a tight, standard national agreement was the homogeneity of firms in the industry in terms of product, labour, and technology. Without a sufficient degree of homogeneity, there was inadequate basis for collective action. Another important factor was the ability and desire of the employers to control competition by taking wages out of contention. Where this was not possible, because, for example, of the large numbers of firms in an industry or its openness to foreign competition, it was difficult to fix standard wages and conditions and in these circumstances there were always undercutters. Where control was feasible and where firms felt the need to stabilise the labour and product market, it was more likely that wages and conditions would be uniform between firms.

A number of contrasting examples may be cited. In engineering, there existed a minimum time rate and a minimum piecework standard. National bonuses were added straight on to earnings. This form of across-the-board increase was favoured by the EEF because it allowed equal additions to be made to timeworkers and pieceworkers without substantially upsetting plant earnings structures and necessitating adjustments in piecework times and prices. National bargaining during the interwar years was about additions to and subtractions from the national bonus. There was no further grading of workers and no attempt to fix maximum wages at national level. Although periodically considered, this was always rejected because of the complexity of the industry in terms of firms, products, and types of labour and its openness to international competition.[66] Standardisation would, moreover, have meant increases in unit labour costs for some firms which they could not have covered by increasing their selling price. Thus, only certain basic conditions were standard – the length of the working week, overtime arrangements, and shift premiums. The national wages system was therefore skeletal. During periods of upswing, earnings rose both because of national increases *and* workplace additions. At these times the tendency was for earnings to deviate increasingly from the minimum time rates and from the minimum piecework standard. The divergence tended to be greatest for pieceworkers, especially, from the 1930s onwards, in sectors such as motor vehicles and aircraft.[67] During periods of downswing, deductions were made at both national and local levels and undercutting occurred. Thus, the employers, acting collectively, provided a national framework, but did not try to equalise wages between firms or to fix the actual structure and level of earnings internally within the firm. A similar skeletal structure existed in other industries such as shipbuilding, iron and steel, printing, pottery, and chemicals.[68] The national framework in all these industries was loose, and there was a gap between minimum rates, as set for certain categories of workers, and actual earnings of workers in the industry. Within each plant, earnings were determined by unilateral management action, unwritten custom, and shopfloor bargaining depending on local circumstances.

By way of contrast, there were other industries where over the interwar period the national system of wages and conditions became more uniform and complete. Citing building as an example again, the wages fixed at national level for each particular region were intended to be standard as was the framework of working rules. There was some payment above the standard in periods of high economic activity, and below in periods of depression especially where non-federated firms posed a competitive threat. However, the relative absence of pieceworking in the building industry and the greater uniformity of methods of production helped sustain a tighter national system.[69] In another section of construction, the rapidly expanding electrical contracting industry, wages and conditions became particularly comprehensive and uniform over the interwar period. Here, despite a large number of small firms, both product and labour markets were homogeneous and it suited both sides jointly to control under- and over-payment. As the boundaries of product and labour markets extended in this industry over the interwar period, so did the geographical area of standardisation.[70] In cotton textiles, excepting the set-backs of the early 1930s, the system of wages and conditions was also tight, as also were similar national piecework price lists in footwear. Other examples of tight national agreements were to be found in both shipping and railways, where a relatively small number of big firms cooperated with highly centralised trade unions to fix increasingly standard rates. Finally, there were a number of small compact industries including flour milling, electrical cablemaking, papermaking, cement, and bricks, dominated by a few firms and characterised by various collusive product market arrangements, where also there developed tight national systems of wage fixing.[71]

The consequences of multi-employer bargaining

What, then, were the consequences of national multi-employer bargaining as it operated in Britain in the first half of the twentieth century? In terms of its impact on the level of wages, it may have had a small effect, slowing down increases during periods of upswing and prosperity. However, against this must be set the possibility that employers may have been *more* willing to make wage concessions under industry bargaining since it was easier to pass these on throughout an industry in the form of higher prices. The existence of earnings drift also compels some scepticism about the effectiveness of multi-employer bargaining in holding down wages. The system may have had more effect in slowing down the rate of decrease during downswings and depression by reducing the flexibility of employers to adjust wages downwards. Though there were many instances of wage cuts forced by employers' associations, it must be remembered that after 1923 there were few changes in wage rates and money earnings remained almost constant until 1937.[72] Certainly some contemporary economists attributed the maintenance of wages, in a situation of high unemployment, to the development of national collective bargaining.[73]

In many industries, the system was also intended to take wages out of competition between firms. In some cases it did this, either by equalising wages or wage costs. In the small flour-milling industry, for example, it was stated that:

As a result of a national scale of hours and wages, there ceased to be competition among employers as regards their labour costs and each employer, by looking at the list of classified towns and areas, can easily calculate his competitor's labour costs. This became a factor of considerable importance in the development of the industry when commercial competition between firms became so acute that the absence of competition in labour conditions was appreciated.[74]

As market-sharing and price-fixing became stronger in this and other industries, and as tariff protection grew from the early 1930s onwards, employers often saw multi-employer wage fixing as a way of reinforcing their product market arrangements.[75]

Collective employer offensives, as in engineering in the early 1920s or cotton in the early 1930s, may have improved manpower utilization for a time. But the assertion of managerial prerogatives by these means had its limitations: it elicited coerced compliance for a time rather than willing cooperation. Against any positive effect must also be set the fact that under a system of external bargaining there was less scope for trading off pay rises for productivity increases within the firm. Moreover, under this multi-level system, in prosperous times, employers often paid twice, making concessions at workplace level and again at national level. In the latter case, increases were unrelated to differential rises in productivity and prosperity between firms. Many employers were thus giving money increases at national level for nothing in return, a situation which became clear from the late 1930s onwards. One commentator noted in the late 1940s:

The sense of responsibility for finding and applying the best incentives has been removed from the hands of individual managements along with the responsibility for them. Workers obtain increases in wages without having played any real part in formulating the changes... Most managements are uneasily aware that, despite all national efforts, the problems of providing adequate incentives remains in their hands. But they are equally aware that the means to a solution have been taken from them. Hence management's lack of lasting interest in the possibility of increasing output by providing stronger incentives for their workers, and their prevailing feeling of frustration.[76]

Two further effects on industrial relations may be singled out. First, the system may have helped contain disputes by mobilising collective employer strength against the unions. However, with the advent of depression these would have fallen anyway. On the other hand, it is likely that industry bargaining increased the likelihood of both big national disputes, as occurred in coal, engineering, and cotton, *and* of short strikes outside the procedure, especially during economic upswing and where the procedure was slow. Second, national recognition and industry-level bargaining did nothing to deal with the inheritance of multi-unionism in British industry. On the contrary, it encouraged it, since some employers' organisations pursued a 'divide and rule' strategy. A group of food manufacturers, for example, held that 'it was desirable to have as many unions as possible to deal with, in order that, with competition in this direction power should not be concentrated in the hands of one union or one official'.[77] Membership of an employers' organisation entailed recognition of any of the trade unions which that association recognised, and reliance on national machinery and failure to develop domestic arrangements meant that employers did not have to think about sorting out representational questions within the firm. Though employers and their organisations did not create multiunionism and its allied jurisdictional and demarcation problems, equally during this period they did little to reshape trade union representation within the firm.

Alternative choices

It is relevant to enquire whether there was an alternative way of organising representational and collective arrangements and whether some firms developed their own internal arrangements within their companies.

Many medium-sized and small firms did not belong to employers' organisations and, for such companies, all their dealings with employees were internal within the firm. However, the majority of small firms did not recognise trade unions and had no representational arrangements of any kind. In some larger firms, there was also a tradition of dealing exclusively or at least primarily with their own employees, without the intermediary of an employers' organisation. Again, this included large firms which refused to recognise unions. In this category are the gas and railway companies before the First World War. In the case of the South Metropolitan Gas Co., its in-house system of employee representation and labour relations remained strong throughout the interwar years. In the case of the railways, once they had recognised unions, the companies established both a national system and an elaborate internal system of company, station, and depot machinery.[78] Another category of firms included those which recognised trade unions, but which dealt with them exclusively or primarily without being members of employers' organisations. This included Brunner Mond, Lever Bros., Cadburys, Imperial Tobacco, and the large Lancashire engineering firm of Hans Renold & Co.[79] In some cases these arrangements consisted only of informal factory meetings, usually of an *ad hoc* nature. In other cases there were more elaborate committees of worker representatives to which trade unionists could be elected, but which were not exclusively trade union based.

During the First World War, as we have already noted, there was a growth of shop stewards' committees which periodically met with management for negotiating purposes, and, in some instances, joint standing works committees were created. The most radical recommendation of the Whitley Report was for the establishment of joint works committees to discuss a wide range of issues internally within the workplace, and over a thousand such committees were created under Whitley auspices.[80] In the engineering industry, the 1919 shop stewards agreement provided a formal basis for works committees, though very few were established. However, after 1920, many such wartime bodies ceased to function. From the outset, national unions had been distrustful both of committees which might be dominated by management and of those which might be dominated by shop stewards to the exclusion of the national union. With the advent of depression, union leaders did little to sustain these arrangements. However, a more important reason for their lack of success was the hesitancy on the part of the employers, who at best saw works committees as a way of dealing with production problems and containing the upsurge of shopfloor activity during the war. The majority of employers saw them as a potential threat to managerial prerogatives and as unnecessary given the existence of external machinery. They therefore did little to maintain them.[81] G. D. H. Cole summed up contemporary attitudes in this way:

The trade unions feared that workshop bodies might fall under unofficial control, subverting the influence of the national unions; and the employers had mostly no intention of granting any real control and therefore would have none of it in the sphere in which it was likely to be most real and effective.[82]

Again during the Second World War there was an expansion of internal representation and consultative machinery. The number of shop stewards and works committees negotiating directly with management increased. From 1941 onwards, joint production committees were established in many factories for discussing wartime production and welfare matters. Mainly with the prompting of union activists and government, these were established in engineering, aircraft production, shipbuilding, and coal mining. By 1943, over 4,000 existed in the engineering and allied industries covering over 2.5 million workers.[83] Often they operated in parallel with joint shop stewards committees, sometimes under the control of the latter. The success of the committees was mixed: some met only irregularly and discussed marginal matters, while others provided an effective addition to representational machinery within the plant. After the war, some survived intact, others remained with more limited functions, while others were integrated into shop steward machinery. However, many just ceased to exist, and managements, some of whom had only reluctantly agreed to committees in the first place, made little attempt to develop them into permanent internal institutions.[84]

By this time, a distinction had been established in Britain between collective bargaining and joint consultation. It was held that collective bargaining between employers and unions was best concerned with adversarial matters, such as wages and conditions, and that overall these were best dealt with outside the firm. In contrast, there were topics of mutual interest between employers and their workers which should be handled in a cooperative manner. Relations within the plant should be predominantly or entirely confined to such matters as were outside the scope of collective bargaining. In fact, both conceptually and practically, this was a difficult distinction to make and it had deleterious consequences for the development of plant-based institutions in Great Britain. However, the distinction suited most employers because it seemed to take dealings with trade unions outside the firm while leaving consultation restricted to a narrow range of issues and subject to the final decision of management.

Despite this overall pattern, there were always some firms which had the organisational capability and which chose to deal internally with trade unions, often in addition to having their own consultative arrangements. In this category were the food firms of Cadburys, Rowntrees, and Frys, which had consultative machinery but which also recognised trade unions and for the most part dealt with them internally within the firm. The same applied to J. & J. Colman, Reckitt & Sons, and Imperial Tobacco. Pilkingtons dealt directly with trade unions without belonging to an employers' organisation or national industrial council. After the collapse of the national agreement in rubber in the early 1920s, Dunlop developed their own factory council, though in this case the clear aim was to reduce trade union power. The classic case in the interwar years of a large modern firm developing its own internal arrangements was ICI. From 1926 onwards it constructed an elaborate consultative system of works councils while also recognising trade unions. Its policy was always to deal with the unions at company level through its Central Labour Advisory Council. In the mid-1930s it left its employers' organisation and ceased to be a party to national agreements. Another large

merged company which left its employers' organisation in the 1930s was
the Lancashire Cotton Corporation, which established its own personnel
department and procedures specific to its own needs.[85] In addition, by
the late 1930s firms such as Unilever and Courtaulds, though still connected with employers' organisations, had outgrown them or dominated
them to such an extent that membership did not matter. They in turn
were groping towards their own internal arrangements. Finally, it should
be added that many of the American firms which located in Britain in
the interwar years followed the pattern which their American parent
companies were establishing at this time — they chose not to join
employers' organisations and developed their own internal systems.
Singers on Clydebank and British Westinghouse in Manchester were two
such examples which refused to recognise trade unions and developed
their own internal systems. In the motor industry, Ford, for example,
gave the EEF a wide berth and, even after recognising unions in 1944,
refused to join the Federation. Vauxhall Motors left the Federation in
1921 and, after it was taken over by General Motors, never rejoined.
Briggs Bodies remained outside the Federation and it was only strong
pressure which induced Pressed Steel to join in the early 1930s.[86] These
and other firms had the capability to manage their own industrial relations
and wanted autonomy to determine wages and conditions as they wished.
There was, therefore, an alternative path which some big firms, often
leaders in terms of organisational development, were able to choose.
Overall, however, British employers found it easier to deal through
employers' organisations rather than develop their own plant, let alone
company, arrangements.

Conclusion

By 1920 a system of management–union relations had been created in
Britain which remained dominant into the 1950s. Through their asssoci-
ations, employers recognised trade unions for manual workers but, in
turn, tried to exclude union activity and bargaining from the workplace
and insisted on dealing with unions primarily through external procedures. In this way they created a framework of wages and conditions
at industry level. The economic and business circumstances of the interwar years tested the system, which on the whole survived. Indeed
depression sustained the system for it meant that power lay with the
employers, who were content to maintain what they had created;
similarly, increasing collusion between firms and trade protection reinforced these arrangments. In addition, the nature of company organisation encouraged this strategy: small, medium-sized, and loosely co-

ordinated larger firms, with weak managerial structures and hierarchies, meant that most firms relied on the services of their employers' organisations. It was only a few exceptional firms which pursued alternative strategies and tried to develop stronger internal arrangements.

However, the system was never as stable as it might have appeared. It relied through the interwar years on economic depression and was sustained by restrictive and protectionist tendencies in the product market. Moreover it was built on a weak infrastructure. The machinery did not usually provide detailed regulation at plant and, even less, at company level. At the workplace, the employers' policy of seeking to externalise management-union relations was never entirely successful - traditional shopfloor practices survived or re-emerged when market conditions became favourable. Such a multi-level system reflected both the deep roots of workplace trade unionism in Britain and the inability of management to follow through its national strategy of externalisation. As early as the recovery of the 1930s, there were signs of instability which took the form of wages drift and unconstitutional action. It was not until the post-Second World War period, however, that the full strength of this problem became clear and that employers were forced to develop new strategies for dealing with industrial relations internally within their companies.

Part 3

Challenges and adjustments in the post-war
years

6 Markets, firms, and the organisation of production

This book has set the history of labour management in Britain in a broad economic and business context. It has argued that the legacy from the nineteenth century had a profound effect on the management of labour in the twentieth century. The first half of the twentieth century witnessed considerable changes in the structure of British industry which in part modified that traditional pattern of labour relations. Markets, which had at first been open and expanding, became subject in the interwar years to growing restrictive and protectionist tendencies. Newer industries based on mass-production technologies became firmly established. Corporate structures also changed and there was a growth of large firms and managerial hierarchies. However, there were also significant continuities from the nineteenth century. Britain remained heavily committed to the older staple industries and markets often remained highly fragmented and differentiated. With the exception of the two world wars, the labour market continued to be characterised by elastic labour supply. The large firms which emerged at the turn of the century and in the interwar years often remained loose federations of constituent companies with weak managerial hierarchies. In this environment, it was argued, many British employers retained traditional forms of work relations which were labour intensive, which afforded skilled workers considerable autonomy, and which constrained productivity growth. In terms of employment and industrial relations firms, for the most part, chose strategies of externalisation and failed to develop strong internal structures of labour management. Only a few exceptional firms, usually characterised by different market, structural, and managerial configurations, pursued different labour strategies and developed stronger internal structures of labour management.

This chapter outlines changes in the economic and business context of the post-Second World War period which led to more substantial adaptations of the traditional system of labour management. The effects of increased product market competition and full employment in the postwar years are stressed. The chapter outlines the growth in company size and developments in corporate structures and managerial hierarchies, but it stresses that, well into the postwar period, these remained weak and continued to constrain the development of managerial strategies. The chapter also examines the management of production where the Second World War and the postwar years revealed critical weaknesses in work relations. Finally, it considers attempts by employers to deal with the pressing problems of low productivity and to restructure the organisation of work.

Changes in the market context

From an economic point of view, the postwar years may be divided into three parts. The first, covering the phase of postwar adjustment from 1945 to 1951-52, was a period of severe economic and financial problems, when people were unsure how long the recovery and full employment would last. In important respects, however, British industry was well placed in terms of world markets in that most of its productive capacity was intact, demand was growing at home and abroad, and its European and Japanese competitors had suffered much greater economic disloca-tion. The second period covered the long boom from the early 1950s to the early 1970s. These were years of unprecedented growth for the British economy, interrupted only by short and relatively minor setbacks. Through the 1950s, full employment came to be taken for granted and an expectation of rising living standards was firmly established. However, from the late 1950s onwards, British industry was subjected to more severe competition in domestic and overseas markets. Through the 1960s, among informed opinion, there was a growing awareness that in terms of growth rates Britain was lagging behind other industrial countries. In the mid-1960s, further problems began to accumulate as both inflation and unemployment rose. The late 1960s marked the beginning of the end of the boom period, though at the time this was only dimly perceived. The third period may be taken as beginning in the early 1970s when economic buoyancy came to a more decisive end. Thereafter, industrial output fell in two major recessions, 1974-75 and 1979-81, the latter of which was followed by a long period of recovery up to 1989. These two recessions had world-wide origins but, in Britain, the problems they caused had to be absorbed by an economy which for many years had been growing relatively slowly and whose firms had been losing market share both at home and abroad.[1]

Over the postwar period, structural change was considerable. At the beginning of the period, the old staple industries of coal, textiles, shipbuilding, and heavy engineering were still very important in terms of output and employment. Thereafter they declined, while the newer industries which had grown in the interwar period – motor vehicles, electrical products, synthetic fibres, and food processing – expanded, especially in the 1950s. To these were added the still newer industries of petrochemicals, pharmaceuticals, and consumer electronics. Both employment and output in manufacturing rose up to the mid-1960s, but from then on declined, steeply after 1979. This decline proceeded at a faster rate in Britain than in other countries, reflecting increasing import penetration and declining share in world exports of manufactured goods.

In historical perspective it is necessary to stress two further major features of postwar markets which profoundly affected employers' labour policies. One relates to the nature of the product market, the other to the state of the labour market.

In terms of product markets, the most striking feature of the postwar period was the increase in competition. Lower transportation costs and better communications effectively widened the area of potential competition, in both domestic and international markets. The postwar international economic settlement involved a liberalisation of international trade and an erosion of the protection which most British industries had enjoyed since the 1930s. Each successive 'round' of trade liberalisation involved a progressive opening of the markets of one country to another.[2] Partly because of this, but also because of the import substitution policies of newly independent states, traditional colonial and commonwealth markets ceased to give preference to British goods. The creation of the European Free Trade Association and the European Economic Community, and Britain's subsequent entry into the latter in 1974, also widened the scope and intensity of competition. In all markets, the growth of American, European, and Japanese competition meant an intensification of competitive pressures. In these circumstances, British exporters had to face the difficult task of trying to maintain their position in traditional markets while progressively reorienting themselves to more dynamic and competitive markets in Europe and N. America. At the same time, within the British market, domestic forces were at work increasing competitive pressures. The Monopolies and Restrictive Trade Practices Act of 1948 stimulated a climate of opinion critical of restrictive business behaviour which, as was argued in previous chapters, had been a long-term feature of many British industries. The passage of the Restrictive Trade Practices Act in 1956 and the Resale Price Act in 1964 led to a dismantling of many market-sharing and price-fixing arrangements which had grown up, especially in the interwar period.[3] These circumstances together created a much more competitive market environment which put strains on the national system of industrial relations and prompted firms to pay attention to their systems of labour management.

In terms of the labour market, the long thirty-year boom from the end of the Second World War was the first time ever in British economic history that there was extended full employment. Comparing adjusted figures, during the years 1874–1914 unemployment probably averaged around 5 per cent; during the interwar years from 1920 it never fell below 10 per cent; whereas in the first twenty years after the Second World War unemployment averaged 1.5 per cent.[4] Postwar full employment resulted both from a slowdown in the growth of the male workforce and high and stable demand for goods and services. Shortages of labour, especially skilled labour, became a feature of manufacturing industry at each cyclical peak in the 1950s and 1960s. It is true that over the postwar period unemployment rose, but the rate of increase was slow until the early 1970s, when unemployment first exceeded one million or 4 per cent of the insured working population. A quarter century of full employment and high demand for labour had profound consequences for industrial relations, in particular threatening the stability of workplace relations and the industry-wide system of collective bargaining. It also had an important effect on employment relations, encouraging the growth of internal labour market-type arrangements in British firms.

The further growth in company size

Growth in aggregate demand and the size of markets led to a further increase in the large-firm sector in Britain. Some of the increase in company size came from internal growth as markets and technological developments offered opportunities for firms to expand. At the same time the increase in market competition and opportunities also led to a further growth of mergers and, in Britain more than in other countries, firms grew by acquisition. From the mid-1950s the number of mergers fluctuated around a rising trend with peaks in the mid-1960s and the early 1970s.[5] As a result of the mergers and acquisitions of this period some of the largest British firms in the electrical engineering, aerospace, motor vehicle, and food, drink, and tobacco industries were created.[6] A particular feature of this period of mergers was the growth of the multi-product firm, as companies diversified in order to reduce their reliance on a single product range and in order to take advantage of market opportunities in several industries. In Channon's sample of the largest 100 British companies, for example, only one quarter were diversified in 1950, whereas the proportion had risen to nearly half by 1960 and to around two-thirds by the early 1970s.[7]

Growth by both internal expansion and acquisition led to an increase in employment in the largest enterprises. The average size of the top 100 firms increased from 20,300 employees in 1958 to 31,180 in 1972, and the number of manufacturing enterprises with employment in excess of 5,000 rose from 180 in 1958 to 210 in 1963.[8] ICI and Unilever, which before the war had been the largest manufacturing employers with 50,000 or more employees, had by the early 1970s been joined by around 25 other firms in the same size category and by that date ten firms employed 100,000 employees or more.[9] In terms of manufacturing net output, the share of the top 100 firms rose from 26 per cent in the early 1950s to 41 per cent in 1968.[10] A similar picture is shown by the evidence on market concentration as represented by the proportion of net output accounted for by the top five firms in an industry: by the end of the 1960s the five largest firms accounted for 90 per cent or more of net output in nearly a quarter of all industries.[11] Indeed, by then the degree of concentration in Britain had surpassed that found in the USA and Germany. However, taking the size of individual firms, Britain's largest companies were still smaller in terms of turnover than their American counterparts. In sectors such as motor vehicles, electrical and electronic products, and chemicals and pharmaceuticals, the largest British firms were also smaller than those in Germany and, by the 1970s, in industries such as steel, shipbuilding, motor vehicles, and electrical products, they had been overtaken in size by the Japanese. Moreover, in these sectors, plant size in Britain tended to be smaller and many British firms had a large number of plants. In 1958 the 100 largest manufacturing companies had an average of 27 plants; by 1972 this number had risen to 72 and was spread over a larger number of industries. This reflected the defensive nature of many British mergers and the failure to rationalise organisation and production.

Problems of organisational change and continuing managerial weaknesses

The growth in company size and the increase in merger activity from the early 1960s created severe organisational and managerial difficulties for British firms. The speed and size of acquisitions and mergers posed coordination problems as the number of subsidiaries and plants increased and the various layers of managers grew.[12] Horizontal and vertical mergers raised problems of integrating and rationalising formerly competing and overlapping units, and diversification created particularly complex problems of coordination and control across a number of industries. All these problems had to be confronted by managerial hierarchies which in Britain continued to be less well trained and integrated than in many foreign countries.

In the immediate postwar period, most firms retained their traditional organisational structures. Thus, the majority of the largest firms remained loose-knit, decentralised holding-companies, with weak management hierarchies and control systems. Acquisitions usually meant the addition of further units to already loose federations without thoroughgoing structural reorganisation. Where firms were previously centralised and organised on functional lines, merger and acquisition often resulted in the grafting on of new subsidiaries. In this way, some hitherto centralised firms became more like holding-companies, with newly acquired subsidiaries subject to little central control.[13] Before the mid-1960s, very few British firms had adopted the multidivisional form of organisation where a company was separated into product divisions, each allowed operating autonomy, but subject to head office strategic monitoring and control.[14] Such a form of organisation had been tentatively developed by a few firms in the interwar years but, as Channon has shown, only about a dozen of the largest firms operating in Britain had a divisional structure in 1950 and a number of these were subsidiaries of American parent companies. In the 1960s the number of firms organised on these lines increased, but by the end of that decade still only about one third of the largest British firms had developed multidivisional structures.[15] However, growing competition and reduced profitability through the 1960s and 1970s made organisational change even more urgent[16] and, by the mid-1970s, around three quarters had adopted a multidivisional form of organisation of some kind, while others strengthened their more centralised, functionally departmentalised structures.[17] These changes allowed growth to be more effectively managed and allowed new strategic initiatives to be taken, including in the area of labour management.

However, two major sets of reservations must be registered concerning improvements in corporate structure in Britain. First, growing as they often did out of holding companies, these new structures tended to be weaker than their American counterparts – with smaller senior management hierarchies, less well-defined and articulated divisions, and weaker head office planning systems. They were also weaker than their German and Japanese counterparts which tended to maintain more centralised, functional forms of organisation.[18] In some cases, in Britain, divisionalised firms tended to act like financially driven conglomerates with insufficient integration of production and marketing strategy. In the 1980s financial pressures have led in some cases to what is probably an excessive devolution of responsibility with only financial control remaining at the centre. This has raised doubts about the feasibility of the development of strategy in the labour management area.[19] Second, at about the same time that structural reforms were taking place, a new set of challenges had arisen. A further wave of mergers and acquisitions in the late 1970s and 1980s, the increased importance of institutional investors, and the growth of what has been termed a 'market for corporate control' began to have important implications.[20] Senior managers had increasingly to worry about the threat of hostile takeover; more importance has had to be placed on short-term profits and share prices rather than long-term growth and market share; and takeovers have led to British firms, often still groping towards improved corporate structures, being bought, dismembered, or reconstituted as subsidiaries of bigger, often foreign, companies. These phenomena also occurred in the US, where they are generally thought to have had deleterious consequences on company performance. They have not happened to the same extent on the Continent or in Japan where firms have concentrated more on strengthening their corporate structures and long-term capabilities.

To manage the increase in size and complexity, through the postwar years there was a growth in the number of managers at all levels. As we have seen, this was part of a long-term trend. The ratio of administrative, technical, and clerical staff in manufacturing industry rose from 19 per cent in 1948 to 27 per cent in 1958 and 34 per cent in 1968.[21] By then, British firms had caught up with, and even surpassed, foreign firms in terms of the size of their managerial hierarchies. However, in terms of quality there were still considerable deficiencies.[22] In firms which retained a loose holding-company form of organisation, family management often persisted, both at main board level and in the constituent companies. Even in some of the better organised companies structured on functional or multidivisional lines, there were vestiges of family control and, when smaller firms were acquired, family members were often retained on subsidiary boards.[23] Though some family members could provide real benefits to firms in terms of experience and commitment, by no means all family managers were trained or knowledgeable, and family background often meant the existence of a considerable gap between senior and lower level management. The overall impression given by various surveys of senior British managers in large companies in the 1950s and 1960s was that they continued to come largely from the top social classes; about half of them had been to private school; and, of the minority who had been to university, they tended to have been to Oxford or Cambridge where they were more likely to have studied arts subjects rather than science, engineering, or business-related subjects.[24] Herein lay a contrast with other major industrial countries. In the US, family control declined earlier and firms had long been run by university-trained professional managers. Other countries, especially Germany, Japan, and France, also made more rapid strides in the postwar period towards developing well-trained professional managerial hierarchies.[25] Of course, there were British firms which were well managed at the top and which had effective management development programmes. The ability of such firms to recruit and develop graduate managers would suggest a demand side failure rather than a supply side constraint: most British firms did not seek to recruit or develop their managerial cadres in the manner of Japanese, German, and American firms.[26]

However, there were some signs of improvement, especially from the mid-1960s onwards. Along with the merger movement and structural reorganisation, there was an attenuation of family participation at main and subsidiary board level. Increasingly at main board level, full-time professional directors replaced owner-directors. The educational attainment of British management also improved as younger managers, with better formal qualifications, began to work their way up the management hierarchy.[27] This included an increase in the numbers trained in science, engineering, and business administration. Again a caveat must be registered. Though there were some improvements in the quality of British management, considerable problems still persisted in terms of training. Management training in Britain probably came to overemphasise general business management and to place less emphasis on technical training as was stressed in Germany and Japan. In Britain the finance function often dominates and accountants are more likely to get to the top of firms than engineers or production managers.[28] Studies in the 1980s have shown that British management on the whole still remains less well educated and trained than its American, European, and Japanese counterparts.[29]

These weaknesses may have been particularly acute at lower levels in the management hierarchy. Middle managers in Britain were likely to have worked their way up through the company's ranks and, in the production area, in industries like engineering and shipbuilding, many were ex-craft apprentices. These were less well educated and formally trained than their overseas counterparts and probably on the whole less open to new management techniques.[30] At the base of the management hierarchy, the position and status of the foreman had for some time been progressively eroded and encroached upon by line managers and specialist departments. In Britain this continued through the Second World War and postwar period, despite some attempts at the training and upgrading of supervisory staff. Overall, the vast majority of foremen in British industry were recruited mainly from manual jobs, were usually selected in an *ad hoc*, casual manner, and received little further technical or managerial training.[31] Moreover, higher level management seems to have been less concerned to integrate them into the management team. One recent study suggested that, 'The major break in the vertical structure of British companies comes between shopfloor supervision and management proper, rather than between supervision and shopfloor.'[32] The weakness of supervisory staff in Britain posed problems for the management of production and industrial relations. For example, it has often been observed that foremen have acquiesced in or colluded with various shopfloor customs and practices. Though this phenomenon is to be found in many countries, it was probably more pronounced in postwar Britain, given the weakness of managerial control systems above and the strength of shopfloor trade unionism below.[33]

Turning finally to personnel management, this was given a considerable boost by the Second World War when, in large part at government prompting, more personnel managers were appointed and specialist labour departments established.[34] The numbers of managers with this title rose substantially from about 2,000 in 1939 to over 5,000 by 1945. Thereafter, through the next two decades, there was a slow increase in their number. However, not all firms employed formally qualified specialists and few gave the personnel function board-level representation.[35] Overall, the majority of personnel managers in Britain lacked formal qualifications and personnel management remained relatively low status in the management hierarchy. Their role was usually administrative and reactive rather than strategic or proactive and, in dealings with trade unions, much was still left to employers' organisations. It was only later in the 1960s, as labour problems accumulated, that the number of personnel managers again rose, increasing from about 15,000 in the mid-1960s to around 50,000 by the late 1970s.[36] By the late 1970s, most large firms employed specialist staff and many had for the first time appointed main board directors with responsibility for personnel management.[37] However, smaller and medium-sized firms often still did not have personnel managers, and foreign-owned firms were more likely to have specialists both at plant and board level than their British-owned counterparts.[38]

Weaknesses in corporate structures and managerial hierarchies lay behind many of the labour management problems of the 1960s and 1970s and constrained managerial labour strategies. Such improvements as there were in structure and hierarchy in those decades provided a basis for changes in labour strategies in the 1970s and 1980s. Continuing weaknesses, combined with an excessive decentralisation and an emphasis on short-term financial considerations, have remained a constraint on the development of labour strategies.

The changing technological context

The Second World War had accelerated change in both old and new industries engaged in war production. In this respect the speed and scale of change in war-related industries was much greater than during the First World War. In the key engineering sector new factories were built and many more extended and reorganised. Along with this went a considerable introduction of new machine tools, many imported from the US. Better practices in terms of standardisation, quality control, and flow line production spread from government 'shadow' factories and from larger firms to smaller firms and sub-contractors.[39] More than during the First World War there was cooperation between management and labour and a willingness to relax traditional practices.[40] One historian of the war economy has gone so far as to conclude that, 'The technical changes in production processes during the Second World War went a long way towards ending the distinction between "artisan" and "workman".'[41] However, the Second World War also highlighted many of the weaknesses of British industry. There were severe problems of scheduling production and inefficiencies in industries such as machine tools, aircraft production, and shipbuilding. In the coal mining, steel, and shipbuilding industries, new equipment and changes in work organisation were limited.[42] Increases in production were often obtained by an increase in the labour force and a more extensive (longer hours) and more intensive (speed-up) use of labour. But this had its limits. At the end of the war, the reports of the Anglo-American Productivity Council showed graphically that productivity per head was much lower in the UK than in the US and that this could in large part be ascribed to the slower introduction of new labour-saving technologies.[43]

In the first quarter century after the war economic circumstances combined to bring about a period of technical change more rapid than in any previous period in British history. Investment in plant and equipment was higher than ever before and British firms had the opportunity to catch up with a backlog of technological advances, many imported from the US. There were substantial changes in machines and processes and in the flow and transfer of materials. In steel making, electric arc and, later, basic oxygen furnaces took over from open-hearth methods of production; in engineering, there was a further introduction of more sophisticated machine tools; in coal mining, machine cutting and power loading were extended throughout the nationalised coal industry. In consumer-goods industries there was also rapid technological change. In artificial fibres high-speed spinning of new fibres such as nylon and polyester were introduced; in the rapidly growing pharmaceutical industry new mass-production and packaging techniques were adopted; and in brewing and baking new faster processes made possible the larger-scale production of more standardised foodstuffs. In the case of material and product flow, there was an extension of assembly-line techniques; in motor-vehicle plants automatic transfer machines were introduced which moved parts through various operations and improved the speed and accuracy of machining; and more mechanical and pneumatic handling was installed throughout industry. There occurred an accelerated movement from batch to continuous process production in industries such as glass, cement, paper, sugar, soap and detergent manufacture. In the chemical, oil-refining, and petrochemical industries, more sophisticated instrumentation was introduced which increased the volume and speed of throughput. At all stages of production a greater degree of automation and control was achieved with the more extensive use of electronics and, from the 1960s onwards, computer-controlled processes.[44]

However, two qualifications relevant to the themes of this book must be added to this overview of technological change in postwar Britain. First, most of the new production techniques were introduced from abroad, especially from the US, and in terms of the diffusion of technical processes Britain often lagged behind best-practice technologies abroad.[45] In older industries such as textiles, many firms continued to rely on spindles and looms which foreign firms had long since abandoned and British firms were slow to introduce new automated machinery. In shipbuilding, the installation of mechanical handling, welding, and pre-fabrication systems and standardisation lagged behind Britain's main competitors. In steel making, British firms did not lead in the introduction of basic oxygen processes, continuous casting, and other new methods of integrated steel production.[46] In newer areas such as machine tools, British firms failed to capitalise on a promising start in the development of numerically controlled machines, and the same occurred in the increasingly important computer industry.[47] Second, the main advantages which manufacturers had to gain from technological innovation were increased quantity and quality of output, reductions in costs, and improvements in productivity. Where labour considerations were important, it was usually in terms of savings in manpower and in most cases simple deskilling was not an objective.[48] Of course, there was some deskilling, especially with the introduction of mass-production methods in industries such as motor vehicles and electrical products and in continuous-process industries such as steel and glass making. On the other hand, much heavy manual work disappeared and the introduction of new plant and machinery often meant more skilled operative, maintenance, and technician jobs. However, it was felt by a growing number of managers and policy-makers that there was a labour problem for British manufacturers and this was how to match competitors in terms of productivity growth.

The productivity problem

The postwar years saw the most rapid and sustained growth in production and productivity in British economic history. Over the quarter century 1948-73, gross domestic product grew at an annual rate of about 2.8 per cent and productivity (as measured by gross domestic product per employee hour) at about 2.4 per cent. By comparison, over the years 1870-1914, output had grown at approximately 1.9 per cent per annum and productivity increased by about 1.1 per cent. In the interwar years 1922-37, output had grown by about 2.3 per cent and productivity by 2.0 per cent per annum.[49] Not only was there an improvement over earlier periods, but also through the postwar period up to 1973 productivity growth was on a rising trend. Thus, in the manufacturing sector, productivity accelerated from 2.2 per cent annually in 1955-60, to 3.2 per cent in 1960-64, to 3.4 per cent in 1964-69, and to 4.5 per cent in 1969-73.[50] This came to an end, however, with the onset of recession in 1973. Between 1973 and 1978, productivity increased at only around 1.0 per cent per annum and, between 1979 and 1980, disappeared altogether before recovering strongly from 1981 onwards.[51]

However, the problem for Britain was that, though productivity growth over the postwar years was good compared to earlier periods, it lagged significantly behind other major competitor countries. The productivity gap between Britain and the US, with its origins in the late nineteenth century, had widened significantly in the 1920s and 1930s, and other industrial rivals, such as Germany, had developed a clear tendency to improve productivity more rapidly. The Anglo-American Productivity reports after the war showed that most British firms were less well-equipped with up-to-date machinery and less well-laid out than their American counterparts and the gap between the good and the bad was very wide indeed in Britain.[52] Contemporary academic studies confirmed these findings and showed that, though the US productivity advantage varied from one industry to another, there was an absolute lead in almost every industry and this was particularly marked in the mass-production industries.[53] In the post-1945 period, industries in Germany, France, Japan, Italy, and a number of other countries successively passed Britain in terms of productivity growth, and progressively, in the 1960s and 1970s, this opened up a significant gap in absolute levels of productivity. Though the origins in these disparities may be traced back before the war, the relative deterioration was greater and more sustained during the postwar period.[54] By the early 1970s manufacturing output per head in West Germany and France was about 50 per cent higher, and in the US over 100 per cent higher, than in Britain.[55] The productivity gap was particularly large in the important metal-working and engineering group of industries – steel, motor vehicles, shipbuilding, mechanical and electrical engineering.[56] Aggregate measures of productivity differences have been confirmed by more detailed comparisons of matched firms and plants. All these studies, both macro and micro level, have problems of data collection and reliability and some may overstate the productivity shortfall. However, cumulatively they show significant differences in productivity growth.[57]

Increasingly through the postwar period these productivity problems came to be seen by many as a problem of labour. Of course, labour productivity is merely a measure of output over labour and it implies nothing about the causes of productivity. However, among employers, politicians, and public opinion formers, Britain's poor performance was increasingly attributed to labour inefficiencies and inadequate industrial relations. From the 1960s onwards, these beliefs, reinforced by a further perception that profits were being squeezed,[58] induced employers to search for changes in the management of production.

Employer strategies and the organisation of production

It was argued in Chapters 2 and 3 that through the nineteenth century traditional work methods persisted or changed only slowly, reflecting the structure of markets, the nature of firms, and an employer preference for labour-intensive methods of production rather than investment in new plant and equipment. The late nineteenth century and the interwar years saw important process innovations and changes in work organisation and the spread of mass-production methods. However, overall, the rate of change was gradual and patchy. This is not surprising given the exceptional fluctuations of demand during these years and the reluctance of the many small and medium sized firms to risk the heavy investment and overheads implied by large-scale modernisation and reorganisation of their production processes. Even larger firms often lacked the organisational capability to push through changes in production. Moreover, in Britain the relatively plentiful supplies of unskilled and skilled labour encouraged the maintenance of labour-intensive methods. Where British employers did try to deal with the problems of productivity, they often resorted to an intensification of work within existing technologies and relied on other employment policies and strategies of externalisation to control and motivate labour.

During the Second World War management sought to raise productivity in various ways. As already stated, there was an extension of scientific management techniques in the war industries involving the application of work study and the introduction of payment-by-results systems. In addition, there was a greater use of motion and method study directed at problems of standardisation, lay-out, scheduling, and quality control.[59] From 1941 onwards managements accepted the establishment of joint production committees whose aim was to deal with production problems and improve productivity and wartime circumstances enabled management to obtain the suspension or abandonment of many restrictive practices.[60] However, in qualification, it should be stressed that wartime changes were uneven between and within industries. For example, in shipbuilding and iron and steel, reorganisation was limited, and outside of the armaments industries, change was minimal. Much of the increase in production during the war came from longer hours and an increase in the intensity of work. This, however, had its price and wartime conditions simultaneously led to an increase in trade union bargaining power which constituted a real or potential check on management.

After the war there was a growing recognition among more informed and perceptive observers of the shortcomings of British industry as evidenced by the work of the Anglo-American Productivity Council. This body, established at government initiative and with American prompting in 1948, was made up of management and union representatives. Its aim was to investigate the sources of Britain's poor productivity performance and to make recommendations for improvements. To this end, it despatched study teams to the US and produced a series of reports.[61] Overall the various studies identified a real productivity gap between British and American industry which they attributed to slower introduction of labour-saving technologies and new methods of production. Though in part the reports referred to poor employment and industrial relations in Britain,[62] they placed more emphasis on levels of investment and managerial failings, especially in the production area.[63] As one team of managers and accountants concluded, 'the greatest single factor in American industrial supremacy over British industry is the effectiveness of its management at all levels'.[64] Though the findings of the Council attracted considerable interest, in practice they had little effect in stimulating change in industry. Though in some quarters there was a recognition of the problem, there was overall considerable complacency, created by the perceived success of wartime industry and the continued myth of Britain as a great power.[65] There was some union opposition to the reports and the government did little to see that they were implemented. However, the main ambivalence towards the findings was on the part of British management who either did not read the reports or who did not believe what they read. Moreover, in a seller's market immediately after the war and before the removal of many restrictive trading agreements, it was all too easy for British manufacturers to ignore the recommendations and to continue with inefficient practices.[66]

The post-Second World War years were very different from the period after the First World War and certainly the years after 1920. In a situation of rising product demand, continuing full employment, and under a Labour government, British employers were not in a situation where they chose to launch a concerted attack on workplace inefficiencies and trade union practices as a way of dealing with problems of costs and productivity. In part this was because British unions were relatively strong and on the whole were not at first perceived as being strongly opposed to technological change.[67] In large part the failure to confront the unions was on the employers' side: they lacked the organisational capability at both national and company level to mount a frontal attack; moreover, in an economic climate of buoyant demand, sheltered by continued protectionism and restrictive trading agreements, and in a political climate of consensus, they lacked the motivation and determination to press home such an attack. This absence of an employer offensive was in contrast to the situation in the US and Japan where more belligerent employers challenged unions and asserted managerial control over the production process. Equally in Britain, employers did not seek to pursue a more cooperative strategy as was being pursued in some Continental countries such as West Germany and Sweden at the time.[68] This was evidenced by the fact that many employers let their wartime joint production committees lapse and put nothing new in their place.

However, in the 1950s competitive pressures on British firms increased and employers resorted to various measures to increase output and to improve productivity. There was an extension of shiftworking, especially in industries such as chemicals, motor vehicles, and food processing. Shiftwork rose from around 10 per cent of all workers in manufacturing in the late 1940s to 20 per cent in 1964 and 25 per cent in 1968.[69] A more dubious response was the increased use of overtime working which rose from one hour per week above normal hours in 1947 to six by 1965. This often had negative consequences, not least in that it encouraged make-work practices in normal hours.[70] In certain industries, such as textiles, transport, and foundry work, there was increasing recourse to the use of cheap immigrant labour prepared to work long hours often on antiquated production processes. There was also an increased use of women, especially married women, though again employers saw them as a source of cheap labour rather than a productive resource to be trained and developed. In addition there was also recourse to the traditional British management strategy of piecework which seemed to offer immediate returns without any major changes in production processes or methods of working. Payment-by-results systems grew and were extended to industries such as chemicals where they had previously been rare. Again, however, this had disadvantages and caused industrial relations problems as will be discussed in Chapter 8.

In the postwar years the use of so-called scientific management techniques increased in Britain. In a few large firms there was an introduction of operational research involving the application of mathematical techniques to problems of stock control, scheduling, and production.[71] More widespread was the growth of work study and its two main techniques, method study and work measurement. Method study involved the investigation of alternative ways of organising work, on the basis of which, work measurement could then be applied to establish the time taken to carry out a job. In practice, in Britain, however, the method-study stage was given less prominence, and management was more enthusiastic about work measurement as the basis for bonus schemes.[72] Overall, however, it is true to say that the 1940s and 1950s saw the main advance of formal scientific management techniques in British industry. Large companies, such as ICI, Unilever, Pilkingtons, Dunlop, Rolls Royce, and Lucas, set up their own work study and management services departments, while others employed one of the many consultancy firms operating in the area. The professional associations in the field, established during and after the Second World War, such as the Society of Industrial Engineers, the Work Study Society, and the Institute of Industrial Technicians, grew in membership and other more established associations, such as the Institutes of Mechanical and Production Engineers, introduced work study into their exams in the 1950s.[73] Though some of these techniques, such as operational research, were pioneered in Britain and though other aspects of scientific management were well understood, on the whole British industry lagged in the incorporation of such techniques into production engineering and workplace management.[74] The uncertain development of new organisational forms and management hierarchies over the first two postwar decades were an important reason why British firms were slow in adopting new management techniques. At the top, many senior British managers espoused a 'gentlemanly' and 'generalist' approach and talked more about the need to improve 'human relations' rather than production techniques; while middle and lower level managers still prided themselves on being 'practical' men and emphasised 'experience' and 'feel' rather than technique.[75]

A wider recognition of a problem of labour productivity came in the 1960s as international competition and labour market pressures intensified. The belief grew that problems of industrial relations were the main cause of poor performance and this led to the beginnings of new policies in this area, the course and outcome of which will be described in more detail in Chapter 7. One response to the perceived cause of the problems was the development in the mid-1960s of so-called productivity bargaining. In this, a number of large companies, aware of international comparisons, played a leading part. Thus, Esso, prompted by low productivity in its Fawley refinery, was one of the leading firms.[76] Productivity bargaining, as it developed, involved detailed company- or plant-level negotiations and the explicit linking of wage increases to specific changes in working practices. The most common of such changes included reductions in overtime working, reduced manning levels, and greater interchangeability among workers.[77] At the same time, there was also a move away from piecework and towards time-based systems where *inter alia* the intention was to increase flexibility in labour deployment and to reduce resistance to change in working practices. These changes often also involved an extension of work study techniques, with the result that by the late 1970s about half of all manufacturing establishments were making use of them.[78] In the process of productivity bargaining, management came to bargain more openly about matters which it had traditionally regarded, formally at least, as managerial prerogatives and in this way there was an extension of the scope of joint regulation in industry. By 1969, about 3,000 productivity agreements had been signed covering six million workers or a quarter of the labour force.[79]

Some have argued that productivity bargaining in particular, and the more general industrial relations reforms of this period, made little or no contribution to increased productivity. Workers, it is contended, created new restrictive practices and, from the late 1960s onwards, under pressure of incomes policies, productivity bargaining was devalued and subsequently declined.[80] Industrial relations reforms more generally merely increased the power of workplace unionism and constrained management.[81] Though it is true that managements were not always able to take advantage of the changes and though there were incursions into 'managerial prerogatives', such pessimistic conclusions are ill founded. In the circumstances of the time, management was attempting 'to regain control by sharing it'[82] and they felt that the reforms were worth having. Also, it should be remembered that there was some acceleration of productivity growth in the late 1960s and early 1970s and some of this may be attributable to productivity bargaining.[83] Certainly it is possible that the deceleration of productivity growth from 1973 onwards may have been even greater in the absence of such reforms. At the very least, the notion of productivity bargaining and other industrial relations reforms were a prerequisite for productivity improvements.

A somewhat different approach adopted by some firms in the 1970s centred on what came to be known as job redesign. This had its origins in part in concerns about productivity, but also in the 1970s with concerns about absenteeism, labour turnover, and other worker dissatisfactions. Job redesign involved a range of different projects and techniques involving rearrangements in factory production methods. Job enlargement meant combining several tasks into one larger job. Job enrichment involved combining jobs of different levels of skill and responsibility, including work scheduling and quality control normally done by supervisory staff. Other approaches involved an extension of these techniques to a whole work group, allowing the group more discretion in planning and organising their work.[84] All of these started from the premise that the subdivision of labour had been taken too far with deleterious consequences, especially low morale and a lack of adaptability and flexibility. A number of large firms were interested in various forms of job redesign.[85] However, this was usually on an experimental basis, involving one plant or part of a plant. On the whole most British managements were hesitant. For them the costs of introducing such systems included the cost of new machinery and plant layout, the retraining of staff, and the need to develop new relationships with workers. There was also some doubt as to the general applicability of such systems and British managements were probably on the whole more conservative than many of their counterparts overseas. Even at its height the pursuit of job redesign was limited and its effects modest.[86] However, in so far as an important element concerned flexibility, there is a backward link with the productivity bargaining of the 1960s and a forward link with new concerns of the 1980s.

A new era of technological innovation and work organisation?

In recent years it has been argued that, from the 1970s onwards, a set of factors have combined to bring about a period of accelerated technological innovation and a major managerial effort to restructure work relations.

To take technological innovation first. Heightened competition, recession in the late 1970s and early 1980s, and a long recovery later in the 1980s gave firms the incentive and the opportunity to adopt new, best-practice production methods. New techniques, based on microelectronics, have become more readily available with a wide variety of applications. As such technologies have also become progressively cheaper and as foreign manufacturers have increasingly installed them, British firms have had little option but to follow suit. Some observers have gone so far to argue that this constitutes a revolutionary transition from mass-production methods based on so-called Fordist lines, involving the close supervision of machine-paced work, towards more specialised and flexible systems of manufacturing. Firms, it is contended, have to respond more quickly and flexibly to demands for greater variety and quality in more competitive markets. The adaptability inherent in computer-controlled production systems makes such 'flexible specialisation' possible. In terms of work organisation this means a move away from highly fragmented jobs towards more skilled and flexible work.[87]

Current changes in work organisation therefore in part result from technological innovation. However, they have also come about because of managerial efforts to restructure working arrangements quite independently of technological change. In Britain, since the late 1970s, a number of factors have made this both desirable and possible from management's point of view. The need to regain competitiveness, economic fluctuations, and a changed political environment have given management the impetus and have provided the opportunity to restructure working arrangements. Much attention has been given to dramatic changes in working practices introduced by management in certain large public-sector corporations such as British Leyland, British Steel, and British Coal and in a number of private-sector firms in the newspaper printing, television, and shipping industries. Less widely publicised, though more important in a broader perspective, a larger number of manufacturing firms have introduced new more flexible working practices through negotiations with trade unions. These have involved cuts in manning levels, reductions in demarcations, and the enlargement of jobs.[88] There has also been an increased managerial interest in team working and other methods aimed at involving workers in solving production and quality problems.[89]

It is still too early to evaluate such recent developments, but drawing on recent surveys and case studies and with the benefit of a historical perspective, a number of tentative points can be made.[90]

First, it may well be true that microelectronically-based technologies do represent a new stage of mechanisation and automation of production processes and it is clear that such technologies have a wide applicability in much the same way as did the coming of electricity at the end of the nineteenth century. However, in the British case a qualification is necessary. Among the major industrial nations, Britain has not been a leader in the diffusion of new technology.[91] Net new investment in manufacturing plant and equipment was low, relative to gross domestic product, in the 1970s, compared with the 1950s and 1960s; it fell dramatically during the recession of the early 1980s and then increased significantly in the subsequent recovery, though it remained low in terms of levels and growth compared with other major industrial countries. Productivity growth, which should be a consequence of rapid technological innovation, has also been no higher through the 1980s than in the 1950s and 1960s.[92] In the British case, the diffusion of new technology has been uneven between and within industries and often piecemeal within firms.

Second, in the changed circumstances of the 1980s, managements have undoubtedly been able to bring about some significant restructuring of working practices. This has been especially true in terms of the reduction in manning levels and greater flexibility across previous job boundaries. However, in the latter respect, change has often been modest, especially between maintenance and production workers and within maintenance areas and has not resulted in broad flexibility and multi-skilling of the labour force. Major changes in this respect have been confined to a minority of plants, and the gap between these and the majority is often still large.[93] As significant as these changes in the restructuring of work have been reductions in manning levels and a shift in power on the shopfloor. This has led some analysts to draw the following conclusions. Given the uneven and piecemeal diffusion of new technology and the often modest changes in working arrangements, what increase there has been in manufacturing productivity in the 1980s, compared to the 1970s, has come as much from plant closures, reductions in manning, and a tightening of managerial control.[94] In this respect, there are certain similarities with other periods in British history, especially the 1890s and the 1920s and 1930s, when there was also a reassertion of management control and an intensification of work.

Third, to take up the theme of managerial intentions and effects on skill. Most studies suggest that managements have introduced new technologies and methods of working in order to increase productivity, reduce costs, and obtain better quality. Certainly these changes cannot be seen simply as an attempt to deskill and thereby control labour.[95] In some industries, such as printing, it is true that change has eliminated traditional skills, downgraded others, and reduced worker control over the production process. In most industries, however, change has deskilled some jobs but reskilled others. Manual dexterity and electromechanical skills have become less important, but they have been replaced by electronic and diagnostic skills and the need to work across job boundaries. However, between firms there has been considerable variation in how skills are organised, reflecting differences in managerial competence and choice. Where managements have the ability, where training is available, and where good industrial relations exist, there is more likely to be an upskilling of work; where the reverse applies, management is less likely to upgrade staff and more likely to retain customary patterns of hierarchical control.[96] There is also evidence of variation between countries in the application of new technologies: in Britain it would appear that managements have attempted to retain tighter control over new processes and have been less likely to upskill than in West Germany or Japan.[97] In part this might be explained by low-trust industrial relations in Britain. However, though adversarial industrial relations are stronger in Britain and though British unions have put a price on the introduction of organisational change, most evidence suggests that unions have not opposed technological change.[98] More important constraints shaping the introduction of change would seem to be national differences in management and training. New technologies and flexible methods of working require sophisticated managerial competencies, including understanding among top management and technical and organisational expertise among middle and lower managers. They also require well-qualified and trained workers to operate the new systems flexibly and effectively. In Britain lower levels of managerial competence and skill deficiencies on the shopfloor have been major constraints on the introduction of new technology and working practices.[99] It may therefore be best to see recent developments in Britain not as a new era, but as a further stage in the long history of attempts to improve work relations and increase productivity performance.

Conclusions

This chapter has argued that in the post-Second World War period, there were significant changes in the environment within which British employers pursued their labour policies. The 1950s and 1960s were decades of rapid technological innovation; however, long-standing weaknesses persisted in the management of production technologies and the organisation of work. In the product market British firms faced heightened competition both at home and abroad. In the labour market, for nearly three decades, employers had to contend with full or near-full employment. The labour market situation eased from the mid-1970s, but product markets became more volatile and competition continued to intensify. At firm level there was in the 1950s and 1960s a growth in company size and complexity in part resulting from a new wave of mergers. Initially, this led to limited change in corporate structures and managerial hierarchies: loose holding-company arrangements predominated and managerial hierarchies remained weak. It was only from the mid-1960s onwards that significant improvements have occurred in these areas, though still insufficient relative to major competitor countries. Throughout the predominant problem facing British industry has been relatively low productivity growth. To overcome this, over the years, British managements have tried in various ways to restructure working arrangements, with some success, especially from the 1960s onwards. However, this has been constrained by lower levels of investment by British firms in production facilities and in organisational capabilities. It has also been constrained, though to a lesser extent, by continued shortcomings in terms of industrial and employment relations. These are the subject of the next two chapters.

7 Industrial relations: challenges and responses

Industrial relations are considered in this chapter before employment relations because of the importance which they assumed in British labour management in the period after the Second World War. It is true that in the early post-war years there was considerable complacency about industrial relations arrangements. However, industrial relations slowly emerged as a major problem for British management and assumed serious proportions for employers from the 1960s onwards. This chapter will analyse the nature of that problem, the employers' response, and the changes which occurred in the institutions of industrial relations.

The industrial relations pattern which had been established in the late nineteenth and early twentieth centuries was based on employer recognition of trade unions and collective bargaining with them through the agency of employers' associations external to the firm. In this way national agreements were established for most British industries laying down procedures and setting basic wages and conditions. By 1945 there were about 500 separate national institutions in which employers' organisations negotiated with trade unions.[1] Internally, within the firm, in many industries, there had long existed rudimentary shopfloor bargaining with work groups and their representatives, but the strength of these varied with economic circumstances and arrangements were seldom formalised. During the upswing from depression and the war years, trade union membership grew considerably, reaching a peak in 1948 of 9.4 million or 45 per cent of the workforce.[2] This was accompanied by an increase in union organisation and bargaining activity at the workplace. The wartime introduction of joint production committees and the more general need to consult workers strengthened workplace bargaining. Simultaneously the war extended and consolidated the national or external system of collective bargaining. Between 1939 and 1946, as many as 56 joint industrial councils or similar bodies were established or reestablished.[3] The wartime Conditions of Employment and the National Arbitration Order of 1940, familiarly known as Order 1305, also encouraged industry bargaining in that it allowed nationally agreed terms and conditions to be imposed on non-federated firms. This in turn assisted recruitment to employers' organisations and strengthened national agreements.[4]

There were, however, gaps in the structure and strains had emerged from the mid-1930s onwards. With the revival from depression, there was an upward drift of earnings over and above national rates with the result that, in a number of industries, national agreements less effectively regulated actual pay.[5] Along with this went an increase in the number of unofficial strikes. Despite this there was little criticism of the system nor much attempt to reform it. During the war there was little time for reform, and immediately after the war there seemed little need for an industrial relations system fundamentally different to that in place. Thus, as has already been suggested in Chapter 6, there was after the war no attempt by British employers to reform or redirect the system of industrial relations such as occurred in the US, Japan, and West Germany.[6]

Trade union membership and organisation

Total trade union membership rose more slowly in the two decades after 1948 than the labour force, with the result that density fell slightly from 45 per cent in 1948 to 43.7 per cent in 1967. Underlying these aggregate figures were important changes. Manual union membership remained more or less stable throughout the 1950s and 1960s, but since there was a reduction of employment in strongly organised industries such as coal, textiles, and railways, this reflected an increase in organisation in other newer industries such as motor vehicles and chemicals. Ford, and its body supplier Briggs, two of the last industrial bastions of non-unionism, recognised unions in 1944. The oil and chemical companies which were building new refineries and petrochemical plants during and after the war recognised rather more willingly. Only a few large firms held out against recognition for manual workers. White collar union membership increased throughout the post-war period, though because this was less than the rate of growth of employment until the late 1960s, density among white collar workers fell.[7]

An important feature of trade unionism in the war and early post-war period was the development and diffusion of shop steward organisation. As has already been noted, shop stewards had long existed in craft situations and had even been formally recognised by the Engineering Employers in 1919. Elsewhere recognition was accorded more informally, but both formal and informal recognition increased considerably during and after the war. By the early 1960s, shop steward organisation was firmly established beyond its craft and engineering bases. Overall the number of stewards increased faster than union membership. Between 1947 and 1961, for example, the number of stewards accredited by the AEU rose by 56 per cent as compared with a 30 per cent increase in membership of the union.[8] The result was that, by the mid-1960s, there were probably 175,000 shop stewards in British industry.[9] In most medium-sized and large plants in manufacturing, management had come to bargain with them over a widening range of issues. Indeed, given the weakness of managerial hierarchies and control systems in many British firms, employers sometimes relied upon them for the effective management of industrial relations at plant level.

From the early 1950s, a number of factors combined to produce a set of industrial relations problems. First, high levels of employment strengthened the bargaining power of workers and curtailed the power of employers who were increasingly in competition with one another for labour. Second, in a situation of buoyant product demand, employers were prepared to make concessions to their work forces since they preferred a rise in labour costs to a loss of output. Third, increased product market competition, as a result of the factors described in Chapter 6, meant that employers were on the whole less willing to cooperate with one another and were under pressure to deal internally with labour cost competitiveness. In terms of the conduct of industrial relations, this had fundamental consequences in four areas – collective bargaining structures, restrictive work rules, strikes and procedures for handling disputes, and the level of wages and labour costs. Each of these will be examined in turn.

Collective bargaining structures

The structure of collective bargaining, as it had developed in Great Britain, was skeletal and subject to recurrent strain in periods of economic upswing. In terms of wage arrangements, in many industries, only rates for certain classes of labour were fixed nationally – usually a rate for skilled men and for labourers, while other rates were fixed at workplace level. The tendency in the post-war period was for nationally determined rates to be exceeded in the form of wage drift, that is a widening margin between formally negotiated rates and actual earnings.[10] This growing disparity came about in a number of ways. In a situation of full employment and high demand, employers were prepared to offer various supplements above national rates in order to attract and retain labour and to secure effort. The increased use of payment by results, during and after the war, accentuated this tendency. Since incentive schemes could rarely be devised at national level, they had to be worked out and implemented within the factory. Here the fixing of piecework times and prices provided ample opportunity for bargaining, and piecework rates tended to work loose and drift upwards.[11] Increased product market competition pressed directly on bargaining structure in several ways. The weakening and abandonment of collusive market arrangements reduced the solidarity of employers and increased competition.[12] In turn, the extension of the market to include foreign competitors made it difficult to bring in all producers and this put pressure on employers to search more for plant-level cost-minimising solutions. In addition, in many British firms, bargaining levels were further complicated by the existence of multiunionism. Employers confronted by different unions for adjacent or even the same group of workers encountered difficulties in coordinating bargaining, problems of demarcation, and leapfrogging wage claims. This was in contrast to countries such as the US, West Germany, and Japan where, in their evolving collective bargaining systems, the levels and units of bargaining were better defined and more formal.[13]

Wage drift fluctuated between and within industries and varied over time with changing economic circumstances. In general, the gap between negotiated rates and actual earnings tended to widen.[14] This was most pronounced in the engineering, shipbuilding, and metal manufacturing industries where national agreements had been the most skeletal, where wage structures were most chaotic, and where shop steward organisation was best developed. From the war years onwards, earnings in these industries greatly exceeded basic rates.[15] Studies of the engineering industry show that the level of earnings and the degree of drift also varied within the industry between sectors and firms.[16] Interfirm variations may in part have been due to differences in labour productivity and profitability and differences in the bargaining power of work groups between firms. However, various studies suggested that a large part of wage drift was caused by reliance on piecework systems and the tendency for these to work loose. This in turn often reflected weaknesses in managerial hierarchies and control systems.[17]

In other industries, for example building, general printing, textiles, and papermaking, the degree of workplace wage drift was less. Here national agreements were more comprehensive and work groups and stewards were less powerful. In cotton textiles and footwear, the national system was supported by the fact that national piecework price lists were in operation.[18] In a few industries, for example shipping, baking, and cement, national agreements remained strong well into the post-war period or, as in electrical contracting, even became stronger.[19] These tended to be relatively homogeneous industries, sometimes with administered prices and where strong relations had grown up between national unions and employers' organisations. Overall, however, in the main sectors of manufacturing industry, national agreements became more and more ineffective at least in large and medium-sized firms and increasingly the purported advantages, both market and managerial, of multi-employer bargaining were not realised.

Restrictive work rules

A second main problem area for management, which grew in the 1950s and became more serious in the 1960s, was restrictive job control. In previous chapters it was suggested that there was some diminution in customary labour practices in the 1920s and early 1930s, and later during the Second World War there was some relaxation of job controls to meet wartime production needs.[20] On the other hand, from the upswing of the 1930s onwards and through the Second World War, there was more opportunity for work groups to impose restrictions on management, and these activities spread to new industries such as motor cars, aircraft production, and electrical engineering. Overall, the impression is that, in the postwar period, under the pressure of buoyant demand and full employment, job controls and restrictive labour practices were extended, reestablished, or newly created. National agreements could not deal with details of work organisation which were therefore left to plant and shop arrangements. In traditional craft industries, such as shipbuilding and printing, rules on apprenticeship, demarcation, output, and the use of new equipment remained strong.[21] In the newer motor-car industry, workers were gradually able to impose restrictions on manning levels and line speeds.[22] Even on a greenfield site, away from the main centres of the industry, and in a well-managed company like Ford, management could not prevent the growth of restrictive job controls at its Halewood plant.[23] In an entirely new industry, oil refining and petrochemicals, restrictive practices grew up covering matters such as work rules and overtime.[24] Here, and in other continuous process industries such as chemicals and steel, one of the main problems was in the maintenance area where manning levels were high and craftsmen insisted that they alone should do certain jobs. Along with higher labour costs, this frequently meant high levels of down-time with plant and equipment.[25] Throughout industry in the postwar period, there was a considerable growth of overtime working, with levels rising from an average of one hour per week above normal hours in 1947 to six by 1965. The fact that overtime in part fluctuated with demand would suggest that it existed for good economic reasons. But, since it fluctuated within only a narrow range and, by most international standards, was high in Britain, there is reason to believe that much of it was created and maintained as a form of job control and a way of boosting earnings. Workers, often with management collusion, spun out work during normal hours in order to ensure overtime with its associated premium rates of pay.[26]

It is difficult to say how widespread and how harmful these practices were in terms of economic efficiency. In many firms in industries such as shipbuilding and printing, they constituted real problems for management. In other firms the extent and effect may well have been exaggerated by managers.[27] However, for a growing number of employers, they were perceived as a serious problem and in popular discussion it became common to blame such practices on trade unions.[28] In fact, outside of craft areas, official unions usually played little role in their creation or maintenance and they were rarely the subject of formal agreements.[29] It is more correct to see them as the creation of work groups and shop stewards. In addition, numerous studies have also shown that management action and inaction contributed significantly to the existence of restrictive practices. Where senior management were uninterested or ignorant about the shopfloor, where company structures were weak, and where lower level managers were inadequately trained and coordinated, there was often a failure of management control and shop stewards took advantage of this.

Generalising from the famous case of the Fawley oil refinery, where a range of restrictive practices had grown up in the 1950s, Flanders commented, 'The truth is that the vast majority of managers in British industry prefer to have as little as possible to do with labour relations'; when problems occurred, their reaction was 'to play for safety and to let well alone'.[30] In the steel industry, a US Steel Company delegation sent to investigate the relatively tranquil industrial relations enjoyed by the British industry in the 1950s concluded that relations were good precisely because British managers refused to face up to the real issues and allowed inefficient working practices to proliferate.[31] In national newspaper printing (admittedly an extreme case) an official enquiry concluded about restrictive practices, 'We consider that the employer must carry his share of the responsibility for failing to remove the sense of insecurity which accounts in large measure for the workers' attitude.'[32] Studies in the engineering industry suggested that the weakness of managerial control systems was crucial in creating and sustaining restrictive practices. In Lupton's study of an electrical engineering firm, various restrictions on output and perversions of the company's piecework system had grown up in the 1950s. In a buoyant market and protected by collusive trading arrangements, top management was insufficiently aware of, or concerned about, what was happening on the shopfloor. In these circumstances, lower level management and foremen were susceptible to pressure from, and able to make concessions to, the shopfloor.[33] In a later study of a number of engineering firms, Brown showed how weak managerial control and information systems and plain errors of management at all levels allowed restrictive customs and practices to emerge. Once precedents had been set, the power and determination of workgroups and their shop stewards ensured their continuation.[34]

Strikes and disputes procedures

Though immediately after the war the number of strikes fell, there were ominous signs of impending conflicts since, in some of the main export industries such as motor vehicles, parts of engineering, and chemicals, strike activity rose.[35] From the early 1950s there was an upward trend in the number of stoppages, triggered initially by the collapse of the Labour government's incomes policy, the subsequent change in government, and price rises initiated by the Korean war. Between 1953 and 1959 stoppages outside coal mining rose by 79 per cent; 1960 saw a massive increase in stoppages, when the non-mining total first exceeded 1,000, and throughout the 1960s there was a more or less continuous growth in the number of stoppages. Between 1960 and 1968 non-mining strikes rose by 85 per cent, working days lost by 83 per cent, and the number of workers involved by 283 per cent, and by 1968 the total number of strikes had exceeded 2,000.[36]

Though there were some large national stoppages in the late 1950s in engineering, printing, and transport, most strikes during this period covered only a single plant or department and were of short duration, reflecting the changes in bargaining structure referred to above. In addition an increasing proportion of the strikes in these years were unofficial (in that they took place without the prior authorisation of the national union) and unconstitutional (in that they took place before an agreed procedure had been exhausted). The average strike in the early 1960s directly involved around 500 workers and led to the loss of about 1000 working days; it was estimated at the time that unconstitutional and unofficial strikes made up 95 per cent of all stoppages and accounted for two thirds of the total number of days lost.[37]

Underlying the rising strike trend were economic factors such as full employment and rising prices and social factors such as rising expectations and a less deferential workforce. The trend also reflected institutional factors such as the growing organisation and assertiveness of shop stewards and the weakness and inability of collective bargaining procedures to cope with the changed circumstances.[38] The fragmented nature of workplace bargaining, as we have described it, led to sectional stoppages over matters such as relative wages, the application of incentive schemes, and working arrangements at shopfloor level. Meanwhile, national disputes procedures were unable to contain the growing number of such disputes, and increasingly both management and unions found these procedures cumbersome and remote.[39] In engineering, for example, from its initiation on the shopfloor, through both formal and informal meetings at works level, to local conference and to central conference, with possible reference back, the hearing of a dispute could take several months. With a larger number of cases going through procedure, the time taken to go through the various stages rose, the disposal rate fell, and the number of breaches of procedure grew.[40]

Industry-wide procedures were not designed for particular issues or individual firms. As a study of the motor-vehicle industry concluded: 'One reason for the high strike level of car firms and of the federated firms in particular, seems to be that the present organisation, attitude, agreements and conciliation procedure of the employers' association provide no effective basis for the settlement of the major issues in dispute between the firms and their workers.'[41] Few plants had their own internal procedures other than those laid down in national agreements, and even fewer companies had procedures which allowed disputes to be taken up through the company.[42] The absence of company procedures was in part because membership of employers' organisations was usually on an individual plant rather than a company basis, and the practice was for each factory management to process its own disputes through the procedure. It was thus difficult for management in multi-plant companies to coordinate their activities. Again to take the motor industry, the study previously mentioned concluded:

Procedure requires that formal reference from the plant management concerned should be not to the company's head office but to the local engineering employers' association and then to the Engineering Employers' Federation itself.... Even in some big recent stoppages, it has been unclear whether the company concerned or the employers' association was handling the matter at issue.[43]

Despite the above, a word of caution must be added. It is possible to exaggerate the deleterious effects of strikes on British industry through these years. For example, it has been pointed out that most British employers in the 1950s or 1960s were never confronted by a strike or the threat of a strike. Employers most likely to be affected were in mining, motor vehicles, shipbuilding, and port transport and within these industries strikes tended to be concentrated in a few large plants.[44] Differences in reporting the incidence of strikes make international comparisons hazardous, but they do broadly show that Britain was not too badly placed in terms of the proportion of working time lost through strikes. The USA was always higher; Japan was higher for a time in the late 1940s and early 1950s; and Canada and Italy also tended to be higher through most of these years. However, some of Britain's main European competitors, W. Germany and France, were consistently lower. Moreover, over the course of the 1960s, Britain's relative position deteriorated.[45] In addition there was a growing feeling in Britain, at least among employers, that small 'wildcat' strikes were more damaging in that they were less predictable than the larger official strikes which took place, for example, in the US or W. Germany. As one British employers' representative noted: 'The impact of a strike of this character is much less severe than the more frequent unconstitutional strikes which are so typical of the British situation.'[46]

Levels of wages and labour costs

The final problem area for management concerned wages and their effects on costs, prices, and profits. These effects were threefold. First, for the firm, an increase in money wages, which was not offset by a commensurate improvement in productivity, meant higher costs. Where prices could be increased, without loss of market share, this was less of a problem, at least for the firm. But, in a hard market environment, rising unit labour costs and price increases threatened the firm's competitiveness. Second, where labour costs were rising faster than productivity and where a firm could not pass on its growing costs in higher prices, its profit margins were squeezed. In turn, this could discourage investment and threaten the longer term viability of the enterprise. Third, frequent changes in wages and prices caused greater uncertainty for the firm, uncertainty about how the wages and prices of competitors would adjust and about the future demand for the firm's products. In these circumstances it became increasingly difficult for the firm to price its products and to assess its rate of return. In addition, frequent adjustments in wages involved other costs, not least of which was the possibility of strike action.

For a long time, British manufacturers had been unaccustomed to dealing with the consequences of a strong upward pressure on costs and during the war many operated under cost plus contracts which meant that commercial pressures on them were weak. After the war, in the new market conditions of high demand, firms were at first able to cover higher costs by higher prices without appreciable loss of business. Overall, during the early 1950s money wages rose no faster in Britain than among its main competitors. But, since productivity growth in Britain was lower, unit labour costs rose more rapidly. From the late 1950s to 1964 money wages abroad rose faster than in Britain and though the productivity differential remained, unit costs in Britain grew less rapidly than in Germany, France, Italy, or Japan, but faster than in the US. However, from the mid-1960s, wages began to rise faster in Britain while relative productivity lagged and, as a result, relative costs in Britain increased rapidly. Devaluation in 1967 provided a temporary respite. However, as earnings in Britain began to accelerate from about this time and as relative productivity growth did not improve, competitiveness had been largely lost by 1973.[47] Through these years also, as was shown in Chapter 6, the product market was becoming more competitive. Increasingly these factors, together with growing trade union wage pressure, began to affect profits.[48] The profit rate, which had been falling slowly since the mid-1950s, fell more rapidly from the mid-1960s, and it has been estimated that, between 1964 and 1973, net profits fell by nearly a half.[49]

Of course all this is not to say that industrial relations factors were the only, or indeed the main influences on costs, competitiveness, and profits. However, from the mid-1960s onwards British employers increasingly saw industrial relations as crucial.

Reforming industrial relations

Between the late 1960s and the late 1970s important changes took place in British industrial relations which constituted a significant transformation of the system. In terms of one of the themes of this book, this may be seen as a movement away from strategies of externalisation and a movement towards a growing internalisation of activities within the firm. It was a slow and unsteady transformation, since the problems were deep-rooted and in some respects getting worse. The economic situation, while it acted as a spur, also compounded the problems. After 1969, wage and price increases accelerated to higher levels and fluctuated considerably, and productivity growth lagged behind the growth of wages by more than in any other peacetime period. Together, the rapid rise in money wages, lower productivity growth, and increased competition combined further to reduce profits.[50] In the face of accelerating price inflation, from 1969 trade union density began to increase, especially among white-collar workers. By 1974 it passed 50 per cent of the labour force and by 1979 had risen to an all-time maximum of 55 per cent.[51] Along with this, shop steward organisation spread and became more assertive in challenging management, and workers showed a greater willingness to use strike action. This was the background to reform in these years.

The origins of reform can be traced back at least to the early 1960s. Though, after the war, employers' organisations and national bargaining were taken for granted, there was a growing questioning of their role and function in some large firms. For example, Samuel Courtauld voiced this view in the 1940s when he said, 'Employers are not by any means always well represented by their existing associations, many of which are quite out of date. They were created long since to meet conditions now vanished, but they are very difficult to replace or reconstruct.'[52] Courtaulds itself had outgrown the employers' organisation which served its industry. Other large firms which were similarly only loosely connected with their employers' organisations were ICI, Unilever, Imperial Tobacco, Pilkingtons, Distillers, the large breweries, Cadburys, Tate & Lyle, British Sugar Corporation, and some of the other large food and drink companies.

In the engineering industry there was also some questioning of the role of the EEF and the usefulness of national bargaining. The 1950 national agreement was an attempt to get away from national across-the-board increases for all workers and to confine industry-wide increases to the lower paid actually on or near minimum rates. This proved unsuccessful in the face of opposition from trade union members who received no national increase and so pushed for one at workplace level. In these circumstances, there was an increase in the number of federated firms which favoured the national agreement becoming a looser safety net.[53] In 1957 the Engineering Employers again attempted to stand firm against an annual general wage claim but, faced with a strike and the lack of government support, the Federation backed down.[54] After this a number of large firms, including Vickers, AEI, Standard Motors, Rootes, Rolls Royce, English Electric, Bristol Aeroplane, and General Electric, combined to criticise the bargaining arrangements and wage structure in the industry and some of the federated motor-car companies considered leaving the national agreement.[55]

A number of official enquiries drew attention to the problems of national bargaining and complicated wage structures. Academic commentators also began to point to the growing significance of plant bargaining and to suggest that wage determination should be confined largely to that level.[56] This was a difficult message for the employers' organisations to accept since it implied a diminution of their powers and raised the spectre of leapfrogging. It also came up against vested interests on the union side. However, through the 1960s a number of employers' organisations came to accept the changed situation, partly at government prompting, but mainly because this was what their members wanted. The 1963 'package deal' in engineering represented a departure: it covered a three-year period; while giving small general across-the-board increases to all, it provided for a minimum earnings level which gave an increase only to those who fell below it; and it attempted to link pay increases to productivity increases. This latter was not particularly successful because, as one representative of the Federation said, 'whilst the money has been conceded nationally, the changes which we were trying to buy were largely changes at the level of the factory'.[57]

Developments were also taking place in other industries. In 1967 the British Rubber Manufacturers' Association negotiated a new type of agreement for their industry. This abandoned across-the-board increases of the 'something for nothing' kind and fixed a minimum earnings level which was not be used as the basis on top of which plant additions were calculated. The explicit objective of the agreement was to transfer wage determination inside the plant, and to relate earnings increases more closely to internal productivity.[58] Similarly, in 1968 the Chemical Industries Association signed an agreement with the unions which stated that company and plant arrangements should govern how national agreements were to be applied.[59] Other employers' organisations came to recognise, albeit grudgingly in some cases, that national agreements were increasingly to be 'safety nets' rather than 'floors' – in other words, when raised they would only affect those actually earning the minimum rate and would not jack up the rates of everyone else in the industry.[60]

Another important development in the early 1960s was the growth of productivity bargaining, to which reference has already been made in Chapter 6. The origins of this type of bargaining are usually attributed to the agreements signed at the Esso oil refinery at Fawley in 1960. In an international productivity comparison, the American parent company had discovered that Fawley showed up badly in terms of labour productivity. Faced with growing competition in the industry, consultants were brought in and the outcome was a series of wide-ranging productivity agreements. Management, unfettered by industry agreements, gave substantial wage increases in return for specific changes in working practices, including relaxation of job demarcations, reductions in overtime, and greater freedom for management to schedule work. The Fawley agreements attracted considerable attention in employer circles and became widely known through the writings of Allan Flanders.[61] Other employers followed in the mid-1960s, led initially by American companies or British firms in capital-intensive industries, such as Mobil Oil, ICI, British Oxygen, Shell Chemicals, in which firms the need for high and continuous throughput was of vital importance. By the end of 1966, 73 major productivity deals had been signed and up to half a million workers were affected by productivity bargaining.[62] The agreements differed in scale and scope, but essentially were attempts, internally within the firm, to trade off wage increases, higher than would have been possible at national level, for certain specific changes in working practices at plant level. These changes included such things as reductions in overtime working, reduced manning levels, increases in flexibility between workers, and the use of work-study techniques often associated with the rationalisation of pay structures.[63] In these deals management tended to take the initiative and usually attempted to bargain with the unions as a group. The agreements differed from earlier bargaining in that they were more far-reaching, more formal, and attempted more explicitly to link wages and working practices. From the mid-1960s, the Labour government encouraged this kind of bargaining as a means of containing inflationary wage pressures. This further encouraged the spread of productivity bargaining: by the end of 1969 the Department of Employment and Productivity registered some 3,000 agreements covering nearly six million workers or 25 per cent of the labour force. Though some of these later deals were merely a way around government incomes policy and, for a time, discredited productivity agreements, nevertheless during these years internal plant bargaining was given a considerable impetus.[64]

In 1968 the Royal Commission on Trade Unions and Employers' Associations (the Donovan Commission), which had been established in 1965 to examine Britain's industrial relations problems, reported.[65] Briefly, the Commission concluded that key sectors of British industry and many leading firms had serious industrial relations problems. These it attributed to deficiencies in the collective bargaining institutions, in particular the gap between the pretence of the national arrangements on the one hand and the reality of workplace bargaining on the other. In a much quoted paragraph it concluded:

Britain has two systems of industrial relations. One is the formal system embodied in the official institutions. The other is the informal system created by the actual behaviour of trade unions and employers' associations, of managers, shop stewards and workers... The informal system is often at odds with the formal system.[66]

More particularly it argued that wage drift, unofficial strikes, and restrictive practices were the result of the inadequate conduct of industrial relations at company and plant level. 'They will persist', it argued, 'as long as companies pay inadequate attention to their pay structures and personnel policies and the methods of negotiating adopted in the workplace remain in their present chaotic state.' Moreover, it argued, 'They will continue until the confusion which so often surrounds the exercise by management of its "rights" has been resolved by the settlement of clear rules and procedures which are accepted as fair and reasonable by all concerned.'[67]

The Report was especially critical of management, arguing that many companies had 'no effective personnel policy to control methods of negotiation and pay structures, and perhaps no conception of one'.[68] Problems would persist, it suggested, as long as firms did not plan their personnel policies and allowed workplace industrial relations to remain outside the control of the management hierarchy. It argued that the primary responsibility for change lay with managers and it looked especially to boards of directors of large companies to take the initiative.[69] More specifically it recommended that they should seek 'comprehensive and authoritative' agreements within the firm, including the establishment of effective negotiating and disputes procedures, written agreements, and new wage systems and structures.[70] This would be based on negotiations with unions and fuller acceptance of the role of shop stewards and would mean an internalisation of industrial relations.[71]

The Donovan report was criticised at the time for various reasons. Many employers felt it placed too much blame on management and underestimated the role unions and shop stewards had played in creating problems.[72] Employers' organisations felt it underestimated the importance of national agreements and that the recommendation for decentralisation of bargaining threatened leapfrogging. However, in the context of the time, the Report was a remarkably powerful document both in terms of its analysis and its prescriptions. In historical perspective, perhaps the main reservation about the Report is that its actual impact has been exaggerated. Firms and employers' associations were already beginning to act in the way Donovan prescribed – and indeed Donovan recognised this.[73] It seems likely that other firms would have followed even without the report. Donovan and other government interventions in the 1960s and 1970s played an important role in educating and encouraging, but the main instigators in reshaping the system of industrial relations were employers.

The further progress of change

From the mid-1960s, as British firms were attempting to reform their overall organisational structures (as described in Chapter 6), they were also trying to sort out their industrial relations problems. Indeed there was a significant connection between overall organisational change and industrial relations. The merger movement of the 1960s may for a time have accentuated some of the labour problems, for example by complicating bargaining arrangements and generating parity claims between plants. However, the subsequent restructuring of firms, often on multidivisional lines, and the development of managerial hierarchies provided firms with a better organisational capability to act. Such reorganisation simultaneously facilitated the setting of strategic goals and imposed more effective control over lower management.[74] Better organised firms had more of a choice to locate bargaining at the level which suited them best. The development of managerial hierarchies, especially the growth in the number and professionalism of personnel specialists, facilitated the planning and coordination of industrial relations strategies.[75]

Many firms undergoing reorganisation on these lines in the 1960s and 1970s felt less need for employer organisation membership, since they were increasingly able to provide their own services internally.[76] For them employers' organisations no longer performed any real protective function. In fact, as we have shown, for many, membership could be harmful. It exposed them to national claims while at the same time restricting the development of their own domestic policies. Diversified firms, which might be members of two or more separate associations, found it difficult or meaningless to reconcile the different national agreements to which they were parties. A number of large firms therefore left their employers' associations. Some, such as Ford and ICI, had never been members or had left many years previously. Others, for example, Esso, Shell, BP, and Alcan, left their associations or loosened their ties in the mid-1960s. By the time of Donovan others were expressing doubts. In evidence to the Royal Commission, the International Publishing Corporation stated that the value of its membership of the British Federation of Master Printers was 'very slight indeed';[77] the electrical company, Philips, stated, 'It is our view that the Engineering Employers' Federation is far too large and ponderous to continue filling what was once a constructive role';[78] and Cadburys resigned from its employers' bargaining body 'primarily because of the rigidity of the national wage system under which flat wage awards are given without recognition of local needs'.[79] There was a similar trend in the engineering industry, where, finally, after a national strike in 1979, in which many companies felt unnecessarily involved, the two largest firms in the industry, GEC and British Leyland, withdrew from membership.[80]

Thus national bargaining became less important and national wage agreements became more like safety nets, with decreasing relevance to companies. Some agreements, as in rubber and parts of the food-processing industry, collapsed altogether. In the case of national procedural agreements, a significant event occurred in 1971 when the engineering unions terminated the historic engineering industry procedure. The unions had objected to various aspects, especially the managerial prerogatives clause and management's claimed priority of interpretation. When agreement could not be reached on a new *status quo* clause, they therefore gave notice to terminate the procedure and the large firms in the industry did nothing to save it.[81] However, it should be stressed that not all employers' organisations declined in membership or importance. Some large firms remained in membership, though usually in order to obtain advisory and lobbying services rather than for collective bargaining purposes. Many medium-sized and small firms continued to rely on their associations and on national agreements and, for them, there was some justification in terms of administrative economies and protection against trade unions.[82] In some industries, such as parts of printing, building, textiles, footwear, and clothing, employers' organisations remained relatively more important. These tended to be industries dominated by smaller firms which failed to develop internal organisational capabilities and for which national collective bargaining still provided some real benefits in terms of controlling competition based on wage-cutting.

The aim of many large firms through the 1970s was to relocate and formalise collective bargaining. This meant bargaining somewhere *below* the level of the industry but *above* the level of the shopfloor. The intention then was to internalise industrial relations and reduce the number of bargaining points thereby tailoring agreements to the firm's needs and strengthening management's position. There were important differences between firms as to the degree of centralisation and the level of collective bargaining. In some firms, for example, ICI, Ford, Kodak, and the British Sugar Corporation, collective bargaining was highly centralised covering all or most of the firm's activities. These tended to be firms with relatively standardised products, integrated production systems, and centralised, functional forms of organisation. Other firms, such as British Leyland, moved in this direction in the late 1970s. On the other hand, some firms, such as Pilkingtons, Lucas, Philips and Cadburys, began to decentralise their bargaining arrangements. Some diversified companies, such as Unilever, Imperial Group, and Reed International, usually with clear product market categories and multidivisional structures, have chosen to bargain at divisional level for many of their activities. Many firms, where production units were not particularly integrated and where there was more plant autonomy, chose to bargain primarily at plant level. This included firms such as GEC and GKN in engineering and Courtaulds and Coats Vyella in textiles.[83] These differences in bargaining levels in large part reflected differences in corporate structure and showed the growing capability of managements to make new strategic choices in industrial relations.

In the circumstances of the 1970s, when trade union power remained strong, employers saw the need to introduce these changes through collective bargaining with unions. In fact, increasingly they preferred to deal with shop stewards internally within the firm rather than with full-time union officers.[84] The number of stewards rose from roughly 175,000 in the mid-1960s to about 300,000 by the late 1970s. At the same time firms tried to deal with more organised and formal joint shop stewards' committees led by senior stewards and convenors. This was reflected in the facilities which were afforded shop stewards and the growing number recognised as full-time by management which rose in manufacturing from about 1,000 at the time of Donovan to about 5,000 in the late 1970s.[85] In some instances where workplace organisation was less developed, management even took the initiative in order to mould it more effectively from the start.[86]

In the 1970s managements were also prepared to go further in providing union security. There were potential problems for management in going so far as to recognise the closed shop: it reduced management flexibility in recruitment and threatened to increase union strength. On the other hand, it offered the prospects of stability and discipline. In calculating the costs and benefits, an increasing number of managers felt it was best to concede the closed shop. The number of workers covered by such arrangements rose from about one in six in the early 1960s to about one in four by 1978, and the closed shop spread beyond traditional sectors into chemicals, oil refining, and food and drink. In manufacturing industry as a whole about half the union members were covered by closed shop arrangements which also tended to be more formal and more explicitly supported by management than previously.[87] In addition, by the late 1970s in three quarters of workforces where manual unions were recognised employers had agreed to collect union dues through check-off arrangements.[88] Together these developments (the growth in the number and power of shop stewards, management's preference for dealing with them rather than full-time officers, and the development of joint shop steward committees) may be seen as the growth of a form of unionism internal to the firm.[89]

Firms also made progress in tackling problems of internal wage structures and payment systems. From the mid-1960s, there was a movement away from piecework and towards measured daywork schemes – payment by time dependent on the achievement of work-studied output targets.[90] (This and the diffusion of work study techniques were also part of the continuing, though not always successful, effort to deal with restrictive work rules.[91]) In addition, through the 1970s, there was a significant increase in job evaluation for blue-collar workers. This will be examined in more detail in the next chapter. It is sufficient to state here that both measured daywork and job evaluation favoured plant-wide bargaining and involved the reform of internal wage structures.[92]

Inevitably the process of change was not without its problems for management and led to some opposition from the workforce. The extension and formalisation of collective bargaining, though intended to enhance management control, simultaneously increased the number and power of shop stewards.[93] As the scope of collective bargaining expanded, so the area of managerial prerogatives was challenged. Given the strength and self-assurance of the shopfloor, much informality remained and new customs and practices were created. In some situations, after management had bought out restrictive work rules in productivity-type bargaining, they were unable to prevent the creation of new ones.[94] The number of strikes, outside coal mining, rose to 2,930 in 1969 and to 3,746 in 1970. Subsequently the number of working days lost in strikes fluctuated, with high points in 1972, 1974, and 1979.[95] However, a growing proportion occurred in the public sector where they were often a direct or indirect response to government intervention in the form of incomes policies. In the private sector strikes became bigger and longer, in terms of the number of workers involved and the working days lost through each strike, and the small, sectional, unofficial strike fell in relative frequency.[96] This reflected the impact of managerial reform strategies, the move to company- and plant-wide bargaining, and the reform of payment systems.

The growth of white-collar unionism was an issue with which employers had to contend in the 1970s. In some firms union membership for white collar workers had existed for many years; in other firms it was an entirely new phenomenon. The density of private-sector white-collar unionism rose from 12 per cent in 1968 to 27 per cent in 1973 and continued to increase thereafter up to 1979 but at a slower rate.[97] In the face of this, employers' traditional opposition to the unionisation of white-collar staff diminished in the course of the 1970s. Attempts to compete with unions via staff associations continued, though a growing number of firms felt it best to recognise the orthodox unions in order to forestall any further problems.[98] Overall employers established better bargaining arrange-ments and procedures and more effective salary structures with greater use of incremental pay increases than had been the case with blue-collar workers. On the other hand, difficulties did arise. Multiunionism was a problem for some employers and strike activity increased among white-collar workers. Perhaps more important, given the continued weakness of managerial hierarchies in Britain, union organisation spread further up the supervisory and managerial structure than many employers thought desirable.[99]

Through the 1970s, governments offered support with reform, but also created industrial relations problems for employers. In the area of trade union law, the Conservative government's 1971 Industrial Relations Act, with its provision for legally binding agreements, machinery to deal with multiunionism and procedural problems, and legal protection against a number of unfair industrial practices, was designed to be of use to employers. However, most employers were extremely reluctant to use the law. Clearly, the strength of union opposition to the Act was an important factor, but employers also calculated that in the circumstances of the time it was best to rely on their own strategies for reform rather than have recourse to the law. For example, the Act introduced severe restrictions on the operation of the closed shop, but jointly managements and unions evaded them and the closed shop continued to operate.[100] In the late 1970s, the threat of a legal imposition of worker directors at the time of the Bullock Commission of Enquiry on Industrial Democracy was resisted by employers who feared that the trade union channel of worker representation would excessively strengthen union power and extend bargaining into major corporate decisions.[101] The report and the possibility of EEC-inspired legislation, however, made managements realise that some action was required.[102] As a result, some tried to build on existing schemes, while others introduced new consultative arrangements, both often alongside collective bargaining. By the late 1970s more than 40 per cent of manufacturing plants had some sort of consultative arrangements, most introduced during the course of the 1970s.[103] These were necessarily always internal to the firm, organised at plant level as in BP or based on a more complex, hierarchical system as at Cadbury-Schweppes and British Leyland.[104]

Government intervention in the form of the Donovan and Bullock reports, new labour legislation, and the activities of agencies such as the Commission on Industrial Relations and, later, the Advisory Conciliation and Arbitration Service played an important part in the changes of the 1960s and 1970s. Such intervention raised employers' awareness, stimulated action, and encouraged the formalisation of rules and procedures. Overall, however, as the Donovan Commission itself prescribed, employers took the initiative in developing industrial relations internally within their companies. This they did slowly and uncertainly, impelled by economic factors and the need to tighten control. A number of large firms led the way, some with good industrial relations such as ICI or BP, others impelled by pressing problems such as British Leyland and other engineering companies. The move to single-employer bargaining, with plant, divisional or corporate agreements and more formality, was significantly related to larger plant and company size.[105] Also, foreign multinationals played an important part. In the late 1970s about a quarter of the 4,000 largest private companies in Great Britain were foreign owned and in manufacturing around one in five jobs were in such firms.[106] These were often leaders in terms of the employment of personnel specialists, the move to single-employer bargaining, the development of more formal agreements, and the use of new forms of payment system.[107]

As a postscript, the 1980s have seen important changes, but also considerable continuity in industrial relations. In the changed economic, political, and legal climate, trade union membership fell by three million, legislative changes have considerably restrained union activities, and the number of strikes declined. At workplace level the closed shop has been curtailed and shop steward influence reduced. In these circumstances, management seized the opportunity to push through changes in industrial relations practices which resulted in major defeats for unions in sectors such as motor vehicles, steel, coal mining, printing, and shipping. Less dramatic, but more important, employers have enforced concessionary agreements allowing changes in working practices and have sought to reduce collective bargaining as a constraint on their activities. In parallel they have increased the scope of unilateral management action and have extended non-union-based consultation and participation systems. However, there have also been significant continuities with the 1960s and 1970s. There have been relatively few cases of the derecognition of unions and collective bargaining still remains the main form of joint rule-making in industrial relations. Despite a growing formality of industrial relations, in line with long traditions of informality in Britain, shop stewards have retained a degree of influence as evidenced by the price in terms of wage increases which employers have had to pay for change.[108] The trend towards internal, single-employer bargaining has continued, often with a further decentralisation to plant rather than company or divisional level.[109] There has also been a continuing trend towards the insulation of bargaining from outside forces, with pay and conditions more related to inside forces such as productivity and profitability. Thus, many of the changes of the 1980s have been built on the developments of the two previous decades.

Conclusions

By the late 1970s a new industrial relations system had emerged in Great Britain. Internal single-employer bargaining had largely superseded external or national bargaining in importance. In manufacturing industry, in plants employing 50 or more workers, single-employer bargaining was the main method whereby wages and conditions were determined for two thirds of manual workers. Multi-employer bargaining, on the other hand, which before and immediately after the Second World War was a major source of wages and conditions in most industries, remained so for only a quarter of manual workers. In the case of non-manual employees, for whom multi-employer bargaining had never been so important, three quarters had their wages and conditions determined mainly at company or plant level.[110] In parallel with this, informal and fragmented shopfloor bargaining had also been much reduced and agreements tended to be more comprehensive, covering the whole of a plant or a number of plants in a company. Along with this, personnel management had become more professional, procedures and agreements more elaborate and formal, and wage systems and work standards more tightly defined and related to internal company criteria.

Management's overall structures and bargaining preferences in particular market contexts have been the key determinants of the structure of collective bargaining. Multi-employer bargaining was initially the product of small firms or loosely co-ordinated larger firms, often in situations where product markets were administered or protected and where labour markets were loose. The development of fragmented shopfloor bargaining in the post-Second World War period coincided with weak holding-company type firms and weak managerial hierarchies in a context of growing product market competition and full employment in the labour market. The emergence of more formal single-employer bargaining is based on more centralised and better coordinated companies which have attempted to control their industrial relations and improve efficiency to meet the challenge of more competitive markets. Over the period of a quarter century, British firms have, largely in response to market forces and the need to regain control, sought to internalise their industrial relations within the firm.

8 Employment relations in the post-war period

In the area of employment relations the pattern delineated in earlier chapters may be summarised as follows. From the nineteenth century onwards British employers relied to a large extent on market mechanisms and externalised their employee relations; they hired and fired as demand dictated; they provided minimal training; and wages were related in various ways to market criteria, such as the 'going rate' for labour or the selling price of the product. The attachment of the worker to the employer was limited and internal employment systems were rudimentary. In some firms this pattern was tempered by vestiges of traditional paternalism of an *ad hoc*, personal nature. However, this was of decreasing applicability to the large, multi-plant enterprise which emerged during the course of the twentieth century. Yet in only a few such large firms had more complex internal employment systems developed by the end of the interwar period.

In the post-Second World War years, economists have identified and analysed so-called internal labour markets.[1] By this, they mean that employment systems can exist within firms which are relatively insulated from the external market and are regulated by a complex set of internal administrative rules and procedures. Thus firms hire workers into a limited number of entry jobs and then rely upon training and promotion to fill the majority of higher level jobs. To this end, jobs within the firm are ordered into something like a promotional hierarchy and, in competing for these jobs, employees are not subject to strong competition from workers outside the firm. In addition, the firm tries to avoid redundancies and attempts to maintain employment stability for key workers and disciplinary codes and procedures prevent arbitrary dismissal by supervisors. Pay is decided by internal administrative criteria, such as seniority and merit as adjudged by management, and more extensive non-wage benefits are provided. As a consequence of these arrangements, the attachment between the employer and the worker is more complex and longer term.

Various reasons have been suggested in the literature for the growth of internal labour markets or this form of modern, bureaucratic paternalism. First, technology and training are cited as important causal factors. Over time, it is argued, production processes and procedures have become more firm-specific and employers have to train workers accordingly. Because of the investment in firm-specific training, it makes sense for employers to hold on to their labour force and for workers to stay in their jobs. To achieve this, the firm offers its workers greater job security, the prospect of advancement, good wages, and fringe benefits. This, it is argued, is more likely to occur in parts of the economy where demand is particularly stable.[2] A second explanation stresses the need for managements in large firms to control or motivate mass work forces. Radical economists have argued that employers seek to control their labour force by segmenting it into hierarchical categories, by offering the carrot of promotion, and by providing an array of benefits which tie the worker to the firm.[3] More neo-classical economists have suggested that employers can better motivate and monitor their labour force when they offer greater job security, internal promotion, and hierarchical wage and benefit scales which reward employees according to seniority and contribution rather than market forces.[4] In either case, big firms are leaders in this respect because they have both a greater incentive and ability to set up internal labour market arrangements.[5] A third explanation places the emphasis as much or more on workers and their unions. Workers, it is argued, dislike instability and uncertainty: they therefore have good reason to support the development of internal institutional mechanisms for controlling competition, allocating jobs, and rewarding seniority. Through their unions, they press for such arrangements and defend them once established. A variant of this argument is that indirectly the threat of unions forces employers to set up internal labour markets either to keep unions out or contain them once organised.[6] Of course, there are other possible explanations for such arrangements. For example, it could be argued that the state has been a major force, both in terms of providing the example of secure employment in the public sector and by means of legislation setting employment standards.

This chapter explores some of these issues. It argues that, in the period since the Second World War, there have been significant changes in the employment relationship and a faster growth of internal labour markets in Britain. However, there have also been considerable continuities with Britain's past and with policies and practices of externalisation. The following sections deal with patterns of employment and job tenure; recruitment, promotion, and termination of employment; training; and wages and other benefits.

Patterns of employment and job tenure

The background story of the labour market since 1945 can be divided roughly into two parts, the transition point between the two being in the early 1970s. Unemployment averaged 1.7 per cent during the 1950s and 2 per cent during the 1960s. The strong demand for labour during this period was the result of a slowdown in the growth of the workforce and a more stable demand for labour from firms. At each cyclical peak there were shortages of labour, especially skilled labour. Though the overall trend of unemployment was slowly upwards, this was not particularly pronounced until the early 1970s. Unemployment then rose, passing the 1 million level or 4.3 per cent of the insured working population by 1975 and 3 million or 13.3 per cent by 1982. Thus, the first quarter century after the Second World War was one of unprecedented full employment and high labour demand; after a transition period, this was followed by unemployment which in the early 1980s approximated interwar levels.[7] In the first period employers were keen to hold on to labour; in the second period workers were keen to hold on to jobs.

In the 1950s and 1960s, full employment and shortages of skilled workers led employers to hoard labour. In the past there had been a tendency for firms to hold on to a nucleus of core workers through recessions. However, in the context of the post-war economic cycle, this became more pronounced. Employers had a greater incentive to hoard given the expectation of upturn and consequent labour shortages. Such labour hoarding can be roughly gauged by the way, during downturns, the percentage reduction in employment was always significantly less than the percentage fall in output.[8] Various explanations for such behaviour have been offered. Some have argued that technological factors and the inflexible way in which production came to be organised meant that firms needed a certain complement of labour in order to run a plant.[9] Others have stressed the costs of hiring and training skilled workers, pointing out that such employees, with associated higher fixed costs of hiring and training, have shown less variation in unemployment over the cycle than unskilled workers.[10] Undoubtedly, in historical terms, labour hoarding and the stability of employment in the early post-war period were influenced by full employment and economic confidence. It has only been from the early 1970s onwards, as the experience of recession has deepened and lengthened, that firms have more readily adjusted their employment relative to output.

On the employees' side, turnover rose rapidly immediately after the war as wartime restrictions on mobility were eased and people began to move out of munitions and back into their old jobs. In the early 1950s turnover rates fell somewhat while still remaining high through the 1950s.[11] As after the First World War, there was an increased managerial interest in turnover and a huge literature developed on its causes and costs.[12] The realisation grew that, since turnover varied greatly between firms in the same industry and locality, it could not be explained solely by external economic factors, but was partly affected by internal institutional arrangements. Commentators at this time started to write about policies and practices which firms could adopt to increase retention.[13] As one engineering manager commented, the need was to develop arrangements 'to build up a positive loyalty'. He went on:

Such a process takes time, and many experiments must be tried in the course of it. Pension schemes, long-service awards, a clear statement of promotion prospects, careful explanation of wage rates, possibly profit sharing, will have an effect in offsetting the natural tendency to rush off to where a few shillings more a week are being offered, by the confidence in a more solid and secure reward for faithful service.[14]

Writing about policies to reduce turnover one study concluded, 'The true cost of these schemes is not the total outlay on them but this outlay less the savings resulting from the lower turnover.'[15] The costs which were usually identified were the costs of hiring and training, lower productivity of new workers, and the higher costs of supervising a rapidly changing labour force. A later British Institute of Management study put this more positively: 'Surely the main objective of all welfare schemes, pension plans, social clubs and the like is something far more positive than merely to prevent employees leaving the company. They could be said to be undertaken to raise morale and increase productivity.'[16]

Official figures show that hiring and leaving rates in manufacturing industry per month averaged 2.9 per cent and 2.7 per cent respectively through the 1950s and 2.7 per cent and 2.7 per cent through the 1960s. From the late 1960s onwards, the turnover rate declined: it fell from 2.2 per cent and 2.4 per cent respectively in the 1970s to 1.4 per cent and 1.7 per cent in the early 1980s.[17] Though there is a clear inverse relationship between the level of business activity and labour turnover, other studies have also shown a variation between and within industries in the levels of turnover. Industries with low labour turnover have been chemicals, oil refining, and other industries dominated by large firms with more firm-specific production technologies and more sophisticated internal labour policies; those with high labour turnover have been construction, textiles, and clothing.[18] Within the same industry and the same locality turnover has been observed to vary considerably between firms, in large part reflecting size, capital intensity, and the adoption of internal labour market type arrangements.[19]

From the late 1960s, as rising unemployment and restricted job opportunities have reduced turnover, the proportion of long-tenured workers
has risen in most industries. The existence of a 'core' of long-service
employees and a periphery of 'floaters' has long been noted.[20] One study
estimated that, for full-time adult males in 1968, 44 per cent of jobs
lasted for 20 years or more and 69 per cent for 10 years or more. However,
there were significant differences between industries. For example, in the
private sector, 55 per cent of the jobs in chemicals were estimated to last
for 20 or more years, whereas the percentage for textiles and construction
were 35 and 22 per cent respectively. Not surprisingly, white collar sectors
such as banking and finance had the highest proportion of long-lasting
jobs at 71 per cent.[21] Unfortunately, there is no statistical series to prove
that jobs have become longer-lasting over time, but various pieces of
research do support the proposition that the proportion of long-tenured
workers has been increasing in most industries and that average job
tenures are longer than in the US, about the same as in France and
Germany, but shorter than in Japan.[22]

A number of factors may be adduced to explain the changing pattern
of employment stability, labour turnover, and job tenure. Macroeconomic
factors have been important, especially the demand for labour and the
level of unemployment. Technological change and increasing capital
intensity may also in part explain higher levels of labour stability and
retention. However, they alone cannot explain variations, especially
within industries. Other factors of an institutional nature must be
included, such as changes in employment practices, training, pay structures, and fringe benefits between industries and between firms. Each of
these will be examined in turn in the following sections.

Recruitment and job tenure

Since the Second World War, selection procedures for manual workers
have slowly become more sophisticated and formalised, especially in
larger firms. Immediately after the war, in part as a consequence of
wartime military selection practices, there was an increased use of tests
and more extensive interviewing.[23] With the growth of personnel departments, recruitment became more centralised and fewer firms allowed
foremen freedom to hire. Of course, 'word of mouth' and other *ad hoc*
recruitment practices continued, but overall the trend was towards centralisation and systematisation. In the period of tight labour markets and
labour shortages in the 1950s and 1960s, the cost of hiring was high
and many better-managed firms increasingly realised that they had

to pay great attention to recruitment and induction in order to reduce turnover.[24]

In the area of termination of employment, a distinction must be drawn between redundancy and disciplinary dismissals. In both areas British employers had traditionally claimed the right to lay off and dismiss at will. During the Second World War, however, the freedom of employers to discharge an employee from a scheduled employment was restricted (as was an employee's freedom to leave an establishment). After the war, there was a slow but steady growth of procedures and formal rules in this area. The practice of giving notice or making a payment in lieu became more widespread. In the case of redundancy, before the war a few exceptional firms had instituted policies of advance notice and severance payments. After the war these became more widespread in large public- and private-sector organisations and, in the 1950s, the practice of 'last in, first out' became better established when reductions in the labour force were necessary.[25] For example, in the motor industry, particularly subject to employment instability, a strike in 1956 against British Motor Corporation's dismissal of 6,000 workers without notice forced management to agree to pay compensation and to accept the 'last in, first out' formula.[26] In the case of disciplinary dismissals, there was also a development of procedures. Increasingly, line managers and foremen were no longer allowed summarily to dismiss workers without reference to higher management and the personnel department, and this necessitated going through a procedure.[27] The reasons for these changes were complex. Government exhortation and trade union pressures were important. However, in the British voluntaristic tradition, there was no legislation in this area until the early 1970s; and trade unions were ambivalent about formal agreements and procedures on such matters. Much of the initial impetus came from firms which saw personnel advantages in introducing rules and procedures, not least that these offered greater security for employees and thereby improved morale and labour stability.[28]

It is true that through the 1960s the law had an important effect. Three main pieces of legislation must be noted. The Contracts of Employment Act 1963 obliged employers to provide a written statement of the principal terms and conditions of employment, thus ending the informality of purely oral contracts, and it gave employees a right to a minimum period of notice according to length of service.[29] The Redundancy Payments Act 1965 compelled employers to make a payment, based on earnings and length of service, to employees declared redundant after a certain qualifying period of employment.[30] Later amendments obliged employers to give notice of redundancy on a sliding-scale basis according to the numbers involved. The Industrial Relations Act 1971 introduced legal standards and procedures for disciplinary dismissals. It also gave employees the right, depending on a minimum qualifying period, to appeal to an industrial tribunal, where compensation for unfair dismissal could be awarded based on length of service, and from 1976 onwards employees have had the legally enforceable possibility of re-employment.[31]

Legislation on unfair dismissal and redundancy payments had different objectives. The aim of the former was to prevent arbitrary dismissal and to improve job security. The aim of the latter was to give compensation for loss of job security and overall it has probably made workers more willing to accept redundancy. However, to put compulsory redundancy into perspective, it must be stated that this constitutes only a small proportion of total terminations and redundancy is usually the last resort of employers wishing to make reductions in their labour force.[32] When there is a lack of work, employers have increasingly sought to make various adjustments short of redundancy. The practice is usually to cease hiring, reduce overtime, redeploy workers, and to call for early retirement and voluntary redundancies in the hope that natural wastage will sufficiently reduce the labour force. The aim of the legislation on unfair dismissal has been to increase job security and this it has probably accomplished. In 1969 13 per cent of plants employing between 100 and 500 workers sacked more than 6 per cent of their workforce (excluding redundancies); by 1977 the proportion of managers sacking more than 3.5 per cent of their workers had been reduced to 5 per cent.[33] The law has also had a considerable impact on disciplinary procedures: as late as 1969 only 8 per cent of plants had a written disciplinary procedure, whereas by the early 1980s this had risen to over 80 per cent.[34]

Of course employment protection legislation has not created real job property rights. The employer still has the ultimate right to lay off or dismiss; most compensation payments are relatively low; and only a small minority of successful claimants in unfair dismissal cases win re-employment.[35] Overall, the main impact of these laws has been to increase formalisation in terms of written statements and procedures; to make it more expensive to hire and fire workers; and therefore to make firms pay greater attention to the quality of labour they recruit.[36] In these areas the law has given some procedural protection to workers, especially in smaller firms and non-union situations. However, it must be stressed that many of the larger firms were moving in these directions anyway and tended to offer provisions above the statutory base-line.[37]

Traditionally, employers also resorted to temporary lay-offs and short-time working, both in old industries such as textiles and newer industries such as motor vehicles. During the boom years after the Second World War, short-time was used much less than in previous decades in large part because of the greater stability of demand and full employment in the post-war period. A contributory factor may also have been that it became more difficult after the war to use the state unemployment benefit system to support short-time and lay-offs. However, another reason was the growth after the war of guaranteed week arrangements, often negotiated between employers and trade unions. These had their origins in the wartime Essential Work Orders which guaranteed wages if employees were available for work and willing to perform reasonable alternative work.[38] Bevin advocated such agreements to unions at the end of the war:

Does anybody ... want to go back to the hourly payment? I cannot believe it. This standing on and off, this going to the factory door in the morning, and 'Nothing doing, Tom, go home' – surely nobody ever wants to go back to that again.[39]

Guaranteed week agreements have assured workers a proportion of their pay for a specified number of days of short-time or lay-off. The guarantees are usually subject to various qualifications, especially a suspension of the obligation to pay if the lack of work is due to strike action in the firm. Nor do they actually prevent lay-offs and short-time, rather they regulate it by setting a price on its use. By 1980 nine million out of thirteen million workers covered by national agreements were entitled to guaranteed week payments.[40] Over time the provisions have improved both in terms of the proportion of income guaranteed and the duration of their payment.[41]

Turning finally to internal recruitment and promotion. For many manual workers in Britain jobs remained 'dead-end' and promotion prospects were poor. Firms have been slow to develop systematic methods of promotion, and selection for promotion tends to be *ad hoc.*[42] This contrasted with stronger systems of seniority in countries such as the US, Germany, and Japan.[43] However, traditionally in Britain there was always an element of recruitment to higher positions and in a few industries, such as the railways and steel, promotion ladders were highly formalised.[44] Even in engineering, where job structures might be thought to be relatively flat and where craft opposition to the promotion of semi-skilled workers was traditionally strong, there is evidence of an employer preference for internal promotion wherever possible.[45] Over the post-Second World War period promotion systems have, however, become more structured and formalised, with internal advertising on plant notice boards, the right to bid for jobs before outsiders, and some notion of promotion by seniority.[46] In part these developments have come about because of pressure from workers and their trade unions. In part it has been the result of economic pressures, since, in periods of labour shortage, employers will rely more on internal recruitment. However, the practice has continued to grow during periods of labour surplus, suggesting that employers have an interest in developing internal promotion systems.[47]

In conclusion, rules and formal practices have developed on various aspects of employment status which, when taken together, are evidence of the growth of stronger internal labour market-type arrangements. In part these developments were prompted by government legislation and trade union pressure. More, however, they have resulted from the growing pursuit by many employers of strategies of internalisation. This has occurred because, in the post-war period, such firms have had a greater incentive to adopt these practices and a growing capability to administer such arrangements. On the whole, however, these have developed more slowly and are less formalised than in equivalent firms in the USA, Japan, or Germany, and British employers still retain a greater preference for the use of external labour market mechanisms.

Training: limited internalisation and inadequate provision

There are a number of courses of action employers can take to acquire and develop a skilled labour force. They may do no training themselves, but hope to poach labour from other firms and acquire labour from the market. Alternatively, they can provide training for their own workers through external institutions such as technical colleges or government training schemes. Or they can organise their own training internally within the firm, either on-the-job or off-the-job in a special training department, and they may supplement this with day release. Internal training is more likely to be firm-specific and, from an employer's point of view, it is arguable that such training is more efficient and effective:[48] it can be geared to the firm's needs; it can draw on internal specialists and use company plant and equipment; and workers trained in this way may be more attached to the firm since their skills are more closely bound up with it.[49]

As we have seen in earlier chapters, British managements were not particularly well trained themselves and in part because of this they did not value the training of those below them. In addition, because of the availability of labour, including skilled labour on the external market, British employers failed to develop strong internal training arrangements. The main formal method of training in Britain had always been the craft apprenticeship. This was served within the firm, but was always intended to provide a significant proportion of training in all-round skills general to a trade. However, it also involved a firm-specific element which may have increased during the interwar years when employers increasingly misused the apprenticeship system as a form of cheap labour. After the Second World War, apprenticeship was increasingly combined with some form of day-release for attendance at classes in a technical college and this may have enhanced the proportion of general skills.[50] On the other hand, the diffusion of firm-specific technologies and the increased costs of training resulting from higher apprentice wage rates, may have led to an increase in the proportion of firm-specific skills.

In the post-war period the apprenticeship system was subject to growing criticism. Experience during the Second World War had shown that it was possible to train a labour force more effectively and in a shorter time than had previously been thought possible.[51] The apprenticeship system was criticised for failing to provide proper training, for restricting entry into jobs, and for creating a defensive set of attitudes on the part of workers concerned to protect their investment in traditional skills. As the Donovan Commission stated, 'the knowledge that they have virtually committed themselves to a craft for life makes men alert to guard what they consider to be their own preserve and to oppose relaxations in practices which, however desirable and even essential for efficiency, may seem to constitute a threat to their whole way of life'.[52] Thus, in Britain, through the post-war period, the apprenticeship system remained highly resistant to change and was neither modernised as in countries such as Germany and France nor replaced with other forms of in-house training as in Japan and the US.

However, there were some exceptions and some large firms were famous for the training which they provided for both apprentice and non-apprentice labour. Examples were English Electric, Metropolitan Vickers and AEI in electrical engineering; Rolls Royce and Babcock & Wilcox in the manufacture of engines and turbines; Stewart & Lloyds and Richard Thomas & Baldwin in steel; and ICI, Courtaulds, and Dunlop in their engineering workshops. But such firms were in a minority: a survey in the mid-1950s cited only 200 firms with systematic training programmes of a good standard.[53] As a result, in the late 1950s and early 1960s there was a continuing criticism of training in Britain and, in particular, of the inability to overcome shortages of skilled labour.[54]

In response to such criticisms, in 1964 the government introduced the Industrial Training Act. This instituted a levy-grant system whereby firms paid a percentage of payroll into a fund and were rebated if they spent an equivalent amount on approved training. The intention was both to encourage training and to spread the costs. For the main sectors of the economy, industrial training boards were established to administer the system and to promote training. Overall, the legislation probably had a small positive effect on the quantity and a larger positive effect on the quality of training, as an increased number of firms developed training programmes, established special departments, and appointed training officers.[55] Though the training boards were organised on industrial lines, on the whole they probably encouraged a growing element of firm-specific training, especially in non-apprenticed areas.[56]

Despite the initial positive effect of the industrial training boards, from the mid-1970s, there was renewed criticism of the training system in Britain. The anomaly occurred of shortages of skilled labour in a period of rising and high unemployment.[57] In part this was because, with the passage of time, the impact of the legislation lost its effect.[58] However, it was more because, with the advent of recession, British employers cut back on training expenditures and saw little need to develop new training arrangements. The number of apprentices declined from the late 1960s and in the 1980s most of the training boards were abolished by the Conservative government, which replaced them with a more market-orientated set of schemes and an emphasis on general transferable qualifications.[59] This occurred despite a greater awareness of international comparisons which suggested that Britain's main competitors did more and better training. Certainly studies show that in West Germany, the USA, and Japan employer-sponsored and employer-organised training is more extensive than in Britain and foreign firms are more likely to see training as an investment and not a cost.[60]

Overall, over the post-war period there has been a slow but unsteady internalisation of training provision in Britain. However, investment in firm-specific training has, for the most part, been insufficient to encourage the development of strong internal labour markets intended to deter turnover and protect investment in training. Similarly, it might be argued that the slow growth of internal labour markets in Britain and the attraction of external labour markets explains much of the failure on the part of British firms to invest in skill formation and to treat training as an integral part of manpower policies.

Wage and benefit systems

The system of wages and benefits is a central aspect of the employment relationship. Historically, it has been argued in this book that British employers had a preference for fixing wages according to external market criteria. Also, increasingly, from the late nineteenth century onwards, they came to rely on piecework as a method of controlling and motivating workers through short-term incentives. Internal wage structures were largely unplanned and rudimentary. Similarly, non-wage benefits were limited and were very unevenly distributed among the labour force. During the Second World War trends in wages and benefits were somewhat contradictory. On the one hand, external considerations in wage fixing such as cost-of-living and comparability were strong. There was also a further extension of piecework, especially in the munitions industry.[61] On the other hand, there was much greater security in terms of pay and an extension of benefits in areas such as sick pay, canteens, and other facilities. After the war, external elements in wage fixing remained strong, especially with continuing, albeit at first low, levels of inflation and with the growing assertion of external comparability claims in plant bargaining. But, in the post-war years, payment by results grew more slowly. Moreover, increasingly piecework systems had some sort of fall-back guaranteeing basic rates and the tendency was for the variable bonus element to be consolidated into an enhanced base rate.[62]

From the mid-1960s, there was a move away from piecework towards various fixed, time-based systems of payment.[63] Private-sector firms, and especially larger firms and foreign multinationals, increasingly recognised the disadvantages associated with piecework, such as restriction of output, constant haggling over rates, and wage drift. Employers also began to see that piecework was no longer suitable in more automated plants where the pace of work was largely beyond the control of the worker and where more stable systems of remuneration might have a more positive effect on employee relations.[64] Thus in the late 1960s there was an increase in various forms of fixed day rates such as measured daywork, under which workers were paid a fixed time rate conditional on the achievement of a performance standard set by work measurement techniques. By the early 1970s, it was estimated that about 10 per cent of manual workers were covered by measured daywork, with a higher proportion in larger plants. In the motor industry the proportion covered was particularly high. Ford, following the practice of its American parent company, had long used a form of measured daywork; Vauxhall went over to this system in 1956; Chrysler made the transition in the late 1960s; and British Leyland followed in the 1970s, though, because of managerial weaknesses and union strength, this was with considerable difficulties. Management had various objectives in converting to such systems. One was to remove some of the disadvantages of piecework by providing greater stability in earnings while hoping to maintain a high level of effort. Another important aim was to reduce the number of wage rates within a plant and to reform internal wage structures.[65]

Of great importance was the growth of job evaluation, especially in the 1970s. Job evaluation is a set of techniques for analysing and assessing the content of jobs in order to place them in a hierarchy which can then be used as the basis for wage structures. Under one popular method, jobs are analysed in terms of their component factors, for example, skill, responsibility, effort; points are awarded for each factor according to a scale; and the total number of points determines a job's place in the wage hierarchy. Job evaluation had been used in the US in the 1930s and 1940s, and American firms played an important part in bringing it to Britain. It was used by a few large British companies from the late 1930s onwards, though mainly for white-collar jobs.[66] However, in the 1960s and 1970s the techniques came to be used to reform blue-collar wage structures. Between the late 1960s and the late 1970s, the number of manual workers covered by job evaluation rose from about a quarter to around a half.[67] Leaders were large firms in such sectors as chemicals, oil refining, the more modern parts of engineering, and food, drink, and tobacco. It was also significantly more common among foreign multi-nationals than British companies.[68] Management's main objective in introducing job evaluation was to bring order into the wage structure and to produce a hierarchy of jobs within a plant. In this respect job evaluation was intended to harness workers' notions of fairness, and trade union representatives were often involved in the evaluation process. It was also intended to overcome 'opportunistic' attitudes associated with piecework and to encourage a 'stable' view of remuneration, thereby perhaps increasing identification with the firm.[69] There is also some evidence that job evaluation and other fixed wage systems lead to lower labour turnover.[70]

In the 1980s employers have experimented with other payment systems. There has been some interest in plant- and company-wide bonus plans based on internal performance measures such as value added. These are intended to introduce an incentive element into pay, while avoiding the disadvantages of piecework and promoting identification with the firm.[71] There has been a renewed interest in profit-sharing schemes and, to a lesser extent, shareownership plans, in part encouraged by government changes in tax laws. The intention behind such schemes has again been to introduce an incentive which can be plant- or company-wide and which may foster employee identification.[72] There has also been an extension to blue-collar workers of performance-appraisal techniques, hitherto used mainly for white collar workers. These are either intended to provide individual merit bonuses or are used to determine progression up incremental or promotion scales.[73] As of yet, these various pay systems are still only limited in application and their effects are uncertain.

However, they share two important characteristics: they are an attempt by management to assert greater control over wage systems and to stress criteria internal to the firm, such as performance, productivity, and profitability.

Studies in the 1950s and 1960s had pointed to the chaotic state of payment systems and wage structures in many British firms, reflecting a legacy of loose managerial control systems and fragmented bargaining.[74] By the late 1970s, there had been considerable reform of payment systems and rationalisation of wage structures. The spread of new time-based payment systems played a significant part in this trend which was also facilitated by the development of single-employer bargaining. These changes have enhanced individual management's control over the wage structure and have also provided workers with more stability in earnings. Two further consequences need to be mentioned. One is that wage structures within firms have tended to become more insulated from outside pressures. Single-employer bargaining has meant that national agreements have had a decreasing effect and job evaluation emphasises internal relativities rather than external comparabilities.[75] There is some evidence that the level and rate of increase of an individual's pay is now related less to external factors such as the 'going rate' for a particular occupation in the external market and more to internal factors within the firm, such as job structure, seniority, and corporate performance.[76] A second, and related, consequence may have been to create something more like formal job hierarchies within British firms. Of course, job hierarchies always existed, but they had historically tended to be *ad hoc* and less under management control. With the introduction of job evaluation and other techniques, management is in a better position to plan a job hierarchy. Though incremental scales for manual workers are rare, and though promotion ladders are short, there is some evidence that wages rise with seniority in Britain, more than might previously have been thought to be the case.[77]

Non-wage benefits also constitute an important aspect of the employment relationship and, here also, there have been significant changes over the post-war period. By the end of the Second World War, the vast majority of manufacturing firms provided holidays with pay for manual workers and this has since been a taken-for-granted aspect of the employment relationship. Subsequent progress has been in terms of the level of pay and the length of the holiday.[78] Formal sick-pay schemes for manual workers also grew rapidly during the war and in the post-war years. Typically, eligibility required a minimum period of full-time employment with the firm and benefits were related to length of service. By the early 1960s, about half of firms had such schemes for manual workers, with a higher proportion among larger firms. Since then, there has been a slow increase in coverage and improvements in provisions.[79] Pension schemes for manual workers grew rapidly in the first two decades after the war. In 1936 about 2.5 million employees belonged to employer-based schemes; by 1963 this had risen to over 11 million. Of this total, 7.2 million were private-sector employees of whom 5.7 million were manual workers.[80] Membership was higher among white-collar than manual workers, among men than among women, and in the public than in the private-sector.[81] Since the mid-1960s, the growth of coverage has been less rapid, but there have been improvements in the provision of schemes.[82]

A number of points need to be made about the growth of such non-wage benefits. First, benefits have risen significantly over the post-war period. Taking total benefits, including payments in kind and various subsidised services, these have risen in manufacturing industry, as a proportion of average pre-tax remuneration, from 11.1 per cent in 1964 to 19.4 per cent in 1981.[83] For the firm, such payments are fixed rather than variable costs in that the employer is committed to pay them to full-time employees regardless of fluctuations in output or hours.[84] As such they symbolise a longer term commitment by the employer to the labour force. Second, with the exception of paid holidays, they did not come about as a result of trade union pressure. Government intervention had some effect: for example, changes in taxation provisions in the post-war years may have encouraged pensions; on the other hand, it might be argued that the existence of state schemes may have slowed down the growth of fringe benefits in Great Britain. Overall, the main impetus seems to have come from employers.[85] Since benefits tend to be seniority-based and are non-portable between firms, this would seem to suggest that a prime objective, on the part of employers, was to attract and retain labour and to encourage loyalty to the firm. A third point to stress is that fringe benefits are very unequally distributed, with clerical and managerial staff enjoying more and better benefits than manual workers. Thus paid holiday entitlement is less for manual workers; fewer are covered by employer sickness schemes and these tend to be less generous; and fewer are members of pension schemes and, again, these are less generous.[86]

In recent years, however, reflecting the growing, albeit slow, internalisation of the employment relationship, there has been some planned movement towards 'harmonisation'. By this is meant the gradual narrowing of differences between manual and staff employees (at least those below managerial level) in terms and conditions of employment. Sometimes this is referred to as staff status where staff benefits and conditions are gradually extended to manual workers. In some cases, it takes the form of single status, where all employees are treated on a uniform basis. The 1960s saw some movement in this direction, connected in part with productivity bargaining, and the trend has continued slowly through the 1970s and up to date.[87] Over time, there has been some narrowing in conditions such as holiday entitlement and more recently in working hours. Within many firms there has been some, though a less marked, equalisation of pension and sickness provisions. However, considerable differences still exist with respect to liability to lay-off and short-time, redundancy arrangements, time keeping, and other facilities.[88] Firms which have led in the movement towards harmonisation, as in other aspects of employment relations, have tended to be large companies, especially in capital-intensive and technologically advanced sectors such as oil refining, chemicals, pharmaceuticals, and electronics, and among these have been a significant proportion of foreign companies.[89] The initiative for such harmonisation has not come from the government; nor has it usually come from trade unions which have often had an ambivalent attitude. For the most part, as a recent report has stressed, 'the initiative for harmonisation has nearly always come from management'.[90] Aims may have varied at different times: in the 1960s an important aim was to improve recruitment and retention of labour; since the 1970s the desire to improve the flexibility of working has been more important. However, in all cases a significant factor has been to increase commitment and common purpose and to bind workers to the enterprise through an extension of non-wage benefits.[91]

Conclusions

In the years since the Second World War there have been significant changes in the employment relationship. These may be seen as an accelerated decline of old-style paternalism and the development of a more modern bureaucratic paternalism; or they may be seen as a movement from a 'commodity' to a 'welfare' concept of employment, with workers becoming less of a 'variable' and more of a 'fixed' cost; or they may be seen in terms of the development of strategies of internalisation and the growth of more structured internal labour markets. In whatever way they are appraised, they have represented, for many workers, a lengthening and deepening of the employment relationship which, when seen in long-term historical perspective, has become more stable and more complex. However, again, it needs to be stressed that these developments in Great Britain in the direction of internalised employment systems. have been slow and unsteady, certainly in comparision with the larger firm sector in the US, Germany, and Japan, where for the most part internal labour markets are stronger and more structured.

This poses two interrelated questions: why has there been a growth of such arrangements in the post-Second World War period in Britain and why has it been relatively slow and unsteady?

Trade unions have played some part in shaping these developments. They have had a positive effect on the growth of internal labour markets both directly and indirectly. Directly they have pressed for certain types of arrangements, such as 'last in, first out' procedures, guaranteed week agreements, fall-back wages, and internal promotions. Indirectly, it is arguable that the threat unions have posed led employers to react by developing certain countermeasures which facilitated the growth of internal labour markets, such as single-employer bargaining, new day wage systems, and procedures for handling discipline and redundancy. Moreover, once such arrangements were in place, trade unions have defended them, though often at the expense of less well-organised and less advantaged groups.[92] On the other hand, British trade unions have had a retarding effect on the growth of internal labour markets. Unions were traditionally suspicious of management-initiated changes in pay systems and fringe-benefit schemes and they preferred to look, for welfare and health benefits, to the state rather than to employers. Moreover, the existence of multiunionism and the fragmented nature of trade unions in Britain may also have militated against some internal labour market-type arrangements by making it difficult to institute promotion and transfer systems and plant- or company-wide systems of wages and conditions. In particular, craft unions, with their insistence on apprentice-ships, traditional demarcations, and craft rates, may have impeded the growth of internal labour markets in Britain. Overall, it might be con-cluded that the motives of trade unions have been too mixed and their strength insufficient to be the predominant determinant of internal labour market arrangements.

Governments played some part. During the Second World War, govern-ment regulations and interventions in industry set new standards of job security and welfare facilities. In the 1960s and 1970s legislation on contracts of employment, redundancy, dismissals, and employment pro-tection helped formalise arrangements and, for a time, statutory support for training may have encouraged firm-based provision in this area also. However, governments may also have retarded the growth of internal labour markets. The extension of welfare provisions such as pensions, sick pay, and unemployment benefit may have made corporate provision less likely than in countries such as the US and Japan. Paradoxically, in the 1980s, the reversal of some of these policies, the removal of employment rights, and the emphasis on a more market-orientated approach to the employment relationship may also have discouraged the growth of internal labour markets. Overall, the argument presented above has been that government action tended not to initiate changes in the employment relationship, but rather to extend and formalise them.

The conclusion must therefore be that it was employers who took the main initiative as they increasingly adopted strategies of internalisation, especially during the first three decades of post-war full employment. Leaders were large firms in certain sectors of the economy, especially chemicals, oil refining, and some modern sectors of engineering and, among these, foreign multinationals played a significant role. Such firms had both the motivation and the capability to establish and administer internal labour systems. Different considerations may have motivated different aspects of internal labour markets. Thus, for example, liberal paternalist concerns may have been behind the provision of welfare and sick-pay schemes by some employers; in other firms concern to retain labour may have been more important in the introduction of benefits such as pension schemes; considerations of industrial relations and labour discipline may have been behind the establishment of dismissals procedures and the reform of pay systems. It was difficult for employers *ex ante* to calculate the costs and benefits of different policies and only later have the efficiency advantages of certain arrangements been recognised. Thus the *ex post* reasons for maintaining arrangements may have been different from the initial reasons for establishing them.

It was also on the employer's side that substantial barriers to change were to be found. Many British firms continued to prefer policies of externalisation and were disinclined to develop internal labour market arrangements. Among managements, conservative attitudes persisted, and there was a reluctance to see labour as a fixed rather than a variable cost, let alone as an asset. In part this may have been rational given that firms had to weigh any advantages against potential losses in terms of costs and reduced flexibility. There was also a reluctance among British employers to give anything away at a time when unions were pushing for concessions anyway. In addition, fragmented structures and policies in weakly co-ordinated British firms were an obstacle, slowing down the introduction of plant- and company-wide wage and benefit systems.

Two major qualifications need to be registered against this account of the growth of internal labour markets. In the first place such arrangements have not covered all the workforce. In industries characterised by small firms, highly competitive product markets, low capital-to-labour ratios, and low skill requirements, such as textiles and clothing, they are less common. Within industries there are also differences, according to size, corporate structure, and ownership. Within firms there are differences between managerial, clerical, and blue-collar workers and between skilled and less skilled workers.[93] Within multidivisional firms, differences can also exist between different divisions of the company, with stronger internal labour markets in divisions where skills are higher or more specific than in other divisions where skills are less or more general in nature.[94] On the basis of such observations, some have suggested that there is a growing duality within the labour market between primary and secondary sectors. In the primary sector of the market, workers tend to enjoy relatively secure jobs, some chance of advancement, high basic wages and the provision of fringe benefits. In other words, structured internal labour markets exist. In the secondary sector, turnover (voluntary and involuntary) is higher, there is less training, promotion opportunities are poor, and wages and benefits inferior.[95] For the most part workers are unable to move from secondary into primary jobs and economic forces prevent the convergence of the two sectors. However, one must be sceptical about the growth of such a duality,[96] since it may be no more marked today than in the past and, when viewed in long-term historical perspective, the overall tendency has been towards an internalisation of the employment relationship.

The second qualification is that in the 1980s, as a consequence of recession, increased competition, and technological change, internal labour market arrangements in many individual firms have come under strain. The economic situation led to an increased number of redundancies and plant closures and a heightened sense for many of job insecurity. Employers, it is argued, have sought increased employment flexibility and have organised jobs within the firm into a core of primary workers and a periphery of less secure and more disadvantaged workers. This view is consistent with the growth of part-time female employment, temporary work, and subcontracting. However, again some scepticism is required. Much of the growth of externalised types of employment is a result of structural changes in the economy and the growth of sectors where such forms of work have always been more common. It may also reflect supply-side preferences on the part of female workers rather than demand-side strategies on the part of employers. There are also limits to this form of externalisation and important countertendencies.[97] Redundancy for some may strengthen the attachment of remaining workers and it may also make employers more careful in their hiring practices. Employees, with rising expectations, demand greater security and benefits; unions oppose casualisation or impose a cost on its introduction; and, despite amendments to legislation, the law imposes certain constraints. Above all, employers see certain efficiency and control advantages in maintaining internal labour markets. Overall, taking a long-term perspective, the tendency has been towards an internalisation of the employment relationship. However, change in Britain has come about slowly and unevenly, reflecting the *ad hoc* approach of most British employers, and traditional attitudes and practices towards the employment relationship remain strong.

Part 4

Conclusions

9 Markets, firms, and the management of labour

The purpose of this book has been to examine the development of labour management in Britain from the late nineteenth century more or less up to the present. It has argued that historically most British employers externalised many aspects of labour management and only slowly and hesitantly built strong internal structures. The fact that there were always exceptions to this general pattern and that a few large firms pursued strategies of internalisation is explained in terms of different market contexts, corporate structures and managerial hierarchies, and production technologies. In the following section the argument is summarised chronologically. The next section then reformulates the conclusions in more thematic terms. A final section reverts to the propositions outlined in Chapter 1 and draws some broader conclusions.

A chronological overview

The British economy in the late nineteenth and early twentieth centuries was characterised by a large number of small, family-owned and -managed enterprises catering for highly differentiated markets at home and abroad. Internally within most firms managerial hierarchies were weak, and owners often relied on various forms of sub-contracting and on largely independent foremen for workplace control. Some large enterprises existed, notably the railway companies, the gas companies, and a few manufacturing firms, and these had more extensive managerial hierarchies. From the 1870s onwards, British entrepreneurs witnessed an intensification in foreign competition, especially from Germany and the US, and there was a growing recognition of this competitive threat. One response was the merger wave at the turn of the century. However, this mainly resulted in loose defensive amalgamations held together as holding companies and there was a failure to develop more sophisticated managerial hierarchies. Another response to competitive pressures took the form in many industries of periodic attempts at market collusion via trade associations.

Control over work tended to be delegated: inside subcontracting persisted in some industries; foremen had wide discretion in organising and monitoring production; and in craft industries skilled workers had considerable control over the production process. Given the lack of standardisation in many products, there were substantial inputs of both unskilled and craft labour at various stages of production. In part because of the ready availability of labour, including skilled craft labour, technological change came relatively slowly and, by the late nineteenth century, Britain had already fallen behind the US and Germany in certain key industries such as machine tools, electrical products, and motor vehicles which were more physical- and human-capital-intensive. However, in some sectors, such as chemicals and food processing, there were substantial changes and a more extensive division of labour emerged. Overall the main formal method whereby skills were acquired was the traditional apprenticeship system. This entailed delegation of training responsibilities to senior workers and training in all-round skills intended to produce workers who were craft- and not firm-orientated. In these circumstances craft workers acquired centrality and had a considerable degree of control over production processes.

For the most part employers pursued a *laissez-faire* approach to the employment relationship; confronted by a buyer's market for labour, they accepted little responsibility for employment security and welfare; job tenure was precarious for most workers, and benefits were minimal. It was expected that wages would fluctuate with market forces or with levels of output and, from the late nineteenth century, there was an increased reliance on payment by results. However, in many firms traditional forms of paternalism persisted on a personal and *ad hoc* basis. More significantly for the future, in a few large firms, on the railways and in some areas of manufacturing, there were the beginnings of more complex bureaucratic employment systems with longer-term jobs, promotion hierarchies, and more extensive benefits.

A significant development in the late Victorian period was the increased recognition by employers of trade unions for male manual workers. Along with recognition, employers took the initiative in developing a system of regional collective bargaining based on membership of employers' organisations. The resulting collective agreements established rudimentary machinery for negotiating and handling disputes, set basic wages and conditions, and attempted to uphold managerial prerogatives. Though such agreements were mainly regional, before the First World War there were already a few which had attained a national scope. Yet most of the agreements remained skeletal and, at workplace level, a combination of unilateral management regulation, autonomous craft control, and informal customs and practices were more important.

The First World War saw an increased division of labour in the munitions industries, but also revealed continued employer dependence on skilled workers and the economic weakness of certain sectors. During the war, there was an extension of employee welfare programmes, some of which continued into peacetime. Of greatest importance in terms of labour management, wartime conditions brought about a significant growth of collective bargaining: shopfloor bargaining grew in importance and, in an attempt to contain it, employers sought to extend formal bargaining through employers' associations at the industry level.

The interwar economy was marked by sharp fluctuations in demand, and from 1920 the labour market was characterised by persistently high unemployment. Through the interwar years, there were important changes in the structure of the economy, with significant growth of industries such as motor vehicles, electrical products, chemicals, and food processing. The importance of large firms increased, especially after the merger wave of the 1920s, and along with this went some elaboration of managerial hierarchies. However, most large firms continued to be managed by family members and remained loosely coordinated with weak managerial structures. In the product market general protection was introduced in 1932 and restrictive agreements grew both in numbers and effectiveness. Together these developments weakened competitive pressures on firms.

In terms of work relations, in the interwar years, there were considerable continuities, especially in the old staple industries, but also some important changes in production techniques and work organisation. Reliance on unskilled-labour and craft-intensive production remained strong in many industries. Rather than opting for rationalisation and mechanisation, employers, for example in coal and cotton, pursued policies based on work intensification and wage reductions. In other industries, such as engineering, there was a further extension of payment-by-result systems aimed at increasing productivity by the use of simple financial incentives. It was mainly in the newer industries, such as motor cars and electrical products, that there was a spread of mechanisation and assembly-line techniques, although, even here, British employers relied more on labour-intensive methods, indirect control, and piecework than did their American counterparts.

In the area of employment practices, changes also came slowly. Among those who kept their jobs during the interwar depression, turnover was lower and, in this sense at least, attachment to firms stronger. Old-style localised paternalism declined, not least because of the development of large multi-plant enterprises. In contrast to this, there was some growth in a more bureaucratic paternalism, with the advent, for some workers, of fringe benefits such as paid holidays, pension schemes, and sick pay. Overall, however, high unemployment provided little incentive to innovation in terms and conditions of employment. The same applied to training, where during the interwar years employers increasingly regarded the apprenticeship system as a source of cheap labour and failed to develop the system or create any alternative arrangements.

Employer recognition of trade unions grew substantially during and immediately after the First World War, and there was a significant extension of industry-wide, multi-employer bargaining. In this way employers hoped to avoid workplace bargaining, to defend managerial prerogatives, and take wages out of competition. Subsequently, through the interwar depression, when they had the power to make changes if they had so desired, the employers chose to maintain this system and did little to develop it further. However, from the recovery of the mid-1930s onwards, the system of industry-wide bargaining showed increasing strains. The enforcement of formal managerial rights became more problematic, unconstitutional strikes occurred, and wages at workplace level began to drift upwards above nationally negotiated rates.

The Second World War brought about an extension of mass-production methods and new techniques in the armaments industries. But again it showed up basic problems associated with traditional methods of production and low productivity in the British economy. As in the First War, there was an extension of welfare arrangements within factories, and workers experienced greater job security. In wartime circumstances, further recognition was accorded to trade unions, especially at workplace level, and there was simultaneously an extension of formal industry-wide bargaining arrangements.

With the peace began thirty years of economic buoyancy and full employment, during which the economy experienced faster growth than ever before, though this proved to be slower than in other industrial countries. In product markets there was a significant increase in competition, resulting from trade liberalisation, legislation curtailing restrictive trading practices, and the emergence of foreign competitors. In the labour market, employers were for the first time over such a long period confronted by full employment and labour shortages. From the 1960s onwards the competitive threat was increasingly recognised and prompted new corporate strategies. In particular the 1960s saw a renewed merger wave and a trend towards diversification. At first many of these larger firms continued to be organised on traditional holding-company lines, but there was a growing recognition of the need to build better corporate structures and improved managerial hierarchies. Significant changes in this respect occurred during the 1970s and 1980s, but weaknesses in terms of managerial structures and hierarchies persisted which constrained the development of strategies in the labour management area.

The postwar years were marked by accelerated technical innovation and changes in work organisation. In addition, management techniques, especially work study, grew in popularity. However, there was simultaneously an increase in restrictive work practices imposed by trade union members in a tight labour market. Among managers, the reason increasingly given for poor productivity performance was labour relations, and from the 1960s onwards this became a subject of growing concern among employers. It became more and more apparent that the formal industry-wide system of collective bargaining was unable to contain the increase in workplace bargaining pressures – growing restrictive practices, unconstitutional strikes, and wage settlements in excess of productivity growth. As a result, from the mid-1960s, employers started to take new initiatives in the reform of the collective bargaining system. This involved a move to single-employer bargaining, the reform of wage systems and structures, and more sophisticated company and plant personnel management. Viewed in longer term perspective, these constituted a significant transformation of the British system of collective bargaining.

In a context of full employment and stronger trade unions, management also had to pay more attention to other aspects of employment policy. In the postwar period there was an extension of non-wage benefits – paid holidays, sick pay, and pensions. In addition, from the 1960s onwards a movement began away from traditional piecework towards time-rated wage systems and more planned wage structures. Protection against arbitrary dismissal and rules governing lay-offs and redundancy grew. In the post-war period there has also been some increase in in-house training, though this has remained insufficient in both quantity and quality and is still a significant weakness of the British economy.

It is still too early to discern the effects of changes in the 1980s under the Thatcher administration. However, a few general points can be made. In industrial relations, the changed economic, political, and legal situation created new opportunities and encouraged employer initiatives. Trade union membership has declined and there have been major offensives against traditional union control over working practices in some sectors – motor vehicles, steel, coal mining, printing, and shipping. Less dramatic, though more significant, initiatives have included a further decentralisation of bargaining structures, especially to plant level, and the negotiation of more flexible methods of working. There has been some, though limited, derecognition of trade unions, and firms have also sought to play down collective bargaining and to develop alternative consultative channels with their employees. In terms of employment relations, the economic conditions and a new political rhetoric of markets and flexibility may have worked against a longer term trend towards internal labour markets. Certainly there has been some growth in part-time, temporary, and subcontract working, though mainly in industries and types of work where it already existed. On the other hand, higher unemployment has reduced labour turnover and increased worker attachment to firms, and employers have continued to develop internal wage and benefit systems tailored to their own domestic requirements. In terms of work relations, under the stimulus of increased competition and taking advantage of high unemployment, there has been both an increase in more flexible forms of working and some intensification of the work process. However, the extent and depth of change in working practices throughout industry as a whole should not be exaggerated. Moreover, the pay-offs in terms of greater productivity have been uneven and limited by continuing weaknesses in managerial capabilities and low levels of investment in physical and human resources. Taking a broader historical perspective, it can be said that in the 1980s British employers have built on the developments of the two previous decades and, in this sense, change has been incremental rather than discontinuous. At the same time, the evidence is that their behaviour has often been opportunistic in nature, in that they have used the combination of economic and political circumstances to force through changes in an *ad hoc* and piecemeal fashion. It is certainly too early to talk about the transformation of employee relations or the development of a new system of human resources management in Britain.[1]

A thematic overview

These conclusions may be reformulated in a more thematic manner. First, the arguments about markets, corporate structures and hierarchies, and technology and the division of labour are recapitulated. Then, attention is given to the three main decision areas which have been identified – work relations, employment relations, and industrial relations. An attempt is also made to draw some conclusions on the long-term economic consequences of managerial policies and practices.

Taking product markets first, a significant characteristic of many British product markets in the nineteenth and early twentieth centuries was their fragmented nature as firms attempted to differentiate their product and often produced for a wide range of markets. This had a profound effect on labour management, slowing down change in production technologies, encouraging labour-intensive methods, and supporting craft unionism. In Commons' term, the extent of the market and the 'competitive menace' grew in most industries in the late nineteenth and early twentieth centuries. Until the 1930s, Britain was committed to free trade and was a particularly open economy. However, a number of qualifications must be made. The markets which British manufacturers served were often highly fragmented and differentiated; British producers had advantages in widespread Empire markets; and, from time to time, in most trades there were periods of collusion in the form of market-sharing and price-fixing. Such collusion increased during the period of protection from the early 1930s to the 1950s. Thereafter, there was a re-opening and extension of markets, a reorientation of trade towards more demanding European and US markets, and an increasing competitive challenge to British industry which has grown through each successive decade. Each of these different stages of market development had important consequences for the management of labour.

In the case of labour markets, it is important to stress that before the 1950s, with the exception of the two world wars, there was usually an excess supply of labour in Britain, including craft labour. This affected labour management in a number of ways: above all, it encouraged reliance on unskilled-labour and craft-intensive methods of production and slowed down the growth of internal labour market arrangements. It also biased the demand for other skills and discouraged the development of managerial and technical improvements. The post-Second World War years saw full employment up to the 1970s and periodic shortages of skilled labour especially at cycle peaks. This stimulated changes in the division of labour and led employers to develop more extensive employment provisions and internal labour markets. Mobility between jobs, though always subject to cyclical factors, has shown a long-term downward trend.

To re-state the argument about corporate structure and managerial hierarchy. The British economy was long dominated by small, single-unit, family-owned and -managed enterprises (S-form firms, to use Williamson's terminology[2]). Even where large, multi-unit firms emerged, as in the merger waves of the 1890s and 1920s, these tended to take the form of loosely coordinated holding companies (H-form) in which family control remained strong, subsidiaries were allowed considerable autonomy, and traditional methods of administration persisted. There were a few large more unified firms with more elaborate managerial hierarchies organised on functional lines (U-form). In most firms managerial and supervisory systems remained weak: personal management often persisted at senior levels; managers were poorly educated and trained; and levels and functions were inadequately integrated. Labour management was left to line managers and foremen within the firm and was delegated to employers' organisations outside the firm. In the early post-Second World War years, there was considerable continuity. Only later, after the mergers and diversifications of the 1960s, did an increasing number of large firms develop multidivisional forms of organisation, with centralised control over strategic matters and devolution of operational decisions to product divisions (M-form). At the same time firms began to pay more attention to management development, not least in the personnel field. However, despite such changes, there is still abundant evidence that corporate structures in Britain remain weak and management is still less well educated and trained than its foreign counterparts, with particular weaknesses at production and operational level. In recent years further moves towards decentralisation and the pressure of short-term financial considerations may have constrained long-term strategic thinking in the human resource management area.

Turning to technology and the division of labour, it was argued that in many sectors technological change developed very slowly and many British firms remained committed to traditional technologies and patterns of work organisation. The continued prominence of the older staple industries before the Second World War meant that such methods continued and even in newer sectors Britain lagged behind some of its main competitors in the introduction of more sophisticated production technologies. There was some catching up during the period from 1920 to 1930, but subsequently Britain fell behind again in terms of technological innovation.

In terms of work relations (defined as the organisation of work and the way workers are organised around technology and processes), from the late nineteenth century onwards, failure to create strong organisational structures and effective managerial hierarchies reduced the ability to take full advantage of integration and rationalisation of production. In addition, the fragmented nature of markets and the availability and strength of labour reduced the incentive to press ahead with standardisation, mechanisation, and a greater division of labour. Many British firms, therefore, continued to rely on relatively labour-intensive methods and looked to reduce labour costs by holding down wages and by an intensification of work. They paid less attention than their foreign counterparts to upgrading the quality of their labour force. On the other hand, this did not mean that there was a strategic management drive to deskill work in a way suggested by Braverman.[3] British management had no such strategy. The demand for new skills was always being created, and labour often retained considerable power in the production process. Weak managerial control over production and poor operational management have been factors contributing to the poor productivity performance of British industry.

In terms of employment relations (defined as covering the way people are recruited and employed, job tenure and promotion, and wage and benefit arrangements), most British employers did not build strong internal labour systems, but relied more on market mechanisms for obtaining labour, fixing its price, and disposing of workers as supply and demand dictated. From managements' point of view, apprenticeship training and informal on-the-job learning usually provided an adequate supply of skilled labour. Yet this lack of attention to employment relations is not to deny the existence of a traditional paternalism in British industry. Over time, however, this became less sustainable, with the growth of large multi-plant and managerially controlled enterprises. Historically, only a few large firms developed more extensive internal employment systems. These tended to be in industries where firms had the incentive (in terms of attracting and retaining skills), the resources (in terms of product market success), and the organisational capability (in terms of corporate structure and managerial hierarchy) to institute and develop such systems. Yet, from the 1930s onwards, accelerating through the post-war period, there was a growth of more bureaucratic internal employment systems with more impersonal rules and formal wage and benefit systems. Along with this went some increase in internal training systems but, on the whole, training has remained a continuing weakness of British firms. Overall internal labour market arrangements are still relatively weaker in Britain than in the USA, Germany, or Japan.

In terms of industrial relations (defined as covering systems of representation, management-union relations, and the process of collective bargaining), at a relatively early date compared to other countries, British employers recognised unions for male manual workers, though usually subject to a formal insistence on managerial prerogatives. From the late nineteenth century, employers in most industries developed systems of regional and then national collective bargaining based on membership of employers' organisations. These systems of industry-wide, multi-employer bargaining were consolidated during and after the First World War. Among their advantages for employers were that they economised on the costs of developing domestic arrangements; they set standards for wages and conditions with the intention of keeping down competitive pressures; and they helped contain conflict and appeared to minimise trade union interference at the workplace. However, the systems were always skeletal and, for the most part, failed to regulate pay, conditions, and working practices at the level of the workplace. In particular they were subject to periodic challenges by shopfloor workers during periods of economic prosperity. In the post-1945 period, as the Donovan Commission showed, they increasingly failed to perform the regulatory functions intended by employers: restrictive practices and unconstitutional strikes grew, shopfloor bargaining challenged managerial prerogatives, and earnings drifted upwards. In their place, therefore, from the 1960s onwards, employers slowly created a different system of single-employer bargaining at plant, divisional, or company levels. This involved the development of internal personnel management, the negotiation of more formal agreements with shop stewards, and the reform of procedures and wage systems.[4]

In the 1980s there have been contradictory trends in terms of employer policies of externalisation and internalisation. On the one hand, economic, political, and organisational factors have induced employers to pursue strategies of externalisation. For example, as already noted, there has been some increase in sub-contracting and other delegated forms of work organisation. Along with this, in terms of employment conditions, employers have resorted to part-time and temporary work. In the early 1980s employers reacted to recession in the traditional manner by making workers redundant; again in the early 1990s' recession, despite much talk about human resource planning and treating employees as assets, employers have again resorted to redundancy to deal with economic fluctuations. The Thatcher government in part encouraged externalisation in areas such as training by emphasising the transferability of training and favouring qualifications which are generally recognised. Training remains a considerable shortcoming, and through the 1980s' upswing firms relied on recruiting in the external labour market and paying whatever wages were necessary to meet labour shortages. The government also sought to increase market forces by such measures as the reduction of employment protection legislation, the promotion of regional pay differences, and the encouragement of portable pensions. On the other hand, there have been continuing trends towards internalisation. In terms of employment relations, labour turnover has fallen and the average length of jobs probably rose through the 1980s. More attention has been given by management to selection, appraisal, and the use of internal transfers and promotions.[5] Where firms have themselves taken the initiative in terms of training, improvements have tended to be of an internal and firm-specific nature.[6] In the case of wage systems there has been a growth in arrangements which stress inside factors such as performance and productivity rather than outside factors such as the cost of living and the rate for the job. In terms of benefit systems there has been a continuing trend towards the harmonisation of terms and conditions of manual and non-manual employees. In industrial relations a number of major trends must be reiterated. The trend towards single-employer bargaining has continued and along with this has gone an increased dependence of workplace trade unionism on the employer for its operation. Alongside this there has been a growth in other kinds of consultative arrangements and forms of employee involvement which are essentially domestic in nature and intended to increase organisational identity and loyalty. Overall, despite contradictory tendencies, the general tendency would seem to be a continuing slow and uneven move towards strategies of internalisation, though the evidence casts some doubt on how consciously or strategically employers are pursuing such policies.[7]

At this stage, it is appropriate to take up two further questions posed in the introduction. First, can the actions of British employers be said to constitute labour strategies and to what extent were their actions congruent with broader business strategies and structures? Second, what effect did labour management practices have on broader business performance?

The benefit of a historical perspective is that it enables one to discern long-term patterns of action. Historically, the vast majority of British employers did not have strategies in the sense of long-term, consciously devised, coherent policies. However, they did act in the long-term with a certain degree of regularity and they did make decisions which when viewed cumulatively reveal a clear pattern of behaviour over time. In Mintzberg's terms, they had strategies which were *enacted* rather than *intended* and which developed incrementally over time.[8] Yet, there were always a few exceptional firms, including always a significant number of foreign-owned companies, which had more planned and coherent strategies, and over the years the number of these increased, especially from the late 1960s onwards. Significantly, the leaders in developing more planned and articulated strategies were often leading firms in their markets, in their organisational structures, and in their managerial hierarchies.

Historically, the predominant strategies, which have been described here as ones of externalisation, had a certain rationality about them – at least in the short- and medium-term. They suited broader business strategies in that they were largely reactive to market conditions. They also suited weak organisational and managerial structures since firms did not have the organisational capability to develop and administer more elaborate internal policies. In this sense, they were both a rational response to market circumstances and a functional necessity given weak

organisational and managerial structures. However, as foreign competitors discovered the advantages of alternative strategies and arrangements, externalisation became less and less appropriate. Much of the
history of labour management over the postwar years may be seen as a
hesitant and uncertain attempt to change direction and develop stronger
strategies of internalisation.

On the effect of labour management strategies on business and
economic performance, in long term perspective, factors other than those
connected with the management of labour were probably more important
in influencing economic performance. In this book a number of these
factors have been stressed. In many sectors of British industry, small or
loosely coordinated larger firms, with weak managerial hierarchies, failed
effectively to manage innovation and production. In part this resulted
from the fact that they relied for too long on fragmented, diverse, and
sometimes captive markets and failed to obtain economies of scale and
scope in production and marketing.[9] Investment levels in Britain fluctuated considerably over time, but at certain key periods, in particular in
the Edwardian period and again in the post-Second World War period,
the growth of investment, especially in key potential growth sectors, was
slower than in other competitor countries.[10] Whilst these factors were
more important than those concerned with labour or the management
of labour, it must be conceded that such factors reinforced one another.
As Ulman commented on the postwar British economy, 'old fashioned
plant and equipment furnishes a most hospitable environment for the
perpetuation of old fashioned working habits and related institutional
arrangements, just as the hardiness of the latter might constitute an
effective obstacle to more ambitious investment projects'.[11]

Turning therefore to problems of labour and its management, it would
be wrong to conclude that British workers through their trade unions
did not at certain periods have an adverse effect on economic performance
in certain industries. It is highly likely that the strength of trade unions
at times in the late nineteenth century, between 1910 and 1920, and again
in the first three post-Second World War decades, affected the performance of certain industries. Recent econometric studies have suggested
that trade unions had a slight negative effect on manufacturing productivity growth in the 1970s and that a reduction of their power in certain
industries contributed to increased productivity growth in the 1980s.[12]
However, outside industries such as coal mining in the first half of the
twentieth century or motor vehicles in the post-Second World War period,
this effect was uneven and has probably been exaggerated. In other
sectors, as diverse as footwear or electronics, where trade unionism was
never particularly strong, it is difficult to attribute poor performance to

the activities of trade unions. The thesis of this book has been that action and inaction on the management side has been more important.

In terms of work relations, it has been argued that British employers showed a preference for labour-intensive methods of production as an alternative to expensive capital investment. Moreover they were often not particularly good at managing more advanced production systems. Senior management relied excessively on delegated forms of control and never showed any great interest in scientific management or production engineering. Rather they attempted to assert broad notions of managerial prerogatives and resorted to an intensification of effort by workers, especially in the 1890s, 1920s, and 1930s, and again in the 1980s. For the postwar period we have evidence that British firms' relative productivity has tended to fall as the need for managerial sophistication has risen and that British firms have had a large productivity disadvantage in industries characterised by large plants and assembly-type operations.[13] Less competent at managing production than their foreign counterparts, they failed to win the respect of their shopfloor workers.[14] Significantly also, in Britain, foreign-owned companies have been more successful than British-owned companies in obtaining high levels of productivity, suggesting that the problem is less one of inefficient workers than of poor management.[15]

In terms of employment relations, one of the main shortcomings of British employers has been their failure to train the labour force at all levels, from management down to the shopfloor. There has been a long-term underinvestment in human capital which continues up to the present and which has adversely affected the ability of workers to improve the quantity and quality of production.[16] The effect of the failure to develop strong internal labour market-type arrangements is more debatable. However, recent theoretical developments in labour economics would lend support to the notion that certain types of employment contracts are likely to elicit more commitment and higher productivity: these are those which offer greater job security, internal promotion, and hierarchical wage and benefit scales which reward workers according to contribution and seniority rather than market forces.[17] Historically, in Britain, job insecurity, the use of variable piecework systems, and limited benefits for blue-collar workers have often been behind lack of trust and cooperation. As one early study of restrictive practices concluded, 'The more the workpeople suffer from unemployment and fluctuating wages, the more restrictive their attitude is likely to be.'[18]

In terms of industrial relations, it must again be stated that unions and their activities have at various times and in various sectors had an adverse effect on productivity growth. However, industrial relations are always a two-way relationship. British employers, for their part, relied too much on employers' organisations and did not for many years develop effective internal systems to meet the representational aspirations of their workforces and to deal with workplace trade unionism. In their rhetoric, they insisted on managerial prerogatives, but in practice they allowed incursions into managerial authority which their counterparts overseas did not tolerate. In the post-Second World War period they were slow to develop new and effective collective bargaining and consultative arrangements which might have encouraged more positive industrial relations. True to market principles, they often approached industrial relations in a short-term and opportunistic manner, for example, taking advantage of trade unions in bad times and having to suffer the adverse consequences of this when circumstances have changed. Taken together, these managerial actions and inactions have played a large part in influencing the productive performance of British industry.

Strategies of externalisation may have given British employers some comparative advantage in the nineteenth and early twentieth centuries. But as the potential of mass markets and mass-production technologies developed in the twentieth century, such strategies became less appropriate. However, the forces of institutional inertia were complex and strong. In the latter half of the twentieth century the demand for higher quality and more flexible production has led to a further need for a change in strategies emphasising more skilled work and more positive industrial relations and permitting employers to use new technologies to their maximum potential. In essence, the argument presented in this book has been that changes in this direction came about only slowly and unevenly in Britain and that this has had major consequences for industrial performance and national competitiveness.

Some theoretical conclusions

In Chapter 1 a number of propositions were outlined. These may be restated as follows. First, markets, for both labour and final products, are key independent variables influencing labour management decisions. Second, corporate strategies and structures are significant intervening variables shaping strategy and structure in the labour field. Third, the nature and quality of the managerial hierarchy is a further important factor influencing labour management. Fourth, technology and the division of labour also shape labour decisions. Finally, firms make labour decisions which can be conceptualised in terms of internalising transactions within the firm or externalising them in the market. Where do these propositions now stand after the presentation of the detailed historical narrative?

The notion of internalising and externalising can be used to analyse managerial strategies in the labour area. It was employed to understand the slow growth of internal labour systems in Britain where employers long relied on external markets for labour supply and wage fixing. It was also used to examine various aspects of work relations. For example, it was employed to describe the historical move from various forms of subcontracting to more direct forms of work organisation. More contemporaneously, in different economic circumstances, it can be used to understand the reemergence of various forms of sub-contracting, temporary, and part-time working. It can be used to focus on one important aspect of training, namely whether training is organised under company control and is firm-specific, or whether it is more market-orientated. The concept, it is hoped, also helped to locate the significance of industry-wide multi-employer bargaining which was analysed as a form of externalisation and the growth of single-employer bargaining which was seen as a form of internalisation.

However, it is necessary to add a number of qualifications and elaborations to this basic proposition. Internalising and externalising should certainly not be seen as outcomes predetermined by economic costs and benefits in a simple neo-classical sense. Employers always had a choice, but their ability to choose was dependent on market and technological constraints and on organisational characteristics and capabilities. This also means that internalising and externalising should not be seen in terms of a precise calculation of costs and benefits. Employers did not have the information on such costs and benefits *ex ante* and, even *ex post*, could usually not assess the effects of different courses of action. However, the fact that they were not known precisely does not mean that employers were not aware that there were costs and benefits of alternative courses of action, especially when market and competitive pressures on them were strong.

Moreover, internalising and externalising should not be seen as a simple dichotomy. There were intermediate forms. Thus the use of employers' organisations may perhaps best be seen as 'coordination by cooperation' rather than by the firm or the market.[19] Within any one firm there could be a mixture of strategies. For example, different strategies often existed for different groups of workers: managerial, technical, white collar, skilled, and unskilled were treated differently usually reflecting different market situations. In addition, it must be added that, over time, there could be backward and forward movement in terms of the use of strategies, depending on the degree of market competition, market change or stability, and organisational capabilities.

This book has tended to stress the benefits of internalisation. It is also necessary to recapitulate some of the disadvantages. For the employer, internalisation can mean heavy fixed costs and inflexibility in terms of the ability to make adjustments to market forces. It can also mean the loss of certain advantages which come from cooperating with other firms through employers' organisations in terms of regulating the labour market and providing joint services. For the employee, internalisation can mean reduced mobility and dependence on the firm, especially where there are inadequate internal systems of representation and due process. Indeed, many years ago the American economist Ross warned of the dangers of internalisation as a new form of industrial feudalism.[20] For peripheral workers and potential employees outside the firm, internalisation can mean exclusion from good jobs, training opportunities, and relatively generous pay and benefits. This can, of course, be a cost for society which should then provide alternative arrangements. In terms of the national economy there may be other disadvantages, especially where insider wage fixing and the lack of coordination between firms create inflationary wage pressures. In Britain in the 1980s, despite high unemployment, insider forces led to annual earnings increases in key industries which were higher than the rate of inflation and higher than in competitor countries; these then spread throughout the economy because of the lack of any coordination of wage fixing. Thus strategies of internalisation, or at least incomplete internalisation, may not always produce an efficient outcome at the aggregate level. This suggests that what is required is a combination of arrangements which include internalisation, market forces, interfirm coordination, and government action. Overall, however, the argument of this book has been that the benefits of internalisation outweigh the costs and that strategies of internalisation have more advantages than disadvantages.

As to the proposition about environmental factors, market forces were important independent variables shaping labour management decisions. Labour markets had a direct effect, product markets a more indirect influence. In the labour market, the relatively abundant supply of labour in Britain during most periods up to the Second World War inhibited the division of labour. It also constrained the development of internal labour market-type arrangements since there was little incentive to by-pass the external market and create elaborate internal labour systems. The state of demand in the labour market directly affected industrial relations in that it shaped the opportunism which was often the hallmark of employer policies, inducing cooperative attitudes in times of prosperity and adversarial attitudes in times of recession.[21] As to the product market, fragmentation constrained the division of labour and held back the modernisation of work and deskilling tendencies in Great Britain. Slow growth and fluctuations in the product market did not provide the conditions for the development of strong internal employment systems. In terms of collective bargaining arrangements, the development of regional and national markets lay behind the emergence of regional and national collective bargaining, and collusion in the product market supported multi-employer bargaining. In the postwar period, as product markets extended internationally, as collusion became more difficult, and as competition intensified, firms changed their bargaining strategies and tried to link changes in wages and conditions more closely to productivity movements within the firm.

The propositions about the firm were that corporate structures and managerial hierarchies also had an important effect on labour management. The traditional small firm and the loosely coordinated holding company, with their weak managerial control systems, went a long way to explain the persistence of a craft division of labour and weaknesses in successfully introducing modern work systems. They also contributed to both traditional paternalism *and* the slow development of more bureaucratic employment systems. In terms of industrial relations, weak corporate structures and managerial hierarchies lay behind the long-term reliance on employers' organisations and the tardy development of domestic industrial relations arrangements. In the early post-war period, their persistence explains the emergence of fragmented shopfloor bargaining. Later, the development of more centralised structures and stronger hierarchies allowed a few firms to pursue a tighter control over the labour process, more bureaucratic employment practices, and more centralised internal dealings with trade unions. Historically, ICI and Ford are good examples of firms which early made these choices.

Thus market, technological, and organisational forms have been important in shaping labour management strategies. However, this is not to deny that there were other forces operating. The influence of the state, both negative and positive, also had an important effect, especially at certain key points in time. At the most fundamental level, from the nineteenth century onwards, the support for *laissez-faire* employment principles and non-intervention in the employment relationship provided the basis for polices of externalisation. Similarly, the provision from the nineteenth century onwards of legal immunities for unions and later the support for collective bargaining, especially during the period of the two world wars and in the post-Second World War years, had an important effect on British industrial relations. In the 1980s the Thatcher administration, with its commitment to market principles and individualism and its introduction of legal restraints on unions, has also had a significant effect on the conduct of industrial relations, by reshaping the agenda and making possible what had previously seemed difficult for employers to attain. However, the argument of this book has been that on the whole, seen in long-term perspective, the role of the state has been less important than that of employers and government activity has tended for the most part to extend and confirm already existing trends.

Some independent effect has to be assigned to the actions of trade unions. In Britain the strength of craft unionism, the persistence of workplace organisation, and the complexities of multi-unionism had an effect on the division of labour, employment practices, and collective bargaining arrangements. However, union impact has tended to be exaggerated in both popular and academic commentary. Employers had initiatory power, while union power was largely reactive and negative. Ultimately employers made the decisions, or failed to make the decisions, which counted most. A corollary worthy of further investigation is that corporate structure and management choice of bargaining arrangements had a substantial effect on the organisation and power structure of trade unions in Britain. Thus, traditional structures provided the basis for craft unionism in the nineteenth century; the resort to employers' organisations led to increasing centralisation of union organisation and decision-making in the early twentieth century; the persistence of loose forms of corporate organisation and the weakness of employers' associations in Britain ensured the strength of fragmented shopfloor unionism through the first three postwar decades; more recently the development of stronger corporate structures has encouraged a more enterprise-orientated trade unionism.

Ideological and cultural factors were also important in shaping labour decisions. In the context of British industrial history, there were certain attitudes which had considerable tenacity: in employment relations a mixture of *laissez-faire* individualism *and* moral notions of paternalism; in work relations a 'gentlemanly' lack of interest on the part of many senior managers and a belief in the 'practical' approach on the part of many lower level managers;[22] in industrial relations a belief in maintaining managerial prerogatives at the cost of developing closer consultative and better bargaining arrangements. Such traditional attitudes were deeply entrenched and affected the choice of labour strategies. However, there are a number of major problems with ideological and cultural arguments: their origins have to be explained and located in historical and institutional contexts: moreover, broad cultural arguments fail to explain the substantial differences between British firms which have been pointed out in this book. Taking a long-term perspective, the best interpretation is one which stresses market and technological contexts, corporate structures and managerial capabilities, and employers' choice of strategies.

These conclusions are drawn from the British experience of managing manual workers in manufacturing and related industries. It is hoped, however, that the framework may have broader uses. For example it could be developed by focusing it more specifically on white-collar, technical, and managerial staff or by extending it to the service sector. It might also be applied to the public sector (though here inevitably political forces would weigh more). Most fruitfully, it could be developed by examining the experiences of different countries. For example, it has been argued in the course of this book that large American firms have historically internalised more activities than their British counterparts. In Japan, large firms have developed a particularly sophisticated mix of internal policies based on elaborate pay systems, extensive welfare benefits, and enterprise trade unionism. In the case of Japan, this internalised system is also supported, however, by strategies of externalisation via the use of temporary workers and subcontracting. In Germany, large firms have also developed extensive internal employment systems, with strong internal labour markets and arrangements for employee representation. However, in the German case, this is also complemented by the use of external multi-employer arrangements for training and collective bargaining.[23]

This prompts a final and more normative conclusion. If large American, German, and Japanese firms have been more successful in securing a more effective and efficient balance between market forces and administrative coordination, then British employers and policy-makers need to examine more closely what they have done. It would certainly be unwise to rely excessively on market based approaches to the management of labour. Already there have been substantial improvements in British corporate structures and managerial hierarchies; industrial relations have experienced major reforms from the late 1960s onwards; and management is, in the final decade of the twentieth century, in a stronger position to bring about further changes. However, the process of adjustment has been slow and many employers have only hesitantly developed strategies of internalisation. There is still much to be achieved, especially in terms of the improved organisation of work relations, in employment conditions and training at all levels, and in terms of more positive industrial relations. Upon this depends to a great measure the future success of British industry.

Notes

1 INTRODUCTION: THE MANAGEMENT OF LABOUR

Except where otherwise stated, the place of publication is London.

1. S. and B. Webb, *Industrial Democracy* (1919) and *The History of Trade Unionism* (1920); E. H. Phelps Brown, *The Growth of British Industrial Relations* (1959) and *The Origins of Trade Union Power* (Oxford, 1983); H. A. Turner, *Trade Union Growth, Structure, and Policy: A Comparative Study of the Cotton Unions* (1962); H. A. Clegg, A. Fox and A. F. Thompson, *A History of British Trade Unions Since 1889. Volume I 1889-1910* (Oxford, 1964); H. A. Clegg, *A History of British Trade Unions Since 1889. Volume II 1911-1933* (Oxford, 1985).
2. See, for example, S. Pollard, *The Genesis of Modern Management* (1965); J. Child, *British Management Thought* (1969); C. R. Littler, *The Development of the Labour Process in Capitalist Societies* (1982); H. F. Gospel and C. R. Littler (eds.), *Managerial Strategies and Industrial Relations: An Historical and Comparative Study* (1983); P. Joyce, *Work, Politics and Society: The Culture of the Factory in Later Victorian England* (Brighton, 1980); R. Fitzgerald, *British Labour Management and Industrial Welfare 1846-1939* (1987); C. Harvey and J. Turner, *Labour and Business in Modern Britain* (1989).
3. R. Coase, 'The Nature of the Firm', *Economica*, 4 (1937).
4. K. Marx, *Capital* (1970), Volume I, especially Chapter 6.
5. A. Marshall, *Principles of Economics* (8th edn, 1946), p. 560.
6. J. Commons, *Legal Foundations of Capitalism* (New York, 1924), p. 285.
7. See, for example, J. Commons, *Institutional Economics* (New York, 1934) and 'American Shoemakers 1648-1895: A Sketch of Industrial Evolution', *Quarterly Journal of Economics*, 24 (1909).
8. Coase, 'The Nature'.
9. See, for example, G. B. Richardson, 'The Organisation of Industry', *Economic Journal*, 82 (1972).
10. O. E. Williamson, *Markets and Hierarchies* (New York, 1975) and *The Economic Institutions of Capitalism* (New York, 1985).
11. A. D. Chandler, *Strategy and Structure: Chapters in the History of the American Industrial Enterprise* (Cambridge, Mass., 1962); *The Visible Hand: The Managerial Revolution in American Business* (Cambridge, Mass., 1977); *Scale and Scope: The Dynamics of Industrial Capitalism* (Cambridge, Mass., 1990).

12. Williamson, *Markets and Hierarchies*, Chapter 8.
13. L. Hannah, *The Rise of the Corporate Economy* (1983) and 'Visible and Invisible Hands in Great Britain', in A.D. Chandler and H. Daems (eds.), *Managerial Hierarchies: Comparative Perspectives on the Rise of the Modern Industrial Enterprise* (Cambridge, Mass., 1980). Lazonick has applied a similar line of argument to technological innovation and business performance in Britain, arguing that the reliance on market coordination and the continued existence of many small firms had adverse consequences for innovation and performance. See, for example, W. Lazonick, *Competitive Advantage on the Shopfloor* (Cambridge, Mass., 1990) and B. Elbaum and W. Lazonick, *The Decline of the British Economy* (Oxford, 1986).
14. These propositions are set out in the same way as in Chandler, *The Visible Hand*, pp. 6-11.
15. For the term 'organisational capability' see Chandler, *Scale and Scope*. Chandler identifies this more with investment in production and distribution and managerial hierarchies. In this book it is taken more to be a combination of organisational structure and managerial hierarchy.
16. This is an extension of Adam Smith's dictum that the division of labour is limited by the extent of the market. See *An Enquiry into the Nature and Causes of the Wealth of Nations* (Methuen, 1904 edn), pp. 9-19.
17. This is taken from G. S. Becker, *Human Capital: A Theoretical and Empirical Analysis, with Special Reference to Education* (New York, 1964).
18. One of the earliest analyses of the internal labour market is to be found in C. Kerr, 'The Balkanisation of Labour Markets', in E. W. Bakke *et al.*, *Labour Mobility and Economic Opportunity*, (Cambridge, Mass., 1954), pp. 92-110. For a fuller analysis see P. B. Doeringer and M. J. Piore, *Internal Labor Markets and Manpower Analysis* (Lexington, Mass., 1971).
19. This term is used in G. B. Richardson, 'The Organisation of Industry', *Economic Journal*, 83 (1972).
20. The handshake can be either 'visible' or 'invisible', the contract can be either 'explicit' or 'implicit'. See A. M. Okun, *Prices and Quantities: A Microeconomic Analysis* (Oxford, 1981), Chapter 3.
21. See H. Mintzberg, *The Nature of Managerial Work* (New York, 1973) and *The Structuring of Organisations* (Englewood Cliffs, New Jersey, 1979), p. 443.

2 MARKETS, FIRMS, AND THE MANAGEMENT OF LABOUR IN THE NINETEENTH CENTURY

1. W. Hamish Fraser, *The Coming of the Mass Market* (1981). For concern about foreign competition see First Report of the Royal Commission on the Depression of Trade and Industry (1896) (Cd. 4621); E. E. Williams, *Made in Germany* (1896); E. A. McKenzie, *American Invaders* (1902); G. R. Searle, *The Quest for National Efficiency* (Oxford, 1971).
2. Adam Smith had remarked on this in *The Wealth of Nations* (1776), E. Cannan (ed.) (6th edn, 1950), Volume I, pp. 68-9. J. Clapham, *An Economic History of Modern Britain: Machines and National Rivalries, 1887-1914* (Cambridge, 1938), Chapter 5.

3. H. W. Macrosty, *The Trust Movement in British Industry* (1907); A. Hunter, *Competition and the Law* (1966); for an example of how collusion in the product market and labour market were interrelated see the Birmingham metal trades alliances of the 1890s, described in Macrosty, pp. 79-81, 155-6, and H. A. Clegg, A. Fox, and A. F. Thompson, *A History of British Trade Unions since 1889. Volume I 1889-1910* (Oxford, 1964), pp. 189-98.

4. L. Hannah, *The Rise of the Corporate Economy* (1983), Chapter 2.

5. P. Payne, 'The Emergence of the Large Scale Company in Great Britain, 1870-1914', *Economic History Review*, 20 (1967); L. Hannah, 'Mergers in Manufacturing Industry, 1880-1919', *Oxford Economic Papers*, 26 (1974).

6. L. Hannah, 'Visible and Invisible Hands in Great Britain', in A. D. Chandler and H. Daems (eds.), *Managerial Hierarchies: Comparative Perspectives on the Rise of the Modern Industrial Enterprise* (Cambridge, Mass., 1980).

7. A. D. Chandler, 'The Development of Management Structure in the US and UK', in L. Hannah (ed.), *Management Strategy and Business Development* (1976); 'The Emergence of Managerial Capitalism', *Business History Review*, 58 (1984); *Scale and Scope: The Dynamics of Industrial Capitalism* (Cambridge, Mass., 1990).

8. Payne, 'Emergence', p. 67, refers to organisational development as 'desperately slow'. See also T. Gourvish, 'British Business and the Transformation to a Corporate Economy: Entrepreneurship and Management Structure', *Business History*, 29 (1987).

9. Business Statistics Office, *Historical Record of the Census of Production 1907 to 1970* (1978), p. 202. For the USA see US Department of Commerce, Bureau of the Census, *Historical Statistics of the United States from Colonial Times to 1870* (Washington, DC, 1975), p. 666; for Germany see J. Kocka, 'The Rise of the Modern Industrial Enterprise in Germany', in A. D. Chandler and H. Daems, *Managerial Hierarchies*.

10. See, for example, C. Erickson, *British Industrialists: Steel and Hosiery* (1959); G. H. Copeman, *Leaders of British Industry* (1955); M. Newcomer, *The Big Business Executive* (New York, 1955); H. Mannrari, *The Japanese Business Leaders* (Tokyo, 1974).

11. D. Jeremy, 'Anatomy of the British Business Elite, 1860-1980', *Business History*, 26 (1984).

12. J. Melling, "Non-Commissioned Officers': British Employers and their Supervisory Workers, 1880-1920', *Social History*, 5 (1980); K. Burgess, 'Authority Relations and the Division of Labour in British Industry, with Special Reference to Clydeside 1860-1930', *Social History*, 11 (1986); R. Coopey, 'Supervision and Industrial Change: The Engineering Industry in Britain 1900-1950', University of Warwick MA, 1985, p. 17.

13. Jeremy. 'Anatomy'; C. Erickson, *British Industrialists: Steel and Hosiery* 1850-1950 (Cambridge, 1959); D. C. Coleman, 'Gentlemen and Players', *Economic History Review*, 26 (1973).

14. Coleman, 'Gentlemen and Players'; R. Locke, *The End of Practical Man: Entrepreneurship in Germany, France and Great Britain* (Greenwich, Conn., 1984).

15. P. L. Robertson, 'Employers and Engineering Education in Britain and the United States, 1890-1914', *Business History*, 23 (1981); D. H. Aldcroft, 'Investment in and Utilisation of Manpower: Great Britain and Her Rivals', in B.M. Ratcliffe, *Great Britain and Her World 1750-1914* (Manchester, 1975).

16. D. C. Mowery, 'Industrial Research', in Elbaum and Lazonick, *The Decline*; J. F. Donnelly, 'Representations of Applied Science: Academics and Chemical Industry in late Nineteenth Century England', *Social Studies of Science*, 16 (1986), pp. 206-7.

17. C. K. Harley, 'Skilled Labour and the Choice of Technique in Edwardian Industry', *Explorations in Economic History* 11 (1974).

18. G. W. Roderick and M. D. Stephens, *Education and Industry in the Nineteenth Century* (1978); J. Wrigley, 'Technical Education and Industry in the Nineteenth Century', in Elbaum and Lazonick (eds.) *The Decline*.

19. D.F. Schloss, *Methods of Industrial Remuneration* (1892) p. 120, stated that subcontracting was 'practically ubiquitous'. For a recent analysis see C.R. Littler, *The Development of the Labour Process in Capitalist Societies* (1982).

20. Littler, *The Development*, Chapters 10 and 11; Melling, '"Non-Commissioned Officers"'; Burgess, 'Authority Relations'.

21. Smith, *The Wealth of Nations*, Volume I, Chapters 1-3.

22. C. Babbage, *On the Economy of Machinery and Manufacturers* (4th edn, 1835) (reprinted 1963), pp. 169-76.

23. K. Marx, *Capital* (1970 edn), Volume I, Part III, Chapter 7, and Part IV, Chapter 15.

24. H. Braverman, *Labor and Monopoly Capital: The Degradation of Work in the Twentieth Century* (New York, 1974); S. Marglin, 'What Do Bosses Do? The Origins and Functions of Hierarchy in Capitalist Production', *Review of Radical Political Economics* (1974).

25. W. Lazonick, 'Factor Costs and the Diffusion of Ring Spinning in Britain Prior to World War I', *Quarterly Journal of Economics* 96 (1981); 'Competition, Specialisation, and Economic Decline', *Journal of Economic History* 41 (1981): 'Production Relations, Labour Productivity, and Choice of Technique; British and US Cotton Spinning', *Journal of Economic History*, 41 (1981); 'Industrial Organisation and Technological Change: The Decline of the British Cotton Industry', *Business History Review*, 57 (1983).

26. J. Zeitlin, 'The Labour Strategies of British Engineering Employers, 1890-1922', in H. F. Gospel and C. R. Littler (eds.), *Managerial Strategies and Industrial Relations* (1983).

27. D. Landes, 'Technical Change and Industrial Development in W. Europe 1850-1914', in H. J. Habakkuk and M. Postan (eds.) *Cambridge Economic History of Europe* Volume VI (1965); B. Elbaum, 'The Steel Industry before World War I', in Elbaum and Lazonick, *The Decline*; B. Elbaum and F. Wilkinson, 'Industrial Relations and Uneven Development: A Comparative Study of the American and British Steel Industries' *Cambridge Journal of Economics*, 3 (1979); D. McCloskey, *Economic Maturity and Entrepreneurial Decline: British Iron and Steel, 1870-1913* (Cambridge, Mass., 1973).

28. M. W. Kirby, *The British Coalmining Industry 1870-1946*, (1977) and R. Church, *The History of the British Coal Industry*. Volume III (Oxford, 1986).

29. E. H. Lorenz and F. Wilkinson, 'The Shipbuilding Industry, 1880–1965', in Elbaum and Lazonick, *The Decline*, and P. J. Hilditch and A. Reid, 'Trade Unions and Labour Productivity: The British Shipbuilding Industry, 1870–1950', Department of Applied Economics, Cambridge, Working Paper 8907 (1989).
30. D. H. Aldcroft, 'The Entrepreneur and the British Economy, 1870–1914', *Economic History Review* 8 (1966).
31. For a similar argument see Lazonick and Zeitlin above.
32. L. F. Haber, *The Chemical Industry During the Nineteenth Century* (Oxford, 1958).
33. See W. J. Reader, *Imperial Chemical Industries: The Forerunners 1870–1926*, Volume I (Oxford, 1979), and C. Wilson, *The History of Unilever*, Volume I (1954).
34. See, for example, J. Clapham, *An Economic History of Modern Britain*, Volume III (Cambridge, 1938), pp. 88–89.
35. A. Hughill, *Sugar and All That: A History of Tate & Lyle*, (1978).
36. See, for example, T. A. B. Corley, *Quaker Enterprise in Biscuits: Huntley & Palmers of Reading, 1822–1972* (1972).
37. B. W. E. Alford, *W.D. & H.O. Wills and the Development of the UK Tobacco Industry* (1973); R. Fitzgerald, 'Employers' Labour Strategies, Industrial Welfare, and the Response to New Unionism at Bryant & May, 1888–1930', *Business History* (1989).
38. S. B. Saul, 'The Engineering Industry' in D. H. Aldcroft, *The Development of British Industry and Foreign Competition, 1875–1914* (1968).
39. I am grateful to A. McIvor for this reference. See also 'The Singer Strike, Clydebank, 1911'. Unpublished Paper, Glasgow Labour History Workshop, June 1988.
40. J. D. Scott, *Vickers: A History* (1962); C. Trebilcock, *The Vickers Brothers: Armaments and Enterprise, 1854–1914* (1977).
41. E. Hobsbawm, 'British Gas-workers, 1873–1914 ', *Labouring Men* (1964).
42. S. Pollard, *The Genesis of Modern Management* (1965); J. Child, *British Management Thought* (1969).
43. See, for example, A. Williams, *Life in a Railway Factory* (1915), pp. 274–6; P. Joyce, *Work, Society and Politics: The Culture of the Factory in Later Victorian England* (Brighton, 1980), p. 100; K. Hudson, *Working to Rule: Railway Workshop Rules* (Bath, 1970), p.48.
44. 'Industrial Reconstruction: An Employer's View', *The Athenaeum* (March 1917).
45. C. More, *Skill and the English Working Class, 1870–1914* (1980); W. Knox, 'British Apprenticeship, 1800–1914', Unpublished Ph.D. Edinburgh University (1980); W. Knox, 'Apprenticeship and Deskilling in Britain, 1850–1914', *International Review of Social History* 31 (1986).
46. D. Bythell, *The Sweated Trades: Outwork in Nineteenth Century Britain*, (1978); G. Stedman Jones, *Outcast London*, (Oxford, 1971).
47. R. C. O. Matthews, C. H. Feinstein, and J. C. Odling-Smee, *British Economic Growth 1856–1973* (Oxford, 1982), p. 83.
48. J.H. Porter, 'Wage Determination by Selling Price Sliding Scales, 1870–1914', *Manchester School of Economic and Social Studies*, 29 (1971).
49. Schloss, *Methods*; G.D.H. Cole, *The Payment of Wages* (1918).

50. D. Roberts, *Paternalism in Early Victorian England* (1979).
51. Joyce, *Work, Politics, and Society*; A. H. Yarmie, 'Benevolence and Labour Management in the Mid-Victorian British Textile Industry', *Europa* 2 (1979).
52. S. Pollard, 'The Factory Village of the Industrial Revolution', *English Historical Review*, 79 (1964).
53. Joyce, *Work, Politics, and Society*; H. I. Dutton and J. E. King, 'The Limits of Paternalism: The Cotton Tyrants of North Lancashire, 1836-54', *Social History* 7 (1982).
54. For a similar discussion see G.M. Norris, 'Industrial Paternalist Capitalism and Local Labour Markets', *Sociology* 12 (1978).
55. Joyce, *Work, Politics, and Society*, Epilogue; M. Savage, *The Dynamics of Working Class Politics: The Labour Movement in Preston 1888-1948* (Cambridge, 1987).
56. C. Kerr, 'The Balkanisation of Labour Markets', in E. W. Bakke *et al.*, *Labour Mobility and Economic Opportunity* (Cambridge, Mass., 1954) pp. 92-110; P. B. Doeringer and M. J. Piore, *Internal Labor Markets and Manpower Analysis* (Lexington, Mass., 1971).
57. This account of the railways is based on P. S. Bagwell, *The Railwaymen*, Volume I, (1963); F. McKenna, 'Victorian Railway Workers', *History Workshop* 1 (1976); P. Nicholls, 'Management Strategies in Early Railway Organisations' (Unpublished Paper, Leeds Polytechnic, 1980); R. Fitzgerald, *British Labour Management and Industrial Welfare 1846-1939* (1988), Chapter 2.
58. Some of the sanctions as used by the railway companies such as fines were also traditional. S. Pollard, 'Factory Discipline in the Industrial Revolution', *Economic History Review* 15 (1963); S. Pollard, *The Genesis of Modern Management* (1965); N. McKendrick, 'Josiah Wedgwood and Factory Discipline', *Historical Journal* 4 (1961).
59. Bagwell, *The Railwaymen*, p. 22.
60. See D. Drummond, 'Crewe - the Society and Culture of a Railway Town, 1842-1914' (London University Ph.D., 1986) for a discussion of the engineering workshops.
61. T. I. Williams, *A History of the British Gas Industry* (Oxford, 1981) p. 47.
62. More, *Skill*, pp. 93, 217-18.
63. Williams, *British Car Industry*, p. 265.
64. J. Melling, 'Industrial Strife and Business Welfare Philosophy: The Case of the South Metropolitan Gas Company from the 1880s to the War', *Business History* 21 (1979) p. 166.
65. *Ibid.* and R.A. Church, 'Profit Sharing and Labour Relations in England in the Nineteenth Century', *International Review of Social History*, 16 (1971).
66. See, for example, Haber, *Chemical Industry*, p. 249; Reader, *ICI*, p. 233; More, *Skill*, pp. 205, 216-17, 219.
67. Wilson, *Unilever* pp. 154-6.
68. Cadbury Bros. Ltd., *Industrial Record 1919-1939* (Bourneville, 1947), pp. 69-75; More, *Skill*, pp. 210-15; C. Dellheim, 'The Creation of a Company Culture: Cadburys 1861-1931', *American Historical Review*, 92 (1987).
69. R. Fitzgerald, *British Labour Management and Industrial Welfare 1846-1939* (1988).

70. *Ibid.*, Chapter 4: J. Melling, 'Employers, Industrial Housing and the Evolution of Company Welfare Policies in Britain's Heavy Industry: West Scotland 1870-1920', *International Review of Social History* 26 (1981).
71. H. Maine, *Ancient Laws* (1861), Chapter 4.
72. O. Kahn Freund, 'A Note on Status and Contract in British Labour Law', *Modern Law Review* 30 (1967).
73. A. V. Dicey, *Lectures on the Relations Between Law and Public Opinion in England During the Nineteenth Century* (1905).
74. R. Currie, *Industrial Politics*, (Oxford, 1979).
75. See Matthews, Feinstein, and Odling-Smee, *British Economic Growth*, Chapters 3 and 4 on unemployment.
76. H. A. Clegg, A. Fox and A. F. Thompson, *A History of British Trade Unions Since 1889* (Oxford, 1964), pp. 1, 466-7. For comparative figures for other countries see G. S. Bain and R. Price, *Profiles of Union Growth* (Oxford, 1980).
77. A McIvor, 'Employers' Organisations and Strikebreaking, 1880-1914', *International Review of Social History*.
78. As cited in P. Bagwell, 'The New Unionism in Britain: The Railway Industry', in W. J. Mommsen and H. G. Husung (eds.), *The Development of Trade Unionism in Great Britain and Germany, 1880-1914* (1985), p 186.
79. E. H. Phelps Brown, *The Origins of Trade Union Power* (Oxford, 1983), p. 22.
80. Adam Smith noted that, 'Masters are always and everywhere in a sort of tacit but constant and uniform combination not to raise the wages of labour above their actual rate...Masters too sometimes enter into particular combinations to sink the wages of labour even below this rate.' Smith, *The Wealth of Nations*, Volume I, pp. 68-9.
81. Between 1895 and 1898 the number of employers' organisations doubled from 336 to 675. Public Records Office/Lab 2/427/256/1918, 'Memorandum on Effect of Organisation on Disputes: Number of Employers' Associations'.
82. H. A. Turner, *Trade Union Growth, Structure and Policy: A Comparative Study of the Cotton Unions* (1962) p. 381.
83. Engineering Employers' Federation (EEF)/23/Management Board/24 June 1924.
84. J. H. Porter, 'Industrial Conciliation and Arbitration 1860-1914' (Ph.D., Leeds, 1968); J. H. Porter, 'Wage Bargaining Under Conciliation Agreements 1860-1914', *Economic History Review* 23 (1970).
85. For studies which stress the advantages to employers see R. Price, *Masters, Unions and Men* (Cambridge, 1980) and K. Burgess, *The Origins of British Industrial Relations* (1975). For an alternative assessment which sees rather more advantages for workers and unions, see R. Tarling and F. Wilkinson, 'Wages and Collective Bargaining in Britain, 1880-1920', *Contributions to Political Economy* 1 (1982).
86. Clegg, Fox, and Thompson, *A History*, Chapters 2-5.
87. For a recent interpretation which sees the employers' strategy as being to 'neutralise' workplace trade unionism, see K. Sissons, *The Management of Collective Bargaining* (Oxford, 1987).
88. Clegg, Fox, and Thompson *A History*, Chapters 4, 5, and 9.

89. Board of Trade, *Report on Collective Agreements Between Employers and Workpeople in the UK* (Cd. 5366, 1910), p. xii.
90. E. H. Phelps Brown, *The Growth of British Industrial Relations* (1959), pp. 358-63, discusses multi-employer bargaining as a way of preventing unfair competition.
91. For the role of the state see *ibid.*, Chapter 4.

3 MARKETS, FIRMS, AND THE ORGANISATION OF PRODUCTION

1. R. C. O. Matthews, C. H. Feinstein, and J. C. Odling-Smee, *British Economic Growth* (Oxford, 1982), pp. 31, 498-9.
2. See, for example, *First Report of the Royal Commission on the Depression of Trade and Industry* (1886) (Cd. 4621); E. E. Williams, *Made in Germany* (1896); the series of articles which appeared in *The Times* in 1901 and 1902 by E. A. Pratt, subsequently published in book form, *Trade Unionism and British Industry* (1904); F. A. McKenzie. *American Invaders* (1902); A. Shadwell. *Industrial Efficiency* (1906); G. R. Searle. *The Quest for National Efficiency* (Oxford, 1971).
3. A. S. Milward, *The Economic Effects of the Two World Wars on Britain* (2nd edn, 1984). C. P. Kindleberger, *The World in Depression* (1973), pp. 31-57.
4. D. H. Aldcroft and P. Fearon (eds.), *British Economic Fluctuations 1790-1939* (1972).
5. S. Pollard, *The Development of the British Economy 1914-1980* (3rd edn, 1983) pp. 138, 144.
6. B. R. Mitchell and P. Deane, *Abstract of British Historical Statistics* (Cambridge, 1971) pp. 272, 329, 477-8.
7. D. H. Aldcroft, *The British Economy Between the Wars* (1983) p. 19.
8. Matthews, Feinstein, and Odling-Smee, *British Economic Growth*, pp. 22-3; R. Garside, *The Measurement of Unemployment* (Oxford, 1980).
9. C. H. Feinstein, *National Income, Expenditure and Output of the United Kingdom 1855-1965* (Cambridge, 1972) Table 57.
10. H. W. Richardson, 'The New Industries Between the Wars', *Oxford Economic Papers*, 13 (1961); B. W. E. Alford, 'New Industries for Old? British Industry Between the Wars', in R. Floud and D. McCloskey (eds.), *The Economic History of Britain since 1700, Volume II 1860 to the 1970s* (Cambridge, 1981); D.H. Aldcroft, 'Economic Progress in Britain in the 1920s', *Scottish Journal of Political Economy*, 13 (1966); N. K. Buxton, 'The Role of the "New" Industries in Britain During the 1930s: A Reinterpretation', *Business History Review*, 49 (1975).
11. I. Drummond, 'Britain and the World Economy 1900-1945', in Floud and McCloskey (eds.), *Economic History*, p. 296.
12. J. M. Rees, *Trusts in British Industry 1914-1921* (1922) p. 27.
13. Committee on Trusts, *Report* (Cd. 9236, 1918) p. 2. See also G. C. Allen, *Monopoly and Restrictive Practices* (1968) Chapter 4.
14. K. Cowling, 'Excess Capacity and the Degree of Collusion: Oligopoly Behaviour in the Slump', *Manchester School* (1983); H. A. Marquand, *The*

Dynamics of Industrial Combination (1931) pp. 5–6, 11–12; A. F. Lucas, *Industrial Reconstruction and the Control of Competition* (1937).

15. Committee on Industry and Trade, *Final Report* (1929), pp. 176–7. See also Board of Trade, *Restraint of Trade* (1931) pp. 6–7.

16. *The Economist*, 'The Cartelisation of England' (18 March 1939); L. Hannah, *The Rise of the Corporate Economy* (1983) pp. 135–6; W. Tudor Davies, *Trade Associations and Industrial Co-ordination* (1938) pp. 1–28; Political and Economic Planning, *British Trade Associations*, Planning No. 221 (12 May 1944); Political and Economic Planning, *Industrial Trade Associations* (1957), Chapter 10.

17. A. J. Marrison, 'Businessmen, Industries and Tariff Reform in Great Britain 1903–1930', *Business History*, 25 (1983).

18. F. Capie, *Depression and Protectionism: Britain Between the Wars* (1983).

19. Political and Economic Planning, *British Trade Associations*, pp. 1–2. A number of later Monopolies Commission and Restrictive Practices Court reports also ascribed inefficiencies to the absence of competitive pressures in the years between the 1930s and the 1950s. See Hannah, *Corporate Economy*, p. 141. In the case of the motor-car industry, for example, one study attributed some of the post-war inefficiencies to the fact that manufacturers were able to sell the vast majority of their output in protected markets. G. Maxcy and A. Silberston, *The Motor Industry* (1959).

20. L. Hannah and J. A. Kay, *Concentration in Modern Industry* (1977) pp. 64–5; L. Hannah, *Corporate Economy*, pp. 92–7, 101–3, 189–90; P. E. Hart and S. J. Prais, 'The Analysis of Business Concentration: A Statistical Approach', *Journal of the Royal Statistical Society* 119/2, (1956); H. Leak and A. Maizels, 'The Structure of British Industry', *Journal of the Royal Statistical Society*, 108/1–2 (1945).

21. L. Hannah, *Corporate Economy*, pp. 75, 95, 99, Appendix 1.

22. *Ibid.*, Chapters 4–5.

23. Leak and Maizels, 'Structure'.

24. A. Armstrong and A. Silberston, 'Size of Plant, Size of Enterprise, and Concentration in British Manufacturing Industry 1935–58', *Journal of the Royal Statistical Society*. Series A, 28, (1965). L. Hannah, *Corporate Economy*, p. 140; S. Prais, *The Evolution of Giant Firms in Britain* (Cambridge, 1976).

25. P. L. Payne, 'The Emergence of the Large-Scale Company in Great Britain, 1870–1914', *Economic History Review*, 20 (1967).

26. A. D. Chandler, 'The Transnational Industrial Firm in the United States and the United Kingdom: A Comparative Analysis', *Economic History Review*, 33 (1980).

27. The railway companies, in particular the LMSR and the LNER, were examples. See G. Crompton, '"Efficient and Economical Working?": The Performance of the British Railway Companies, 1923–1933', *Business History*, 27 (1985).

28. W. J. Reader, *Imperial Chemical Industries: A History, Volume I* (1970), pp. 300–16, 379–424, and *Volume II* Chapter 7; L. Hannah, 'Managerial Innovation and the Rise of the Large-Scale Company in Interwar Britain', *Economic History Review*, 27 (1974).

29. Hannah, *Corporate Economy*, p. 85.
30. See the activities of the Management Research Group, No. 1, through which a number of large firms exchanged information. The Ward Papers, British Library of Political and Economic Science, London.
31. ICI learnt and borrowed from DuPont.
32. D. F. Channon, *The Strategy and Structure of British Enterprise* (1973). In his calculations Channon may have underestimated the number of holding-company examples and exaggerated the spread of functionally organised firms. Estimates are, however, extremely difficult and forms shade into one another.
33. J. D. Scott, *Vickers: A History* (1962).
34. L. Hannah, 'Visible and Invisible Hands in Great Britain', in A. D. Chandler and H. Daems (eds.), *Managerial Hierarchies: Comparative Perspectives on the Rise of the Modern Industrial Enterprise* (Cambridge, Mass., 1980) p. 57. R. Jones and O. Marriott, *Anatomy of a Merger* (1972).
35. A. D. Chandler, *Scale and Scope: The Dynamics of Industrial Capitalism* (Cambridge, Mass., 1990).
36. D. C. Coleman, 'Gentlemen and Players', *Economic History Review*, 26 (1973).
37. Business Statistics Office, *Historical Record of the Census of Production 1907 to 1970* (1978), p. 202; S. Melman, *Dynamic Factors in Industrial Productivity* (Oxford, 1956) pp. 77, 131; US Department of Commerce, Bureau of the Census, *Historical Statistics of the United States from Colonial Times to 1970* (Washington, DC, 1970) p. 666.
38. Melman, *Dynamic Factors*, Chapter 12. W. J. Hiscox, *Factory Lay-Out Planning and Progress* (1948).
39. S. P. Keeble, 'University Education and Business Management from the 1890s to the 1950s: A Reluctant Relationship' (London, Ph.D., 1984); Coleman, 'Gentlemen and Players'; R. Locke, *The End of Practical Man: Entrepreneurship in Germany, France and Great Britain* (Greenwich, Conn. 1984).
40. Coleman, 'Gentlemen and Players'; W. Lazonick, 'Strategy, Structure, and Management Development in the United States and Britain', in K. Kobayashi and H. Morikawa (eds.), *Development of Managerial Enterprise* (Tokyo, 1986).
41. Melman, *Dynamic Factors*, p. 89; R. Coopey, 'Supervision and Industrial Change: The Engineering Industry in Britain 1900-1950', University of Warwick MA 1985; Management Research Group No. 1, Box 14, 'Notes for Meeting of the Works Managers Section of the MRG to be held at St. Helens, 3 May 1939' stated that training and re-training is 'one of the biggest problems facing industry today and it must be tackled immediately if the full benefits of scientific management are to be realised'.
42. M. M. Niven, *Personnel Management 1913-63* (1967) pp. 40-45.
43. C. G. Renold, *Joint Consultation over Thirty Years* (1950) p. 14.
44. Niven, *Personnel Managment*, pp. 45, 79; Reader, *Imperial Chemical Industries*, Volume II p. 60; C. H. Northcott, *Personnel Management* (1945) pp. 106-8.
45. Reader, *Imperial Chemical Industries*, Volume II, p. 60.

46. Niven, *Personnel Management*, p. 79; Northcott, *Personnel Management*, pp. 106-8; A. Briggs, *Social Thought and Social Action: A Study of the Work of Seebohm Rowntree* (1961) pp. 226-7. A. Shaw had worked with the work study specialist Dr L. Gilbreth.

47. Niven, *Personnel Management*, pp. 36, 61, 84. T. G. Rose, *A History of the Institute of Industrial Administration* (1954). Many of the largest British companies were also members of the Management Research Groups, to which they sent board or senior managers with personnel responsibilities to exchange information and to discuss management methods. One of the sections of the Management Research Group, No. 1, was devoted to personnel matters. The active companies were ICI, AEI, Standard Telephones & Cables, Pilkingtons, Metal Box, Dunlop.

48. *Official History of Ministry of Munitions*, Volume 7, Part I (1922) p. 94. Quoted in S. Pollard, *The Development of the British Economy 1914-1980* (1983 edn) p. 26.

49. See Chapter 3 and E. Cadbury *et al.*, *Scientific Management in Industry* (1915) reprinted from *Sociological Review*, 7 (1914).

50. *Official History of Ministry of Munitions*, Volume 7, Part I, p. 87; A. S. Milward, *The Economic Effects of the Two World Wars on Britain* (1984), pp. 19, 37-38; S. Pollard, *The Development*, p. 26; C. Wrigley, 'The Ministry of Munitions' in K. Burk (ed.), *War and the State* (1982).

51. Hannah, *Corporate Economy*, p. 26; J. M. Winter (ed.), *War and Economic Development* (Cambridge, 1975).

52. The so-called Shells and Fuses Agreement of early 1915 permitted women and young persons to work special single-purpose machines, involving little skill, while in the same year the Treasury Agreement between union leaders and the government went further and permitted the employment of semi-skilled workers on tasks and on machines hitherto solely the preserve of fully skilled men. See the Munitions of War Act 1915 s.4(3).

53. Milward, *Economic Effects*, p. 39; G. D. H. Cole, *Trade Unions and Munitions* (Oxford, 1923); C. Wrigley, *David Lloyd George and the British Labour Movement* (Brighton, 1976).

54. S. Webb, *The Works Manager Today* (1917), p. 134.

55. There was an attempt to apply the wartime regulations to private work by the Rochdale textile engineers, Tweedale & Smalley, which triggered off a widespread series of strikes in May 1917.

56. A. Reid, 'Dilution, Trade Unionism and the State in Britain During the First World War' in S. Tolliday and J. Zeitlin (eds.) *Shop Floor Bargaining and the State* (Cambridge, 1985); C. More, *Skill and the English Working Class, 1870-1914* (1980) pp. 30-1; G. Braybon, *Women Workers in the First World War* (1981).

57. The guarantees embodied in the Munitions of War Acts of 1915 and 1916 were fulfilled by the Pre-War Practices Act of 1919.

58. A. Reid, 'Dilution', p. 66.

59. Board of Trade, *Engineering Trade after the War* (Cd. 9073, 1918) p. 95.

60. S. and B. Webb, *The History of Trade Unionism* (1920), p. 642, n. 2.

61. See Cole, *Trade Unions*, p. 214, for this view.

62. Webb, *History*, p. 642, n. 2.

63. See Scrapbook of North East Coast Engineering Employers' Association entitled 'Engineers' Lock-out 1922'; Engineering Employers' Federation /XX/Executive Board/18 March 1921; the pamphlet, 'Maintenance of Right of Employers to Exercise Managerial Functions', issued by the Federation in March 1922, emphasises the importance of the 'machine question' in the dispute.

64. Speech by Sir A. Smith in Commons Debate on 1922 dispute, *House of Commons Debates*, Volume 152, 20 March 1922, Column 122.

65. See A. McIvor, 'Employers Associations and Industrial Relations in Lancashire, 1890–1939' (Ph.D., Manchester, 1983).

66. J. Hilton *et al.*, *Are Trade Unions Obstructive?* (1935) p. 335.

67. B. W. E. Alford, *Depression and Recovery? British Economic Growth 1918–39* (1972) p. 79; B. W. E. Alford, 'Entrepreneurship, Business Performance and Industrial Development', *Business History* 19 (1977) p. 130.

68. Engineering Employers' Federation/XXXII/Management Board. April 1934; H. Gospel 'Employers' Organisations: Their Growth and Function in the British System of Industrial Relations in the Period 1918–1939' (London Ph.D., 1974) pp. 189–90.

69. C. R. Littler, *The Development of the Labour Process in Capitalist Societies* (1982) Chapters 8 and 9.

70. Taylorism implies a more articulated system: the analysis of work as a basis of job redesign; an increased subdivision of labour, including the divorce of direct and indirect jobs and the separation of manual and mental work; an increased planning of jobs and the issuance of detailed instructions; the fixing of piecework rates by time study; and the use of 'functional foremanship' with more specialised foremen and inspectors replacing the old-style foreman. F.W. Taylor, 'Shop Management', American Society of Mechanical Engineers *Transactions* 24 (1903) and *Scientific Management* (1911).

71. There was also an increased interest in the study of fatigue under the auspices of the Health of Munitions Workers' Committee. See E. T. Elbourne, *Factory Administration and Accounts* (1914). In all 10,000 copies were sold during the war. See A. Briggs, *Social Thought and Social Action; A Study of the Work of Seebohm Rowntree 1871–1954* (1961).

72. W. Meakin, *The New Industrial Revolution* (1928); L. Urwick, *The Meaning of Rationalisation* (1929); S. Myers, *Business Rationalisation* (1932); S. Shaw, 'The Attitude of the TUC towards Unemployment in the Interwar Period' (Kent Ph.D., 1980).

73. J. A. Hobson in E. Cadbury, *Scientific Management*, p. 35.

74. The Industrial Fatigue Research Board and the National Institute of Industrial Psychology were involved in time and motion studies in the 1920s. A. J. McIvor, 'Employers, the Government, and Industrial Fatigue in Britain, 1890–1917', *British Journal of Industrial Medicine*, 44 (1987) and 'Manual Work, Technology, and Industrial Health, 1918–1939', *Medical History*, 31 (1987).

75. Group Report (chaired by A. Shaw), 'Time and Motion Study', *British Management Review* (July–September 1938); G. Brown, *Sabotage* (Nottingham, 1977) pp. 248–9.

76. Other consultancy firms offered similar packages from the 1930s onwards. Urwick Orr and Partners were established in 1932; PE Group in 1934; and Personnel Administration in 1943. In 1938 Bedaux changed its name to Associated Industrial Consultants. P. Tisdall, *Agents of Change: The Development and Practice of Management Consultancy* (1982).

77. Trades Union Congress, *Bedaux: The TUC Examines the Bedaux System of Payment by Results* (1933) p. 3.

78. Littler, *The Development*, p. 114.

79. For examples of firms where Bedaux was only partially introduced see ICI, Pilkingtons, Lucas, Rover, and GEC. *Ibid.* chapter 9.

80. Over the interwar years, the industrial consumption of electricity increased by 359 per cent. L. Hannah, *Electricity Before Nationalisation* (1979) pp. 170–4, 420.

81. See, for example, R. Wild, 'The Origins and Development of Flow-Line Production', *Industrial Archaeology* 11 (1974).

82. Morris was a leader in the early 1920s in introducing new machine tools, assembly lines, and transfer machines. Austin was at first somewhat less ambitious. but from the mid 1920s onwards began to reorganise production machinery and methods at Longbridge. Both owed a debt to American ideas and methods. Managers from Morris visited the US in 1924 and Austin bought American machines and used American engineers in reorganising Longbridge. During the interwar years, Ford, which had first established a plant at Trafford Park in Manchester in 1911, considerably expanded production and in 1931 opened its Dagenham plant, probably the best equipped and organised car plant in Europe at the time. General Motors, which took over Vauxhall in 1925, substantially reorganised and mechanised its production facilities in the 1930s. In addition to the assemblers, Briggs and Pressed Steel were two important suppliers of American origin, which introduced machine-fed presses and flow line methods to produce car bodies. W. Lewchuk, 'Fordism and the British Motor Car Employers, 1898–1932', in H. F. Gospel and C. R. Littler (eds.), *Managerial Strategies and Industrial Relations* (1983); W. Lewchuk, *American Technology and the British Vehicle Industry* (Cambridge, 1987); R. Church, *Herbert Austin* (1979) p. 69. P.W.S. Andrews and E. Brunner, *The Life of Lord Nuffield* (Oxford, 1955) pp. 140–1; L. Holden, 'A History of Vauxhall Motors to 1950' (Open University, M.Phil. thesis, 1983).

New mass-production techniques were also adopted in the electrical products industry, especially by firms producing electric light accessories and lamps, telephones and telegraph equipment, and domestic appliances. As in motor vehicles, a small number of leading firms set the pace – GEC, AEI, Lucas, Plessey, Philips, Mullard, Ferranti, Morphy Richards, and Electrolux. Single-purpose machine tools were extensively used along with assembly-line systems. In this sector these resulted in a pronounced sexual division of labour. Skilled men were employed in the tool room and on maintenance work, but most of the more repetitive work on the line was done by semi- and unskilled female labour.

83. W.J. Reader, *Imperial Chemical Industries: A History, Volume II* (Oxford 1975); W. J. Reader 'Chemical Industry' in N. K. Buxton and D.H. Aldcroft,

British Industry Between the Wars (1979); L. F. Haber, *Chemical Industry 1900-1930* (Oxford, 1971) especially Chapter 10.

84. M. A. Glucksmann, *Women Assemble: Women Workers and the New Industries in Interwar Britain* (1990); T. A. B. Corley, *Quaker Enterprise in Biscuits: Huntley & Palmer of Reading* (1972) pp. 222, 232. In biscuits, for example, Peak Frean automated its two plants in Bermondsey in the early 1930s, installing new ovens and conveyor systems. In contrast to Peak Frean, Huntley & Palmer were slower to automate and attempted rather to increase the proportion of women.

85. D. C. Coleman, *Courtaulds: An Economic and Social History*, Volume II (Oxford, 1969).

86. M. Stewart and L. Hunter, *The Needle is Threaded* (1964), p.197.

87. Lewchuk, *American Technology*.

88. See, for example, J. Zeitlin, 'The Labour Strategies of British Engineering Employers, 1890-1922', in H. F. Gospel and C. R. Littler (eds.), *Managerial Strategies and Industrial Relations* (1983).

89. J. McGoldrick, 'Crisis and the Division of Labour: Clydeside Shipbuilding in the Inter-War Period', in T. Dickson (ed.), *Capital and Class in Scotland* (Edinburgh 1987); L. Jones, *Shipbuilding in Britain* (Cardiff, 1957), Chapters 4 and 7.

90. T. H. Burnham and G. O Hoskins, *Iron and Steel in Britain, 1870-1930* (1943), pp. 190-3; D. L. Burn, *The Economic History of Steelmaking, 1867-1939* (Cambridge, 1940) pp. 362-70, 408-13, 427; J. C. Carr and W. Taplin, *History of the British Steel Industry* (Oxford, 1962) parts 4 and 5; Balfour Committee, *Survey of Industries*, Volume IV, pp. 21-32; K. Warren, 'Iron and Steel', in N. K. Buxton and D. H. Aldcroft, *British Industry*; N. K. Buxton, 'Efficiency and Organisation in Scotland's Iron and Steel Industry During the Interwar Period', *Economic History Review*, 29 (1976).

91. P. Pagnamenta and R. Overy, *All Our Working Lives* (1984), p. 40.

92. Pollard, *The Development*, p. 67; A. Taylor, 'The Coal Industry', in D. H. Aldcroft (ed.), *The Development of British Industry and Foreign Competition* (1968); Pagnamenta and Overy, *Working Lives* (1984) p. 179; *Coal Mining. Report of the Technical Advisory Committee* (Cmd. 6610, 1945); E. C. Rhodes, 'Output, Labour and Machines in the Coal Mining Industry of Great Britain', *Economica* (1945); M. Dintenfass, 'Entrepreneurial Failure Reconsidered: The Case of the Interwar British Coal Industry', *Business History Review*, 62 (1988).

93. See footnote above.

94. S. Tolliday, *Business, Banking, and Politics: The Case of British Steel 1918-1939* (Cambridge, Mass., 1987) and J. S. Boswell, *Business Politics in the Making: Three Steel Companies Compared* (1983).

95. T. Manwaring and S. Wood, 'The Ghost in the Labour Process', in D. Knights *et al.*, *Job Redesign* (Aldershot, 1985).

96. W. P. Kennedy, *Industrial Structure, Capital Markets and the Origins of British Economic Decline* (Cambridge, 1987).

97. In 1919 hours fell from 54 to 47. Thereafter the only significant increase was in coal mining. See Matthews, Feinstein, and Odling-Smee, *British Economic Growth*, pp. 64-73.

98. In the period of labour shake-out between 1920 and 1924 industrial productivity rose by 5.6 per cent per annum. The output of mechanical engineering,
for example, rose by 6 per cent in 1920-24, yet the labour force was reduced
by no less than 46 per cent. D. H. Aldcroft, *The British Economy Between
the Wars* (Oxford, 1983). p. 49. Overall, through the interwar years, the
annual rate of growth of productivity per man hour in manufacturing was
2.5 per cent. H. W. Richardson, 'The New Industries Between the Wars',
Oxford Economic Papers, 13 (1961).
99. Rostas in a study of labour productivity in 1936 showed that physical output
per man in Germany was between 10 and 20 per cent higher in blast furnaces,
steel smelting, and rolling mills; between 20 and 25 per cent higher in cotton
spinning and artificial fibres; and 50 per cent higher in coal mines and coke
ovens. Comparative figures with the US were even more striking: productivity was substantially higher in all American industries and enormously
higher in some, with a maximum difference of 200 per cent in blast furnaces.
L. Rostas, *Comparative Productivity in British and American Industry* (Cambridge, 1966).
100. W. E. G. Salter, *Productivity and Technical Change* (Cambridge, 1966) p. 71,
101. N. Crafts and M. Thomas, 'Comparative Advantage in UK Manufacturing
Trade, 1910-1939', *Economic Journal*, 96 (1986).

4 THE EVOLVING EMPLOYMENT RELATIONSHIP

1. D. H. MacGregor, *The Evolution of Industry* (1911) Chapter 5, talks about
a 'loose' or 'incomplete' or 'imperfect' association. C. R. Littler, *The Development of the Labour Process in Capitalist Societies* (1982) talks similarly about
'minimal interaction'.
2. The system of leaving certificates was introduced under s.7 of the 1915
Munitions of War Act and lasted until it was repealed by s.2 of the 1917
Munitions of War Act. Under the system employers were permitted to keep
a man in his job against his will by refusing him a certificate without which
he could not get a job for six weeks after quitting his old employment.
3. Measures on these lines were introduced from the summer of 1940 onwards
and came fully into force with the passage of the Defence Regulations Act
58A of March 1941. Workers in scheduled establishments were not allowed
to leave their employment without giving seven days' notice to both their
employer and the National Service Officer, stating their reasons. Also the
employer was not allowed to discharge an employee (although he could
suspend him) without going through the same procedure or unless the
employee was guilty of serious misconduct. Movement was therefore only
to be for exceptional reasons. In return for this, employers had to pay a
guaranteed week's pay even when there was no work, as long as any stoppage
was due to causes outside the workers' control. A. Bullock, *The Life and
Times of Ernest Bevin*, Volume II, 1967, Chapter 5.
4. N. Whiteside, 'Industrial Welfare and Labour Regulation in Britain at the
Time of the First World War', *International Review of Social History* (1980);
J. H. Richardson, *An Introduction to the Study of Industrial Relations* (1954)
p. 37; P. Inman, *Labour in the Munitions Industries* (1957) Chapter 9.

5. M. M. Niven, *Personnel Management 1913–63* (1967) pp. 40–45; A. Briggs, 'Social Background', in A. Flanders and H.A. Clegg (eds.), *The System of Industrial Relations in Great Britain* (Oxford, 1967) pp. 38–39; A. Briggs, *Social Thought and Social Action: A Study of the Work of Seebohm Rowntree 1871–1954* (1961) pp. 120, 125.

6. Niven *Personnel Managment*, pp. 26,43,46–47,53; Briggs, *Scoial Thought*, p. 120; N. Whiteside, 'Industrial Welfare'; A. Mclvor, 'Industrial Fatigue and Scientific Management 1914–1939,' (Unpublished Polytechnic of Central London Research Paper, 1984).

7. Though compared to pre First World War it may have been less exceptional than is sometimes supposed. See Chapter 3.

8. J. McGoldrick, 'Crisis and the Division of Labour: Clydeside Shipbuilding in the Interwar Period', in T. Dickson (ed.), *Capital and Class in Scotland* (Edinburgh, 1982) p. 151.

9. 'A works could be idle for a month, and the men would be on the dole. Suddenly the news would come around, "[The mill] is going to start, don't know how long". And they would start producing again for maybe two months. Then they closed down again. We called them "umbrella plants" in that they were always opening and closing.' P. Pagnamenta and R. Overy, *All Our Working Lives* (1984) p. 83.

10. P. Bagwell, *The Railwaymen* (1963) pp. 413, 420.

11. P. Smith, 'Seasonal Fluctuations in the Motor Vehicle Industry: A Comment', *Journal of Industrial Economics*, 21 (1973).

12. 'Work was seasonal. One firm had three busy months, three quiet months, three short-time months. There was no arguing then. It was just three days a week, short-time.' Pagnamenta and Overy, *Working Lives*, p. 222.

13. Pagnamenta and Overy, *Working Lives*, Chapter 11; M. A. Glucksmann, *Women Assemble: Women Workers and the New Industries in Interwar Britain* (1990).

14. N. Whiteside, 'Welfare Insurance and Casual Labour', *Economic History Review*, 32 (1979), suggests that in the interwar years, as a result of the existence of unemployment insurance, some casual trades developed structures similar to short-time work.

15. H. Gospel, 'The Development of Management Organisation in Industrial Relations: A Historical Perspective', in K. Thurley and S. Wood (eds.), *Industrial Relations and Management Strategy* (Cambridge,1983); G. D. H. Cole, *The Payment of Wages* (1918); C. R. Littler, *The Development*; R. J. Waller, *The Dukeries Transformed: The Social and Political Development of a Twentieth Century Coalfield* (Oxford, 1983), Chapter 5; R. Goffee, 'The Butty System in the Kent Coalfield', *Bulletin of Society for the Study of Labour History*, 34 (1977). Sub-contracting emerged in some motor car firms in the 1920s, but more in the form of collective piecework organised by the men themselves.

16. E. H. Hunt, *Regional Wage Variations in Britain 1850–1914* (Oxford 1973).

17. P. S. Florence, *Economics of Fatigue and Unrest* (1924), p.177; W. J. Hiscox and J. R. Price, *Factory Administration in Practice* (1939) p.264; J. R. Long, 'Labour Turnover Under Full Employment', (University of Birmingham, Studies in Economics and Society, Monograph A2, 1951); H. Silcock, 'The Phenomenon of Labour Turnover', *Journal of the Royal Statistical Society*

(Series A, 117 1954); A. K. Rice et al., 'The Representation of Labour Turnover as a Social Process', *Human Relations*, 3 (1960); G. Thomas, 'Labour Mobility in Great Britain 1945–49', An Inquiry Carried Out for the Ministry of Labour and National Service (Report 134, 1949) p.59; C. Clark, *National Income and Outlay* (1937) pp.33–4.

18. M. Greenwood, 'Problems of Industrial Organisation', *Journal of Royal Statistical Society*, 82 (1919); M. Greenwood, Committee Report No. 16, 1918; P. S. Florence, *Economics*, Chapter 2; G. N. Miles, *Westminster Gazette*, 10 January 1923; Industrial Fatigue Research Board, *A Statistical Study of Labour Turnover*, No. 13 (1921).

19. After initially rising during the Second World War, turnover declined, but rose from 1944–45 onwards and led to a revived interest and a further series of studies. Long, 'Labour Turnover'; Thomas, 'Labour Mobility', especially pp.28,35,39–40; T. H. Burnham, *Modern Foremanship* (1937), p.7; W. Raphael *et al.* 'Report on an Enquiry into Labour Turnover in the London District', *Occupational Psychology*, 12 (1938); Rice *et al.*, 'The Representation'; R. James, 'Human Waste: An Analysis of Labour Turnover in Industry', *Economic Journal*, 59 (1949).

20. B. W. E. Alford, 'New Industries for Old? British Industry between the Wars',in R. Floud and D. McCloskey (eds.), *The Economic History of Britain since 1700, Vol 2 1860 to the 1970s* (Cambridge, 1981) p. 321; Hunt, *Wage Variations*.

21. D. Baines, *Migration in a Mature Economy* (Cambridge, 1985); J. Stevenson, *British Society 1914–45* (1984).

22. See, for example, A. Williams, *Life in a Railway Factory* (1915) p.276.

23. E.T. Elbourne, *Factory Administration and Cost Accounts* (1929) p.240; Florence, *Economics*, p.111.

24. Quoted in Niven, *Personnel Management* pp. 77–8. It is also quoted in K. E. Wilkinson, *The Employment Department* (1927) and O. Sheldon, *The Philosophy of Management* (1923). Sheldon was in the Labour Department at Rowntrees and was to become a director of that firm.

25. W. J. Deeley, *Labour Difficulties* (Manchester, 1918) p.29.

26. Among the books in use were Sheldon, *Philosophy*; Hiscox and Price, *Factory Administration*; Burnham, *Foremanship*; B. Muscio, *Lectures on Industrial Psychology* (1920); H. L. Hollingsworth, *Vocational Psychology* (1919); H. Munsterberg, *Psychology and Industrial Efficiency* (1913); C. S. Myers, *Mind and Work* (1920). In devising such arrangements firms could, during the interwar years, increasingly draw on the advice of consultants and other specialist bodies. From 1918 the Industrial Fatigue Research Board and from 1921 the National Institute of Industrial Psychology pioneered vocational guidance, testing, and selection techniques. See A. J. McIvor, 'Employers, the Government, and Industrial Fatigue in Britain, 1890–1917', *British Journal of Industrial Medicine*, 44 (1987) and 'Manual Work, Technology, and Industrial Health, 1918–1939', *Medical History*, 31 (1987); Niven, *Personnel Management*, p.74; L. Urmick and E. F. L. Brech, *The Human Factor in Management* (1944) pp. 24–25. During and after the Second World War the use of tests was given a further stimulus by their adoption by the armed forces. See also Richardson, *Industrial Relations*, p. 49 and P. S. Florence, *Labour*, pp. 129–30.

27. Burnham, *Foremanship*, pp. 71-2; T. H. Burnham, *Engineering Economics: Work Organisation and Management*, Volume II (1935) pp. 41-2; M. B. Gilson and E. J. Riches, 'Employers' Additional Unemployment Benefit Schemes in Great Britain', *International Labour Review*, 21 (1930).
28. W. F. Watson, 'The Workers' Point of View: Hiring and Firing', *Human Factor*, 6 (1932).
29. More, *Skill*, pp. 67-8; Richardson, *Industrial Relations*, p. 43.
30. C. L. Goodrich, *The Frontier of Control* (1975 edn) p. 95; Engineering and Allied Employers National Federation, *Unemployment; Its Realities and Problems* (1937) pp.16, 65; Hiscox and Price, *Factory Administration*, p.264; Florence, *Labour*, p.135. A. McKinlay, '"A Certain Short-Sightedness": Metalworking, Innovation, and Apprenticeship', in H. F. Gospel (ed.), *Industrial Training and Technological Innovation* (1991).
31. Florence, *Labour*, p. 136.
32. *Ibid*; T.H., Burnham, *Engineering Economics*, pp.84-7. According to Burnham, p.85: 'In the experience of a number of firms it has been found that the time required for training operatives is reduced by a special department or training supervisor, as the trainees became more rapidly efficient than if they commence work at once in the production department...There appears to be a consensus of opinion that a trainer doing a full-time job will accelerate the training of employees compared with the foreman who already has his hands full with considerations of efficient production.'
33. D. C. Thomson, *Training Worker Citizens* (1949), p. xiii; More, *Skill*, p.86. Metropolitan-Vickers was said to have the best apprenticeship scheme for electrical engineers in Great Britain.
34. Committee on Industry and Trade, *Final Report* (1929), p.208; P. F. R. Venables and W. J. Williams, *The Smaller Firm and Technical Education* (1961); A. Abbott, 'Recent Trends in Education for Industry and Commerce in Great Britain', *International Labour Review*, 32 (1935).
35. More, *Skill* (1980) p.105.
36. *Ibid.*, p.86; *Report of an Enquiry into Apprenticeship and Training in 1925-26*, Volume VI, p. 39, 1927-8.
37. P. Ryan, 'Apprentices, Employment and Industrial Disputes in Engineering in the 1920s', Unpublished paper presented to Workshop on Child Labour and Apprenticeship, University of Essex, 1986; W. Knox, 'British Apprenticeship, 1800-1914', Unpublished Ph.D., University of Edinburgh (1980) and 'Apprenticeship and Deskilling in Britain, 1850-1914', *International Review of Social History*, 31 (1986).
38. W. H. Beveridge, *Unemployment: A Problem of Industry* (1930), pp. 193, 221; A. L. Bowley, *An Elementary Manual of Statistics* (7th edn 1952) p.151.
39. Whiteside, 'Welfare Insurance'.
40. Under the three-day continuity rule employees could draw benefit as a supplement to reduced wages. This led groups of employees to form 'pools' composed of five or six members who arranged with the employer to 'play', i.e. to be temporarily laid off, in turn. In this way members of the pool retained continuous eligibility for insurance benefits. The system came to be known as 'OXO' because of the arrangement of alternating days of work (O) and unemployment (X).
41. Short-time working was also a way of reducing the threat of overproduction

and resultant increased competition, at least where it was organised on an industry basis as in parts of cotton textiles and flour milling. H. F. Gospel, 'Employers' Organisations: Their Growth and Function in the British System of Industrial Relations in the Period 1918–1939', Unpublished Ph.D., University of London (1974), p.251.

42. M. B. Gilson and E. J. Riches, 'Employers' Additional Unemployment Benefit Schemes in Great Britain', *International Labour Review*, 21 (1930), p. 351.
43. *Ibid.* and H. F. Gospel, 'Employers' Organisations'. Contracting out was suspended in 1922 and abolished in 1927 when the national fund went into the red.
44. Gilson and Riches, 'Unemployment Benefit Schemes'.
45. *Ibid.* An agreement in flour milling in 1937, pioneered by Ranks and Spillers, guaranteed workers their full wages when on short-time or laid off. H. F. Gospel, 'Employers' Organisations', p. 250. Both Rowntrees and Boots used casual and temporary workers as a buffer and expected women to leave on marriage or the birth of a first child.
46. Gilson and Riches, 'Unemployment Benefit Schemes'.
47. *Ibid.*; G. T. Schwenning, 'British Dismissal Gratuities' *Social Forces*, 13 (1935). An agreement covering the railways had been included in the 1921 Railways Act. Indeed an agreement covering central and local government dated back to the nineteenth century. S. Shaw, 'The Attitude of the TUC Towards Unemployment in the Interwar Period' (Kent Ph.D., 1980).
48. Schwenning, 'Dismissal Gratuities'; Gilson and Riches, 'Unemployment Benefit Schemes'; Gospel, 'Employers' Organisations', pp. 252–4.
49. This scheme was partly funded by employee contributions and compensation took the form of a weekly payment over a three month period. Schwenning, 'Dismissal Gratuities' and Gilson and Riches,'Unemployment Benefit Schemes'.
50. The 1921 Railway Act provided for statutory compensation payments to railway workers who lost their jobs as a result of merger. G.T. Schwenning, 'Dismissal Gratuities'.
51. However, the practice did gradually develop of paying a lump sum according to length of service. *Ibid.* and Gilson and Riches, 'Unemployment Benefit Schemes'.
52. Schwenning, 'Dismissal Gratuities', p. 449.
53. Richardson, *Industrial Relations* (1933), p. 188.
54. *Joint Interim Report on Unemployment*, 12 March 1929, p. 14.
55. Gospel, 'Employers' Organisations'.
56. E. Hobsbawm, *Labouring Men* (1964); J. A. Hobson, *Wealth and Life* (1929); J. Schoenhoff, *The Economy of High Wages* (1892); A. G. B. Fisher, *Some Problems of Wages and their Regulation in Great Britain since 1918* (1926).
57. B. Austin and W. F. Lloyd, *The Secret of High Wages* (1926).
58. See also the cotton employers who aspired to an extended hours and low wage policy though, in the event, in the industrial relations crisis of the early 1930s they lacked the power to enforce this.
59. W. Lewchuk, 'Fordism and British Motor Car Employers, 1896–1932', in H.F. Gospel and C.R.Littler (eds.), *Managerial Strategies and Industrial*

Relations (1983); S. Tolliday, 'Management and Labour in Britain, 1896-1939', in S. Tolliday and J. Zeitlin, *The Automobile Industry and its Workers* (1985).

60. Fisher, *Problems of Wages*, Chapter 10 and pp. 240-46; Richardson, *Industrial Relations*, Chapter 6.
61. Fisher, *Problems of Wages*, p. 222; G. Routh, *Occupation and Pay in Great Britain 1906-60* (1965) pp. 201-2.
62. Ministry of Labour, *Report on Profit-Sharing and Labour Copartnership in the United Kingdom* (cd. 544, 1920); E. Bristow, 'Profit-Sharing, Socialism, and Labour Unrest', in K. D. Brown, *Essays in Anti-Labour History* (1974).
63. The desire to reduce labour turnover is to be seen in the qualifying period and the length of service recognised in many firms by a bigger share in profits. For example in the case of Associated Portland Cement Manufacturers Ltd, employees of ten years' service or more received five times the bonus of the employee with one year's service. J. Ramage, 'Profit-sharing and Copartnership in Great Britain', in F.E. Gannett and B.F. Catherwood, *Industrial and Labour Relations in Great Britain* (New York, 1939).
64. *Labour*, p. 112 and Ramage, 'Profit-sharing', p. 259.
65. Richardson, *Industrial Relations*, p. 117.
66. G. D. H. Cole makes the point, 'Coal, steel, engineering, and cotton have in the main stood aloof from the movement'. *Modern Theories and Forms of Industrial Organisation* (1932) p. 86.
67. M. L. Yates, *Wages and Labour Conditions in British Engineering* (1937), p. 97 and Chapter 7.
68. H. Wolfe, *Labour Supply and Regulation* (Oxford, 1923), p.266.
69. Yates, *Wages and Labour*, p.97; W. McLaine, 'Payment by Results in British Engineering', *International Labour Review*, 49 (1944); K. G. J. C. Knowles and D. J. Robertson, 'Earnings in Engineering, 1926-48', *Bulletin of the Oxford University Institute of Statistics*, 13 (1951) p. 187.
70. Richardson, *Industrial Relations*, Chapter 6.
71. National Board for Prices and Incomes, *Payment by Results Systems*, Report No. 65 (Cmnd. 3627, 1968), p.76; Ministry of Labour, *Gazette* (September 1961).
72. In some trades the time rate which was guaranteed was the same as that paid to the time worker; in other cases the guaranteed time rate was fixed at a lower rate. R. Wilson, *Methods of Remuneration* (1931), pp. 25-6.
73. E. Wigham, *The Power to Manage* (1973) Chapter 4; Cole, *Payment of Wages*; J. E. Powell, *Payment by Results* (1924), p. 87; R. P. Lynton, *Incentive and Management in British Industry* (1949) p. 84.
74. Wilson, *Methods*, p. 26; Cole, *Payment of Wages*; Goodrich, *Frontier*, p. 79.
75. Lynton, *Incentive*, p. 84.
76. The so-called Taylor Differential Piece Rate. Powell, *Payment*, p. 109; Lynton, *Incentive*, p. 88.
77. There were numerous such systems, differing mainly in how the worker was compensated for time saved. Oversimplifying, the most favourable system to the worker was the Weir system which usually credited the worker with half of the time saved; the Halsey system assigned one third of time savings

to the worker; while the least favourable from the worker's point of view was the Rowan system which credited the worker with a variable amount which was geared in such a way that it usually did not exceed a quarter of the saving. The Weir system was developed by G.& J. Weir at their engineering works at Cathcart on Clydeside. The Halsey system was introduced from the USA in the late nineteenth century. Sometimes elements of the two systems were joined together and proved popular in engineering in Britain. J. J. Gillespie, *Training in Foremanship and Management* (1943). The Rowan system was developed by the Glasgow marine engineering firm of David Rowan & Co. in 1898. It was the most complicated and least generous to the pieceworker.

78. In engineering it came to be accepted that a pieceworker of average ability should be able to earn 25 per cent over the existing time rate for the job concerned. Powell, *Payment*, p. 88. In 1919 the minimum piecework standard was formally fixed by the EEF and the ASE at 33.3 per cent and was reduced to 25 per cent in 1931.

79. Wilson, *Methods*, pp. 76-7; 'Staff-Grading and Promotion Schemes' in *British Management Review*, 11 (1937).

80. Florence, *Labour*, p. 116.

81. L. Hannah, *Inventing Retirement* (Cambridge, 1986), p. 67.

82. *Ibid.*, and F. Green, 'Occupational Pension Schemes and British Capitalism', *Cambridge Journal of Economics*, 6 (1982).

83. Though workers could, of course, still leave or be dismissed. In addition pension schemes could be a way of compulsorily retiring older or less effective staff without damaging morale within the firm. See H. F. Gospel, 'Employers' Organisations', pp. 254-6 on flour milling which had an interesting industry-wide scheme.

84. H. J. Levy, 'The Economic History of Sickness and Medical Benefit Since the Industrial Revolution', *Economic History Review* 14 (1944).

85. Richardson, *Industrial Relations.*, p. 38; J. R. Hay, 'Employers' Attitudes to Social Policy and the Concept of Social Control, 1900-1920', in P. M. Thane (ed.), *The Origins of British Social Policy* (1978) pp. 119-20; W. J. Deeley, *Labour Difficulties and Suggested Solutions* (Manchester, 1918) pp. 89-97.

86. Deeley, *Labour Difficulties*, p. 94.

87. R. M. Titmus, 'The Social Division of Welfare', in *Essays on The Welfare State* (1958).

88. Employers' schemes, of course, built on the state national insurance scheme, in that the employer made up the state benefit to a certain percentage of the wage. H. Keast, 'Sick Leave Pay Under National Insurance', *Industrial Law Review* 3 (1948).

89. G. L. Reid, 'Sick Pay', in G. L. Reid and D. J. Robertson, *Fringe Benefits, Labour Costs and Social Security* (1965).

90. Ministry of Labour, *Holidays With Pay* (1939) pp. 7-18.

91. The EEF tried in 1936 to dissuade the Morris Car Company from conceding holidays with pay. Engineering Employers' Federation /XXXIV/ Management Board/17 June 1936. See also *Minutes of Evidence Taken Before the*

Committee on Holidays with Pay 1937-38, Parliamentary Papers 1937-38
XII *Report of the Committee on Holidays with Pay*, pp. 28-33.
92. Ministry of Labour, *Holidays with Pay*, footnote 1 (1939).
93. J. Melling, 'Employers' Industrial Welfare and the Struggle for Workplace
    Control in British Industry, 1880-1920', in H. F. Gospel and C. R. Littler,
    Managerial Strategies and Industrial Relations (1983).
94. R. J. Waller, *The Dukeries Transformed* (Oxford, 1985).

5 EMPLOYERS, UNIONS, AND COLLECTIVE BARGAINING

1. H. A. Clegg, A. Fox, and A. F. Thompson, *A History of British Trade Unions
   Since 1889*, Volume I (Oxford, 1964), pp. 362-3.
2. Department of Employment, *British Labour Statistics, Historical Abstract
   1886-1968* (1971), Tables 196 and 197. This has been interpreted by some
   as a period of more general political and social crisis in British society. See
   G. Dangerfield, *The Strange Death of Liberal England* (1936), for a classic,
   if exaggerated, statement of this kind.
3. J. Hinton, *The First Shop Stewards Movement* (1973), Chapter 2.
4. Under the so-called York Memorandum, the obligation on workers to work
   under conditions dictated by management while a case went through procedure was taken out, though the obligation to keep the peace was retained;
   a works' conference stage was introduced which allowed workers' deputations to be accompanied by a full-time officer, though when this occurred
   an official of the employers' association was also to be present. See E.
   Wigham, *The Power to Manage: A History of the Engineering Employers
   Federation* (1973), Chapter 4.
5. G. Alderman, 'The Railway Companies and the Growth of Trade Unionism
   in the Late Nineteenth and Early Twentieth Centuries', *Historical Journal*,
   14 (1971).
6. B. Mogridge, 'Militancy and Interunion Rivalry in British Shipping, 1911-
   1929', *International Review of Social History*, 6 (1961).
7. H. Pelling, *A History of British Trade Unionism* (3rd edn 1976) p. 142.
8. J. Hinton, *The First Shop Stewards Movement* (1973); C. Wrigley, *David
   Lloyd George and the British Labour Movement* (Brighton, 1976); I. McLean,
   The Legend of Red Clydeside, (1983).
9. Department of Employment, *Labour Statistics*, Table 196 and G. S. Bain
   and R. Price, *Profiles of Union Growth* (Oxford, 1980) p. 37.
10. H. F. Gospel, 'Employers' Organisations: Their Growth and Function in
    the British System of Industrial Relations in the Period 1918-1939' (Ph.D.,
    London, 1974) Chapters 1 and 3. S. Pollard, *The Development of the British
    Economy 1914-1980* (3rd edn, 1983) p. 30.
11. G. R. Askwith, 'Memorandum on Employers' Associations', 30 August 1917,
    p. 1, in the author's possession. Askwith was the Chief Industrial Com-
    missioner of the Labour Department of the Board of Trade.
12. Public Records Office/Lab 2/427/259/1918; Ministry of Labour, *Eighteenth
    Abstract of Labour Statistics* (Cmd 2740, 1926) p. 191.
13. The Engineering Employers' Federation recognised the National Union of
    Clerks in 1920 and the Association of Engineering and Shipbuilding

Draughtsmen in 1924. The Newspaper Proprietors' Association recognised the National Union of Journalists in 1919 and was followed by the Newspaper Society in 1918 and the Scottish Daily Newspaper Society in 1921. The NPA also recognised the National Union of Printing Bookbinding and Paper Workers for circulation representatives in 1919 and the National Society of Operative Printers and Assistants for clerical workers in 1920. See G. S. Bain, *The Growth of White Collar Unionism* (1970) pp. 142–75. J. Melling, 'Employers and the Rise of Supervisory Unionism, 1914–1939' in C. Wrigley (ed.), *A History of British Industrial Relations, 1914–1939*, Volume 2 (Brighton, 1987).

14. J. Hinton, *Shop Stewards*; G. D. H. Cole, *Workshop Organisation* (Oxford, 1923); *Official History of Ministry of Munitions*, Volume 7, Part 2 (1921). Bargaining about wages and conditions was undoubtedly more important than questions of either dilution or broader political questions.

15. R. Price, *Masters, Unions and Men* (Cambridge, 1980).

16. Ministry of Labour, *Works Committees*, Report No. 2 (1918) p. 13; G. D. H. Cole, *Workshop Organisation*, pp. 3–4 also stresses the positive aspects.

17. EEF/XIV/ *Memo as to the Effects of the Conflict between Industrial Trade Unionism and Craft Trade Unionism* (1918) p. 1.

18. Regulations Regarding the Appointment and Functions of Shop Stewards and Works Committees, York, 20 May 1919.

19. See EEF/XIV/ *Memo as to the Effects of the Conflict between Industrial Trade Unionism and Craft Trade Unionism* (1918) p.1; EEF/XV/Management Committee (19 December 1918); Speech by Sir A. Smith, *House of Commons Debates* (Volume 152, 20 March 1922, Column 124).

20. The leading arbitration tribunal under the wartime system of compulsory arbitration was the Committee on Production set up in 1915 under the chairmanship of G. R. Askwith.

21. See Ministry of Reconstruction, *Interim Report of the Committee on Relations between Employers and Employed* (Cd. 8606, 1917–1918) and *Final Report* (Cd. 9153, 1918).

22. Ministry of Labour, *Works Committees*, p. 37.

23. Figures based on estimate of Board of Trade, *Report on Collective Agreements between Employers and Workplace in the UK* (Cd. 5366, 1910) p. iv and figures on the number of employers' organisations cited above. For the fullest account see R. Charles, *The Development of Industrial Relations in Britain 1911–1939* (1973). See also *Report on the Establishment and Progress of Joint Industrial Councils 1917–1922* (1923) p. 3; J. B. Seymour, *The Whitley Council Scheme* (1932); J. H. Richardson, *Industrial Relations in Great Britain* (Geneva, 1933) Chapter 4. The less formal Whitley-type arrangements were the Interim Industrial Reconstruction Committees. These were a temporary form of joint body established in less well organised industries. In addition in 1919 there were 50 trade boards in industries where organisation on both sides was so poor that voluntary collective bargaining could not be established. The intention behind both the interim industrial reconstruction committees and the trade boards was that, as organisation improved on both sides, collective bargaining would develop and national joint industrial councils would be established.

24. Wage rates fell from 275 in the winter of 1920–21 (July 1914 100) to 173 in the winter of 1923–24, S. Pollard, *The Development of the British Economy 1914–1980* (3rd edn, 1983), p. 136.
25. Bain and Price, *Profiles*, p. 37; H. A. Clegg, A. Fox, and A. Thompson, *A History of British Trade Unionism since 1889, Volume II, 1911–1933* (Oxford, 1985) p. 543.
26. S. Glynn and S. Shaw, 'Wage Bargaining and Unemployment', *Political Quarterly*, 52 (1981).
27. R. Hyman, 'Rank and File Movements and Workplace Organisation 1914–1939' in C. Wrigley (ed.), *A History of British Industrial Relations* (Brighton, 1986). In 1922 the EEF reminded some of the members that shop steward recognition was mandatory on all federated firms. EEF/XXI/Management Committee/30 June 1922.
28. Richardson, *Industrial Relations*, (1938 edn) p. 137. There were 47 national joint industrial councils and interim industrial reconstruction committees in 1926.
29. See scrapbook of North East Coast Engineering Employers' Association entitled 'Engineers Lock-out 1922', pp. 1–25; EEF/XX/Executive Board/18 March 1921. The leaflet 'Maintenance of Right of Employers to Exercise Management Functions' issued by the Federation in March 1922, emphasises the importance of the machine question in the dispute.
30. Speech by Sir A. Smith, *House of Commons Debates* (Volume 152, 20 March 1922, Column 122).
31. Section II (1)(d) of 1922 Memorandum of Agreement between the Engineering and National Employers' Federation and Unions affiliated to the Engineering and Shipbuilding Trades Federation.
32. In 1932 the Patternmakers voted to terminate the provisions, EEF/XXXI/Management Board/26 May 1932 and EEF/XXXI/Management Board/21 July 1932. In 1934 the AEU pressed for changes, AEU *Monthly Journal and Report*, December 1934, p. 1, and EEF/XXXIV/Management Board/21 May 1936. In 1937 the Sheet Metal Workers gave notice to terminate, EEF/XXXVII/Management Board/26 January 1939. See also H. F. Gospel, 'Employers' Organisations', pp. 211–2.
33. EEF/XX/Executive Board/22 April 1921 and 20 May 1921; EEF/XXIII/Management Committee/29 February 1924; XXIX/Management Board/31 October 1929; XXXII/General Council/19 April 1934; XXXIII/Management Board/10 September 1935; XXXVII/Management Board/29 June 1939.
34. EEF/XXXIV/Management Board/26 September 1936; XXXV/Management Board/21 January 1937 and General Council/28 January 1937. For motor vehicles see EEF/XXVIII/Management Board/28 June 1928 and for aircraft see XXXIII/Management Board/23 May 1935 and XXXIV/Management Board/26 September 1936. Machine tools also became something of a wage leader in some areas in the mid 1930s, EEF/XXXIV/Management Board/31 October 1935. See also H. F. Gospel, 'Employers' Organisations', pp. 212, 269.
35. EEF/XXIII/General Council/13 May 1924; XXIX/Management Board/31 October 1929; XXXII/General Council/19 April 1934; XXXV/Management Board/28 January 1937.

36. J. W. F. Rowe, *Wages in the Coal Industry* (1923); A. G. B. Fisher, *Some Problems of Wages and their Regulation in Great Britain Since 1918* (1926); J. R. Raynes, *Coal and its Conflicts* (1928).
37. At the end of the coal dispute G. A. Spencer established the Nottinghamshire and District Miners' Industrial Union to coordinate the drift back to work. This also had some support in Derbyshire and S. Wales and was assisted by the owners in these coalfields. Spencerism ceased to exist in the late 1930s. See A. R. and C. P. Griffin, 'The Non-Political Trade Union Movement', in A. Briggs and J. Saville (eds.), *Essays in Labour History*, Volume III (1977); A. R. Griffin, *The Miners of Nottinghamshire* (1962); R. J. Waller, *The Dukeries Transformed* (Oxford, 1985), Chapter 5.
38. Waller, *Dukeries*, and Griffin and Griffin, 'Non-Political'.
39. G. W. McDonald, 'The Role of British Industry in 1926', in M. Morris (ed.) *The General Strike* (1976). G. A. Phillips, *The General Strike* (1976), Chapter 11.
40. Clegg, *History*, p. 214.
41. A. Anderson, 'The Labour Laws and the Cabinet Legislative Committee of 1926-27', *Bulletin of Society for Study of Labour History* 23 (1971), pp. 39-52, Phillips, *General Strike*, p. 250; McDonald, 'British Industry', pp. 307-8; R. Lowe, 'The Government and Industrial Relations, 1919-1939' in Wrigley (ed.) *History*.
42. The Mond-Turner Talks were named after Sir A. Mond, chairman of ICI, and B. Turner, the TUC President. G. W. McDonald and H. F. Gospel, 'The Mond-Turner Talks 1927-1933', *Historical Journal* (1973), and H. F. Gospel, 'Employers' Labour Policy: A Study of the Mond-Turner Talks 1927-1933', *Business History*, 21 (1979).
43. H. A. Clegg, *The System of Industrial Relations in Great Britain* (Oxford, 1970) p. 133.
44. See Conference on Industrial Reorganisation and Industrial Relations, *Interim Report*, 4 July 1928, p. 9. The main change in bargaining arrangements which was proposed was a national joint disputes procedure.
45. A. J. McIvor, 'Employers' Associations and Industrial Relations in Lancashire 1890-1939' (Ph.D., Manchester, 1983).
46. North West Federation of Building Trades Employers, *Minutes*, 18 February 1925. Quoted in *ibid.* p. 497.
47. See J. W. F. Rowe, *Wages in Practice and Theory* (1928) pp. 145-6; McIvor, 'Employers' Associations'; H. F. Gospel 'The Development of Bargaining Structure: The Case of Electrical Contracting' in C. Wrigley (ed.), *History*.
48. Ministry of Labour, *Report on Collective Agreements*, Volume I (1934) pp. 141-85; J. C. Carr and W. Taplin, *History of the British Steel Industry* (Oxford, 1962), pp. 452-64; F. Wilkinson, 'Collective Bargaining in the Steel Industry in the 1920s', in Briggs and Saville (eds.) *Essays*.
49. B. Mogridge, 'Militancy and Inter-Union Rivalries in British Shipping, 1911-1939', *International Review of Social History* 6 (1961). L. H. Powell, *The Shipping Federation* (1950) Chapter 5.
50. Askwith, 'Memorandum', p. 3. Employers' labour market and product market arrangements could be related in either a *complementary* or *alternative* manner. In the first instance, an effective employers' organisation could add to and strengthen collusive price arrangements. On the other hand,

where such arrangements did not exist, standard wage rates throughout an industry could act as a substitute for price fixing or could at least take wages out of competition between firms.

51. Recognition was, however, subject to certain important qualifications – for the most part only manual unions were recognised and most employers were not prepared to concede the closed-shop principle. On white-collar recognition, see footnote 6 above. Employers tried to keep out trade unionism for foremen and supervisory staff. On the closed shop, informal arrangements existed for some craftsmen in areas of engineering, shipbuilding, printing, iron and steel, and cotton textiles. However, with the exception of the shipowners and the National Union of Seamen from 1921 onwards, more formal closed shops were rare and were opposed by British employers throughout the interwar years. See W. E. J. McCarthy, *The Closed Shop in Britain* (1964), passim.

52. A. Flanders, 'Industrial Relations: What is Wrong with the System?' *Management and Unions* (1970) p. 88.

53. *Interim Report on Joint Standing Industrial Councils* (Cd. 8606, 1917).

54. Richardson, *Industrial Relations,* 1933, pp. 139-51. See also Committee on Industry and Trade (Balfour Committee), *Survey of Industrial Relations* (1926).

55. Introduced in 1914 York Memorandum.

56. Gospel, 'Employers' Organisations', pp. 140-1. This was the case in electrical contracting and flour milling.

57. *Ibid.,* p. 161. See also on engineering A. Marsh, *Industrial Relations in Engineering* (Oxford, 1965); A. Marsh, *Disputes Procedures in Britain,* Royal Commission on Trade Unions and Employers' Associations, Research Paper 2 (1) (1966) and 2 (2) (1968). For cotton see *Britain's Industrial Future: Being the Report of the Liberal Industrial Inquiry of 1928* (1977) p. 161, and A. McIvor, 'Employers' Associations', Chapter 8.

58. H. Phelps Brown, *The Origins of Trade Union Power* (Oxford, 1983) p. 143.

59. *AEU Monthly Journal and Report* (April 1926) pp. 48-9.

60. R. Hyman, 'Rank and File Movements and Workplace Organisation', in Wrigley, *History,* Volume II; McIvor, 'Employers' Associations', pp. 579-90, 607-610; Gospel, 'Employers' Organisations', pp. 179-90.

61. EEF/XXXII/Management Board/19 April 1934.

62. A. McIvor, 'Employers' Associations', Chapter 10.

63. B. W. E. Alford, 'New Industries for Old? British Industry Between the Wars', in R. Floud and D. McCloskey (eds.), *The Economic History of Britain Since 1700, Volume II, 1860 to the 1970s* (Cambridge, 1981); R. Croucher, *Engineers at War 1939-45* (1982) Chapter 1; R. Hyman, 'Rank and File'.

64. In cotton textiles male spinners and weavers retained considerable control, McIvor, 'Employers' Associations', Chapter 8; in coal mining from the mid 1930s onwards the union began to roll back management power; for building see McIvor, op. 526; R. Hyman, 'Rank and File', also cites railways, shipbuilding, and iron and steel.

65. K. G. J. C. Knowles and D. J. Robertson 'Earnings in Engineering, 1926-1948', *Bulletin of the Oxford University Institute of Statistics,* 13 (1951), and 'Some Notes on Engineering Earnings', *Bulletin of the Oxford University*

Institute of Statistics, 13 (1951). M. Dobb, *Wages* (Cambridge, 1946) p. 33; A. L. Bowley, *Wages and Income in the U.K. Since 1860* (Cambridge, 1937) pp. 11-18; Ministry of Labour, *Gazette,* February 1945; Gospel, 'Employers' Organisations', pp. 260-302; McIvor, 'Employers' Associations', pp. 441-2 and 529-31 on cotton and building.

66. EEF/XIV/Interim report by special sub-committee on post-war industrial problems/29 July 1918. This considered grading, but rejected it.
67. See Knowles and Robertson, 'Earnings'; Gospel, 'Employers' Organisations', pp. 260-5; M. L. Yates, *Wages and Labour Conditions in British Engineering* (1937) p. 122; K. G. J. C. Knowles and T. P. Hill, 'The Variability of Engineering Earnings' *Bulletin of the Oxford University Institute of Statistics,* 18 (1956).
68. See, for example, Ministry of Labour, *Report on Collective Agreements,* Volume I (1934); R. Whipp, ''The Art of Good Management'; Managerial Control of Work in the British Pottery Industry 1900-1925', *International Review of Social History* 29, (1984).
69. Ministry of Labour, *Report,* and McIvor, 'Employers' Associations', Chapter 9.
70. H. F. Gospel, 'The Development of Bargaining Structure: the Case of Electrical Contracting', in Wrigley (ed.), *History,* Volume II.
71. For flour milling see Gospel, 'Employers' Organisations', passim; for electrical cablemaking and cement see Ministry of Labour, *Report* and Charles, *The Development,* pp. 175-6; for bricks see A. Flanders, 'Collective Bargaining', in Flanders and Clegg, *Industrial Relations,* p. 282; for papermaking see C. J. Bundock, *The Story of the National Union of Printing, Bookbinding, and Paper Workers* (Oxford, 1959) and A. Barker, *The Employers' Federation of Papermakers and Boardmakers: A Brief History* (1953).
72. Glynn and Shaw, 'Wage Bargaining'.
73. See, for example, A. C. Pigou, 'Wage Policy and Unemployment', *Economic Journal,* 37 (1927), and H. Clay, 'The Public Regulation of Wages in Great Britain', *Economic Journal* 39 (1929).
74. Flour Milling Employers' Federation/I/Management Committee (20 September 1921) and VII/Board (11 May 1922).
75. L.H. Green, 'Labour Problems in the British Flour Milling Industry: An Experiment in Ordering Industrial Relations', in F. E. Gannett and B. F. Catherwood (eds.), *Industrial and Labour Relations in Great Britain* (1939) p. 126.
76. R. P. Lynton, *Incentives and Management in British Industry* (1949) p. 170.
77. Flour Milling Employers' Federation/III/Investigation Committee/16 September 1926.
78. P. S. Bagwell, *The Railwaymen* (1963) Chapters 15 and 16; D. Chang, *British Methods of Industrial Peace* (New York, 1936) pp. 242-52, 279.
79. W. J. Reader, *Imperial Chemical Industries: A History,* Volume I (1970) p. 233; C. Wilson, *The History of Unilever,* Volume I (Oxford, 1954) pp. 277, 292-6; Cadburys Bros. Ltd, *Industrial Record 1919-1939* (1939); B. W. E. Alford, *W. D. & H. O. Wills and the Development of the UK Tobacco Industry, 1786-1965* (1973); C. G. Renold, *Joint Consultation over Thirty Years* (1950) and McIvor, 'Employers' Associations', p. 566.

80. *Interim Report on Joint Standing Industrial Councils* (Cd. 8606, 1917) pp. 4-5; Ministry of Labour, *Works Committees,* Report no. 2 (1918) p. 3; Committee on Industry and Trade (Balfour Committee), *Survey of Industrial Relations* (1926) p. 305.

81. From the beginning the Federation of British Industries voiced employer suspicion: See *Industrial Councils: Recommendations on the Whitley Report Put Forward by the FBI,* 3 August 1917. Some national joint industrial councils never established works committees. See Charles, *The Development,* p. 160, and Richardson, *Industrial Relations,* 1933, p. 130.

82. G. D. H. Cole, *A Short History of the British Working Class Movement, vol. III,* 1900-1937 (1937) p. 139.

83. International Labour Organisation, Studies and Reports, 'British joint production machinery', *Industrial Relations,* 43 (1944) p. 88.

84. *Ibid.;* P. Inman, *Labour and the Munitions Industries,* 1957, pp. 371-92; Industrial Welfare Society, *Works Councils and Committees* (1945); A.E.U., *Enquiry into Production Committees* (1943); Engineering and Allied Employers' National Federation, *Joint Production Committees and Advisory Committees: Summary of Replies to Enquiry* (1943); Croucher, *Engineers,* pp. 161-174, 373. According to H. Phelps Brown, *The Origins.* p. 144. after the war many 'fell back into the ambiguity surrounding consultation.'

85. Cadburys, *Record;* M. B. Gilson and E. J. Riches, 'Employers' Additional Unemployment Benefit Schemes in Great Britain' *International Labour Review,* 21 (1930). T. C. Barker, *The Glassmakers* (1977), pp. 247, 395-6. J. and J. Colman, *The First Fifty Years of the Carrow Works Council 1918-1968* (Norwich, 1968). For Dunlop see Public Records Office LAB2/1295/IR 545/27 Letter from Chief Conciliation Officer to Industrial Relations Department 16 May 1935; and K. E. Dunlop, 'The History of the Dunlop Rubber Co. Ltd 1888-1939' (Ph.D. University of Illinois, 1949); A. McIvor, 'Employers' Associations', pp. 623-4.

86. S. Tolliday, 'Ford and "Fordism" in postwar Britain', in S. Tolliday and J. Zeitlin (eds.), *The Power to Manage* (1991), and EEF/XX/Management Committee/23 July 1921. EEF/XXX/Management Board/30 August 1934 and Gospel, 'Employers' Organisations', pp. 105-6.

6 MARKETS, FIRMS, AND THE ORGANISATION OF PRODUCTION

1. W. W. Rostow, 'The World Economy Since 1945: A Stylized Historical Analysis', *Economic History Review* (1985); R. C. O. Matthews, C. H. Feinstein, and J. C. Odling-Smee, *British Economic Growth 1956-1973* (Oxford, 1982), p. 548; C. H. Feinstein, *National Income, Expenditure and Output of the United Kingdom, 1855-1964* (Cambridge, 1972).

2. J. Foreman-Peck, *A History of The World Economy: International Economic Relations Since 1850* (Brighton, 1983); A. G. Kenwood and A. L. Longheed, *The Growth of the International Economy 1820-1980* (1983).

3. By the mid 1960s well over 2,000 cartels and restrictive agreements had been terminated or abandoned. G.C. Allen, *Monopoly and Restrictive Practices* (1968), pp.55-8; D. Swann, D. P. O'Brien, W. P. J. Maunder, and

W. S. Howe, *Competition in British Industry: Restrictive Practices Legislation in Theory and Practice* (1974), pp. 144–214; Political and Economic Planning, *Industrial Trade Associations: Activities and Organisation* (1957), pp. 248–50.

4. Feinstein, *National Income*, Table 57; Department of Employment, *British Labour Statistics, Historical Abstract 1886–1968* (1971); R. C. O. Matthews, 'Why Has Britain Had Full Employment Since the War?' *Economic Journal*, 75 (1968).

5. For a good review see G. Bannock, *The Takeover Boom: An International and Historical Perspective* (Edinburgh, 1990).

6. S. Aaronovitch and M. C. Sawyer, *Big Business: Theoretical and Empirical Aspects of Concentration and Mergers in the UK* (1975), p. 125.

7. D. Channon, *The Strategy and Structure of British Enterprise* (1973), pp. 24, 45, 50, 238.

8. S. J. Prais, *The Evolution of Giant Firms in Britain* (Cambridge, 1976), pp. 20, 62.

9. GEC, ICI, British Leyland, Unilever, Courtaulds, British American Tobacco, GKN, Imperial Group, Associated British Foods, and Dunlop. L. Hannah, *The Rise of the Corporate Economy* (1983), p. 146; S. J. Prais, *Giant Firms*, p. 222–3.

10. Hannah, *Corporate Economy*, Appendix 2.

11. C.J.M. Hardie, 'Competition Policy', in D. Morris (ed.), *The Economic System in the UK* (Oxford, 1985), p. 801.

12. The problem would seem to have been greater than in Europe or the US. See Commission of the European Communities, *Survey of Multinational Enterprises* (Brussels, 1976). European and Japanese firms were more centralised than British, and American firms had already adopted multi-divisional structures.

13. Channon, *Strategy*, pp. 87, 238.

14. A. Chandler, *Strategy and Structure* (Cambridge, Mass., 1962).

15. D. Channon, *Strategy*, p. 238; P. S. Steer, 'An Investigation into the Managerial Organisation of Firms' (Unpublished MA dissertation, Warwick 1973).

16. Various studies have shown that the mergers of the 1960s created management difficulties and produced poor financial results. See, for example, G. Meeks, *Disappointing Marriage: A Study of the Gains from Merger* (Cambridge, 1977); *A Review of Monopolies and Mergers Policy* (Cmd. 7198, 1978), pp. 100 ff.; G. D. Newbould, *Management and Merger Activity* (Liverpool, 1970), p. 113. In addition to the above see R. S. Thompson, 'The Diffusion and Performance Impact of the M-Form in the UK: An Empirical Investigation', (Unpublished Ph.D. thesis, University of Newcastle-upon-Tyne, 1982).

17. Channon, *Strategy*, p. 238. By 1970 72 of his top firms had adopted a multidivisional form, at least in part. R. S. Thompson, 'Diffusion of the M-Form Structure in the UK', *International Journal of Industrial Organisation* 1 (1983); R. S. Thompson, 'Internal Organisation and Profit: A Note', *Journal of Industrial Economics* (1981); R. S. Thompson, 'The Spread of an Institutional Innovation: The Multidivisional Corporation in the UK', *Journal of Economic Issues*, 17 (1983).

18. Channon, *Strategy*, pp. 239-42; A. D. Chandler, 'The Development of Modern Management Structure in the US and UK', in L. Hannah (ed.), *Management Strategy and Business Development* (1976); A. D. Chandler, 'The Emergence of Managerial Capitalism', *Business History Review* 58 (1984); C. W. L. Hill and J. F. Pickering, 'Divisionalisation, Decentralisation, and Performance of Large UK Companies', *Journal of Management Studies*, 23 (1986).

19. Hill and Pickering, 'Divisionalisation', and M. Goold and A. Campbell, *Strategies and Styles: The Role of the Centre in Managing Diversified Corporations* (Oxford, 1987).

20. A. D. Chandler, *Scale and Scope* (Cambridge, Mass., 1990), pp. 621-8.

21. Business Statistics Office, *Historical Record of the Census of Production 1907 to 1970* (1978), p. 202.

22. S. P. Keeble, 'University Education and Business Management From the 1890s to the 1950s: A Reluctant Relationship' (Unpublished Ph.D. London, 1984), Chapter 10; P. S. Florence, 'The Educational Profile of Management in Two British Iron and Steel Companies with Some Comparisons, National and International', *British Journal of Industrial Relations* (1966); R. Dore, *British Factory - Japanese Factory* (1973); M. Maurice, A. Sorge, M. Warner, 'Societal Differences in Organizing Manufacturing Units: A Comparison of France, West Germany, and Great Britain', *Organization Studies*, 1 (1980); R. Locke, 'The Relationship Between Educational and Managerial Cultures in Britain and West Germany: A Comparative Analysis of Higher Education, From an Historical Perspective', in P. Joynt and M. Warren, *Managing in Different Cultures* (Oslo, 1985).

23. A. D. Chandler, 'The Transnational Industrial Firm in the United States and the Kingdom: A Comparative Analysis', *Economic History Review* 33 (1980); A. D. Chandler, *Business History Review* (1984); P. L. Payne, 'Industrial Entrepreneurship and Management in Great Britain', in P. Mathias and M. M. Postan (eds.) *The Cambridge Economic History of Europe Volume VII The Industrial Economies Part I* (Cambridge 1978), p. 222.

24. There have been numerous surveys. For a good review see Keeble 'University Education', especially Chapter 6. See also G. H. Copeman, *Leaders of British Industry* (1955); Acton Society Trust, *Management Succession: The Recruitment, Selection, Training and Promotion of Management* (1956); R. V. Clements, *Managers: A Study of their Careers in Industry* (1958); D. G. Clark, *The Industrial Manager: His Background and Career Pattern* (1966); D. Hall, H. Cl. de Bettignies, and G. Amado-Fischgrund, 'The European Business Elite', *European Business* 23 (1969); R. Betts, 'Characteristics of British Company Directors', *Journal of Management Studies*, 4 (1967); J. Deeks, 'Educational and Occupational Histories of Owner-Managers and Managers', *Journal of Management Studies*, 9 (1972); P. Payne, 'Industrial Entrepreneurship', p. 224, NEDO, *Management Education in the 1970s* (1970).

25. Keeble, 'University Education'; D. Granick, *Managerial Comparisons of Four Developed Countries: France, Britain, United States and Russia* (Cambridge, Mass., 1972); R. Locke, *The End of Practical Man: Entrepreneurship in Germany, France and Great Britain* (Greenwich, Conn., 1984).

220   Notes to pages 112–113

26. Management development began to spread in Great Britain in the 1950s among a few large firms which tended to follow American business practice. See R. Lewis and R. Stewart, *The Boss: The Life and Times of the British Business Man* (1958); A. Mant, *The Rise and Fall of the British Manager* (1977), p. 122; S.P. Keeble, 'University Education', pp. 167 and 202–20 on graduate trainee programmes. Both Keeble and Chandler, *Economic History Review*, 1980, argue that the problem was more on the demand side than the supply side.

27. See Keeble, 'University Education'. London and Manchester Business Schools were founded in the mid-1960s to develop management education and other departments of management studies were established. For an optimistic view of the improvement in the educational attainment of British managers see British Institute of Management, *Profile of the British Manager* (1975). For a less optimistic view see G. Crockett and P. Elias, 'British Managers: A Study of Their Education, Training, Mobility, and Earnings', *British Journal of Industrial Relations* 22 (1984).

28. P. Armstrong, 'Competition between the Organised Professions and the Evolution of Management Control Strategies', in K. Thompson (ed.), *Work, Employment and Unemployment* (Milton Keynes, 1984) and 'Engineers, Management, and Trust', *Work, Employment and Society*, 1 (1987).

29. I. Mangham and M. Silver, *Management Training: Context and Practice* (Bath, 1986); J. Constable and R. McCormick, *The Making of British Managers* (1987); C. Handy *et al.*, *Making Managers* (1988).

30. See, for example, T. M. Mosson and D. G. Clark, 'Some Inter-Industry Comparisons of the Background and Careers of Managers', *British Journal of Industrial Relations* 6 (1968); A. I. Marsh and J. G. Gillies, 'The Involvement of Line Staff Managers in Industrial Relations', in K. Thurley and S. Wood, *Industrial Relations and Management Strategy* (Cambridge 1983); Commission on Industrial Relations, *Shipbuilding and Shiprepairing*, Report No. 22 (Cmd. 156, 1971), p. 114; S. G. Reading, *The Working Class Manager: Beliefs and Behaviour* (Farnborough 1979).

31. During the Second World War the Ministry of Labour introduced the American system of Training Within Industry. This continued to grow after the war. See H. Ward, 'TWI in the UK 1944–1952', in Ministry of Labour, *Training Within Industry Topics*, January 1953, p. 5; D. Jenkins, *Supervisory Selection and Training in Manufacturing Industry* (1968) pp. 15–16, 41; National Institute of Industrial Psychology, *The Foreman* (1951), pp. 40, 94; J. Child and B. Partridge, *Lost Managers: Supervisors in Industry and Society* (Cambridge, 1982), pp. 30, 98, 166, 212; M. Fores, P. Lawrence, and A. Sorge, 'Germany's Front-Line Force', *Management Today*, March 1978; M. Fores and D. Clark, 'Why Sweden Manages Better', *Management Today*, February 1975; P. Lawrence *Managers and Management in West Germany* (1980), p. 212.

32. Child and Partridge, *Lost Managers*, p. 137. One indication of this is that from the mid-1960s British supervisory staffs increasingly joined trade unions. *Ibid.* pp. 11, 148–9, 169–88.

33. T. Lupton, *On the Shop Floor* (Oxford, 1963), pp. 180–90; D. Roy, 'Efficiency and "the Fix": Informal Intergroup Relations in a Piecework Machine

Shop', *American Journal of Sociology*, 60 (1955); J. W. Kuhn, *Bargaining in Grievance Settlement* (New York, 1961); W. Brown, 'A Consideration of Custom and Practice', *British Journal of Industrial Relations*, 10 (1972); S. Hill, 'Norms, Groups, and Power: The Sociology of Workplace Industrial Relations', *British Journal of Industrial Relations* 12 (1974); W. Brown, *Piecework Bargaining* (1973), pp. 163-5.

The lack of information, if not interest, at senior levels, in the management of labour has been commented upon, including the marked absence of any good statistical information for senior management planning and control. See J. Winkler, 'The Ghost at the Bargaining Table: Directors and Industrial Relations', *British Journal of Industrial Relations* 12 (1974); Royal Commission on Trade Unions and Employers Associations, 1965-68, (Donovan Commission) *Report* (Cmd. 3623, 1968), pp. 25, 44; Commission on Industrial Relations, *The Role of Management in Industrial Relations*, Report No. 34, (Cmd. 1973), p. 9; H. A. Turner, G. Clack, and G. Roberts, *Labour Relations in the Motor Industry* (1967), p. 79; H. A. Turner, G. Roberts, and D. Roberts, *Management Characteristics and Labour Conflict* (Cambridge, 1977) pp. 6, 16; C. F. Pratten, *Labour Productivity Differentials Within International Companies* (Cambridge, 1976).

34. P. Inman, *Labour in the Munitions Industries* (1957), p. 264; L. Urwick and E. F. L. Brech, *The Making of Scientific Management Vol. 2 Management in British Industry* (1964 edn) p. 208; S. Melman, *Dynamic Factors in Industrial Productivity* (Oxford, 1956) pp. 86-7.

35. In 1945 half of the 4,700 factories with over 250 workers employed a personnel manager. See Ministry of Labour and National Service, *Report of Conference on Joint Consultation, Training Within Industry, Works Information and Personnel Management*, Paper No. 4, 'Personnel Management' (1948) p. 42; R. Betts, 'Characteristics of British Company Directors', *Journal of Management Studies*, 4 (1967); A. Marsh, 'The Staffing of Industrial Relations Management in the Engineering Industry', *Industrial Relations Journal* 2 (1976).

36. H. A. Clegg, *The Changing System of Industrial Relations in Great Britain* (Oxford, 1979), pp. 127-8.

37. W. Marks, *Politics and Personnel Management* (1978), p. 183. See, for example, the increased number of textbooks and courses. P. Anthony and A. Crichton, *Industrial Relations and the Personnel Specialists* (1969) p. 222. On the other hand W. W. Daniel and N. Millward, *Workplace Industrial Relations in Britain* (1983) p. 117 suggest that younger personnel managers are not better trained. A. Marsh, 'Employee Relations – From Donovan to Today', *Personnel Management*, June 1981, p. 35, states that 'Full-time divisional personnel directors were more likely to have qualifications than their headquarters counterparts'. See also Brown (ed.), *Contours*, p. 27; A. Marsh, *Employee Relations Policy and Decision Making* (Aldershot, 1982), p. 62.

38. See, for example, discussion in Daniel and Millward, *Workplace Industrial Relations*.

39. W. Hornby, *Factories and Plant* (1958), Chapters 10-13; M. M. Postan, *British War Production*, pp. 206-7; W. H. G. Armytage, *A Social History of Engineering* (1961). pp. 297-8; S. Pollard, *The Development*, p. 204.

40. Croucher, *Engineers*; S. Zweig, *Productivity and Trade Unions* (Oxford, 1951) pp. 21, 30.
41. Milward, *Economic Effects*, p. 37.
42. C. Barnett, *The Audit of War* (1986), provides a vivid, albeit overstated, account.
43. The Anglo-American Productivity Council was established by Sir Stafford Cripps in August 1948. Under its auspices selected teams of managers and trade unionists were sent to visit US industry.
44. G. Nasbeth and G. F. Ray, *The Diffusion of New Industrial Processes* (Cambridge, 1974); G. F. Ray, *The Diffusion of Mature Technologies* (Cambridge, 1984); Department of Scientific and Industrial Research, *Automation* (1956)
45. Matthews, Feinstein, and Odling-Smee, *British Economic Growth*; Nasbeth and Ray, *Diffusion*; Ray, *Diffusion*.
46. As late as the mid-1950s only 12 per cent of Lancashire looms were automatic and 41 per cent of spindles of the ring type. W. Lazonick, 'Competition, Specialisation, and Industrial Decline', *Journal of Economic History*, 41 (1981); W. Mass, 'Technological Change and Industrial Relations: The Diffusion of Automatic Weaving in the US and Great Britain', *Journal of Economic History* (1985). For shipbuilding see S. Pollard and P. Robertson, *The British Shipbuilding Industry, 1870-1914*, (Cambridge, Mass., 1979); E. Lorenz and F. Wilkinson, 'The Shipbuilding Industry, 1880-1965' in B. Elbaum and W. Lazonick, *The Decline of the British Economy* (Oxford, 1986). More generally see Nasbeth and Ray, *Diffusion* and Ray *Diffusion*.
47. See, for example, J. Hendry, *Innovating for Failure* (Cambridge, 1990).
48. Nasbeth and Ray, *Diffusion* and Ray, *Diffusion*. For example, in the case of electric arc and basic oxygen steel processes, these offered advantages in terms of lower energy costs, increased yield from raw material, and improved quality. In the case of the float glass process, this was developed by Pilkingtons in the 1950s because of its lower costs, higher quality, and greater profit potential. In the case of changes in brewing and baking the aim was to use ingredients more cost effectively and to speed up processes.
49. E. H. Phelps Brown and M. H. Browne, *A Century of Pay: The Course of Pay and Production in France, Germany, Sweden, the UK and the USA, 1860-1960* (1968); Matthews, Feinstein, and Odling-Smee, *British Economic Growth*, pp. 546-8; A. Maddison, *Economic Growth in the West* (1964); A. Maddison, 'The Long-Run Dynamics of Productivity Growth', in W. Beckerman (ed.) *Slow Growth in Britain* (Oxford, 1979); A. Maddison, 'Western Economic Performance in the 1970s: A Perspective and Assessment', *Banca Nazionale del Lavoro Quarterly Review* (1980); D. Sapsford, 'Productivity, Growth in the UK: A Reconsideration', *Applied Economics* 13 (1981).
50. R. E. Caves, 'Productivity Differences Among Industries', in R. E. Caves and L. B. Krause (eds.), *Britain's Economic Performance* (Washington DC, 1980), p.138, quoting D. T. Jones, 'Output, Employment and Labour Productivity in Europe Since 1955', *National Institute Economic Review*, No.77, August 1976.
51. See, for example, J. Muellbauer, 'The Assessment: Productivity and Competitiveness in British Manufacturing Industry', *Oxford Review of Economic Policy* 2 (1986); E. R. Berndt and D. O. Wood, 'Energy Price Shocks and

Productivity Growth in US and UK Manufacturing', *Oxford Review of Economic Policy* 2 (1986).

52. The Anglo-American Productivity Council was established by Sir Stafford Cripps in August 1948. Under its auspices selected teams of managers and trade unionists were sent to study American practices. In all 68 reports were produced. In 1952 the British Productivity Council took over much of its work. See Anglo-American Productivity Council, *Final Report* (1952).

53. L. Rostas, *Comparative Productivity in British and American Industry* (Cambridge, 1948), especially pp. 391-8. D. Paige and G. Bombach, *A Comparison of National Output and Productivity in the UK and US* (Paris, 1959).

54. Phelps Brown and Browne, *Century*; E. Denison, *Why Growth Rates Differ* (Washington DC, 1967); Maddison, 'Economic Performance' (1980); S. J. Prais, *Productivity and Industrial Structure* (Cambridge, 1981); Jones, 'Output'; T. Liesner, *Economic Statistics 1900-1983* (1985); 'Productivity and Labor Cost Trends in Manufacturing, 12 Countries' *Monthly Labor Review* 109 (March 1986).

55. See, for example, Jones 'Output' and C.F. Pratten, *Labour Productivity Differentials Within International Companies* (Cambridge, 1976), Appendix 2. For the broader literature see L. Rostas, *Comparative Productivity of British and American Industry* (Cambridge, 1948); W. E. G. Salter, *Productivity and Technical Change* (Cambridge, 1960); D. Paige and G. Bombach, *A Comparison of National Output and Productivity in the UK and the US* (Paris, 1959); *National Institute Economic Review*; I. Elliot, 'Total Factor Productivity' in M. Panic (ed.) *The UK and W. German Manufacturing Industries* (NEDO 1976); R. E. Caves, 'Productivity Differences Among Industries' in R. E. Caves and L. B. Krause (eds) *Britain's Economic Performance* (Washington DC, 1980); Prais, *Productivity*, For a useful survey of some industry level studies see C. F. Pralten and A. G. Atkinson, 'The Use of Manpower in British Manufacturing', *Department of Employment Gazette* (June 1976).

56. C. Saunders, 'Engineering in Britain, West Germany and France: Some Statistical Comparisons', Sussex European Research Centre (1978); Central Policy Review Staff, *The Future of the British Car Industry* (1975); A. Cairncross, J. A. Kay, and A. Silberston, 'The Regeneration of Manufacturing Industry', *Midland Bank Review* (Autumn 1977); Prais, *Productivity*.

57. Some of these disaggregated studies, such as the work of Pratten and the National Institute of Economic and Social Research, are economic and quantitative. C. F. Pratten, *A Comparison of the Performance of Swedish and UK Companies* (Cambridge, 1976); C.F. Pratten, *Labour Productivity Differentials Within International Companies* (Cambridge, 1976). Others are more sociological, for example, the work of Dore comparing British and Japanese factories, Gallie on British and French oil refineries, and Maitland on British and German factories. R. Dore, *British Factory–Japanese Factory* (1973); D. Gallie, *In Search of the New Working Class* (Cambridge, 1978); I. Maitland, *The Causes of Industrial Disorder: A Comparison of a British and a German Factory* (1983). In addition, over the years there have been many official reports. There are various studies by the National Economic Development Office. These are usefully reviewed in D. G. Mayes, 'A Comparison of Labour Practices and Efficiency Between Plants in the UK

and Seven Foreign Countries', paper presented at NIESR Conference on
Competition Policy and Labour Practices, 23 March 1983. For a critical
review, see T. Nichols, *The British Worker Question: A New Look at Workers
and Productivity in Manufacturing* (1986).

58. Profits in Britain may have been declining since the 1950s and the rate of
profit was below that of Britain's major international competitors. A more
serious decline in profits occurred between the mid-1960s and the mid-to-late
1970s. Matthews, Feinstein, and Odling-Smee, *British Economic Growth*,
pp. 177–9; E. H. Phelps Brown, *Pay and Profits* (Manchester, 1968); A.
Glyn and B. Sutcliffe, *British Capitalism and the Profits Squeeze* (1972).

59. Pollard, *The Development*, pp. 200–4; Armytage, *Social History*, pp. 297–8.

60. See Chapter 5.

61. Its work was continued after 1952 by the British Productivity Council.

62. A. Carew, *Labour under the Marshall Plan* (Manchester, 1987).

63. J. Tomlinson, 'The Failure of the Anglo-American Council on Productivity',
Business History (1991).

64. Anglo-American Productivity Council, *Management Accounting*, (1950), p.6.

65. Barnett, *Audit*.

66. J. Tomlinson, 'The Failure'. Zweig's study of productivity in industry in the
immediate postwar period found few employers aware of inefficiences within
their factories. Zweig, *Productivity*, pp. 19–30.

67. Zweig, *Productivity*; J. Mortimer, *Trade Unions and Technological Change*
(Oxford, 1971).

68. For the US see H. Harris, *The Right to Manage* (Madison, 1982); for Japan
see A. Gordon, *The Evolution of Labour Relations in Japan Heavy Industry,
1853–1935* (Cambridge, Mass., 1985) Chapter 9.

69. Thereafter the proportion continued to increase, though at a slower rate.
R. Marris, *The Economics of Capital Utilization: A Report on Multiple Shift
Working* (Cambridge, 1964); D. Bosworth and P. J. Dawkins, *Work Patterns:
An Economic Analysis* (Gower, 1981); F. Fishwick, *The Introduction and
Extension of Shiftworking* (1980). National Board for Prices and Incomes,
Hours of Work, Overtime and Shiftworking Report No. 161, Cmnd 4554,
(1970). However foreign competitors were also increasingly using shiftwork,
and Britain lagged behind the US and West Germany. See National Board
for Prices and Incomes, *Hours of Work, Overtime, and Shift Working*, Report
161 (Cmnd 4554, 1970) p. 68. The extension of shiftworking was one of
the recommendations of the various Anglo-American Productivity Councils.
S. Prais, *Productivity and Industrial Structure* (1981) p. 54 argues that it was
lower than in USA and W. Germany.

70. E. G. Whybrew, *Overtime Working in Britain*, Royal Commission Research
Paper 9 (1968); H. A. Clegg *The System of Industrial Relations in Great
Britain* (Oxford, 1970) pp. 182–85; D. Leslie, 'Hours and Overtime in British
and United States Manufacturing Industries: A Comparison', *British Journal
of Industrial Relations* 14 (1976); National Board for Prices and Incomes,
Hours of Work.

71. In a few large firms such as ICI and British Airways these various techniques
were grouped together under the new title Management Services. A. Fields,
Method Study (1969), pp. 1–7.

72. In the 1950s, in addition to time study with a stop watch, new techniques were introduced from the US and developed by British consultants. Known collectively as predetermined motion-time study, these involved analysing jobs in terms of their basic components and using so-called 'synthetic' times to establish how long it took to carry out a job. Department of Employment, *An Introduction to Predetermined Motion Time Systems* (1976); National Board for Prices and Incomes, *Payment by Results*, Report No. 65, Cmnd. 3627 (1968), pp. 50-1; S. Shimmin, *Payment by Results* (1959)

73. For example ICI was a pioneer. It developed a large Central Work Study Department and by 1956 had 1,200 Work Study Officers. S. J. Dalziel, 'Work Study in Industry', *Political Quarterly* 27 (1956), p. 274. Many of its handbooks became standard works for British management. See, for example, R. M. Currie *Work Study* (3rd edn 1961). For the role of consultants, see P. Tisdall, *Agents of Change: The Development and Practice of Management Consultancy* (1982). For the various professional associations, see the Institute of Management Services, *The History of the Institute of Management Services* (undated).

74. Armytage, *Social History* (1961), pp. 297-8; J.A. Merkle, *Management and Ideology: The Legacy of the International Scientific Management Movement* (Berkeley, 1980) Chapter 7; J. Rosenhead and C. Thunhurst, 'A Materialist Analysis of Operational Research', *Journal of Operational Research*, 33 (1982).

75. See J. Child, *British Management Thought* (1969); J. A. Merkle, *Management and Ideology*, pp. 42-6; S.P. Keeble, 'University Education'; D. C. Coleman, 'Gentlemen and Players' *Economic History Review* 26 (1973); R. Locke, *The End*.

76. A. Flanders, *The Fawley Productivity Agreements* (1964) and B. W. Ahlstrand, *The Quest for Productivity: A Case Study of Fawley After Flanders*, (Cambridge, 1990).

77. For a further discussion of productivity bargaining, see the next chapter.

78. W. Brown (ed.), *The Changing Contours of British Industrial Relations* (1981) pp. 113-14.

79. M. Nightingale, 'UK Productivity Dealing in the 1960s' in T. Nichols (ed.), *Capital and Labour* (Glasgow, 1980), pp. 319-20.

80. R. McKersie and L. Hunter, *Pay, Productivity and Collective Bargaining* (1973); B. Towers et. al. *Bargaining for Change* (1972); E. Batstone, *Working Order: Workplace Industrial Relations over Two Decades* (Oxford, 1984), pp. 146-59.

81. E. Batstone, *Working Order* (Oxford, 1984); E. Batstone, 'Labour and Productivity', *Oxford Review of Economic Policy*, 2 (1986); D. Metcalf, 'Water Notes Dry Up', *British Journal of Industrial Relations*, 27 (1989).

82. This notion is discussed in A. Flanders, 'The Internal Social Responsibilities of Industry' in *Management and Unions* (1970).

83. National Board for Prices and Incomes, *Productivity Agreemeents*, Report 123, (Cmnd 4136, 1969); Department of Employment, *The Reform of Collective Bargaining at Plant and Company Level*, Manpower Paper 5 (1976); W. W. Daniel and N. MacIntosh, *The Right to Manage?* (1973).

84. The literature is very extensive. For useful surveys see J. Kelly, *Scientific Management, Job Redesign and Work Performance* (1982); D. A. Buchanan,

The Development of Job Design Theories and Techniques (Farnborough, 1971). The Work Research Unit has produced some useful bibliographies: see numbers, 5, 6, 10, 11 (1982). For group technology see NEDO Mechanical Engineering Economic Development Council, *Why Group Technology?* (1975).

85. ICI, Philips, Shell, United Biscuits, Associated Biscuits, Scottish & Newcastle Breweries, Carrington Dewhurst, Gallagher, British Oxygen. See, for example, Department of Employment, *Making Work More Satisfying* (1975); L. King Taylor, *Not for Bread Alone: An Appreciation of Job Enrichment* (1980); J. Roeber, *Social Change at Work* (1975); W. J. Paul and K. B. Robertson, *Job Enrichment and Employee Motivation* (Aldershot, 1970); G. L. Buckingham, R. G. Jeffrey, and B. A. Thorne, *Job Enrichment and Organisational Change* (Aldershot, 1975); F. H. Blackler and C. A. Brown, *Job Redesign and Management Control* (Aldershot, 1978).

86. J. Kelly, *Scientific Management, Job Redesign, and Work Performance* (1982); A. Hopwood, 'Economic Costs and Benefits of new Forms of Work Organisation', in International Labour Organisation, *New Forms of Work Organisation*, Part 2 (Geneva, 1979); T. Wall *et al.*, 'Outcomes of Autonomous Work Groups: A Long-term Field Experiment', *Academy of Management Journal*, 29 (1986); Blackler and Brown, *Job Redesign*, for a comparison of British Leyland and Volvo; R. E. Walton, 'From Control to Commitment in the Workplace', *Harvard Business Review* (1985) for a review of the US experience.

87. A strong version of this argument is to be found in M. J. Piore and C. F. Sabel, *The Second Industrial Divide* (New York, 1984). See also C. F. Sabel and J. Zeitlin, 'Historical Alternatives to Mass Production: Politics, Markets and Mass Technology in Nineteenth-Century Industrialisation', *Past and Present* 108 (1985).

88. National Economic Development Office, *Changing Patterns of Work: How Companies Introduce Flexibility to Meet New Needs* (1986); C. Curson (ed.) *Flexible Patterns of Work* (1986); J. Atkinson, *Flexibility, Uncertainty and Manpower Management* (Brighton, 1984); M. Cross, *Towards the Flexible Craftsman* (1985); W. W. Daniel, *Workplace Industrial Relations and Technical Change* (1987); Incomes Data Services, *Flexibility at Work* (Study 360, 1986); Advisory Conciliation and Arbitration Service, *Labour Flexibility in Britain* (1988).

89. See, for example, Incomes Data Services, *Teamworking*, Report 419 (1988) and R. Collard and B. Dale, 'Quality Circles', in K. Sisson (ed.), *Personnel Management in Britain* (Oxford, 1989).

90. For good reviews of the literature, see I. McLoughlin and J. Clark, *Technological Change at Work* (Milton Keynes, 1988); W. W. Daniel, *Technical Change*; R. Martin, 'Technological Change and Manual Work', in D. Gallie (ed.), *Employment in Britain*, (Oxford, 1988); P. Wilman, *New Technology and Industrial Relations*, Department of Employment Research Paper 58 (1986).

91. N. G. Attenborough, 'Employment and Technical Change; The Case of Microelectronics Based Production Technologies in UK Manufacturing Industry' (Government Economic Service Working Paper No. 74, 1984);

J. Northcott and P. Rogers, *Microelectronics in Industry: What's Happening in Britain* (1982); J. Northcott and P. Rogers, *Microelectronics in British Industry: The Pattern of Change* (1984); J. Northcott and P. Rogers, *Microelectronics in Industry: An International Comparison* (1985).

92. J. Muellbauer, 'The Assessment'; L. Mendis and J. Muellbauer, 'British Manufacturing Productivity 1955-1983: Measurement Problems, Oil Shocks and Thatcher Effects' (Centre for Economic Policy Research, Discussion Paper 32, 1984). Though productivity growth rates increased from 1981, trend growth through the 1980s has been about 3 per cent per annum or about the same as before 1973.

93. See, for example, National Economic Development Organisation, *Changing Patterns* (1986); Daniel, *Technical Change*; M. Cross, 'Changes in Working Practices in UK Manufacturing 1981-1988', *Industrial Relations Review and Report*, Number 415 (1988); J. MacInnes, *Thatcherism at Work* (Milton Keynes, 1987); Incomes Data Services, *Flexibility at Work*, Study 454 (1990).

94. For summaries of the debate on this see D. Metcalf, 'Water Notes Dry Up', *British Journal of Industrial Relations* 27 (1989); P. Nolan and P. Marginson, 'Skating on Thin Ice', *British Journal of Industrial Relations* 28 (1990); D. Metcalf, 'Union Presence and Labour Productivity in British Manufacturing Industry', *British Journal of Industrial Relations* 28 (1990); S. Wadhwani, 'The Effects of Unions on Productivity Growth, Investment and Unemployment', *British Journal of Industrial Relations* 28 (1990).

95. Attenborough, 'Employment', p. 23; J. Child, 'Managerial Strategies, New Technology, and the Labour Process' in D. Knights, H. Willmott, and D. Collinson (eds.), *Job Redesign: Critical Perspectives on the Labour Process* (Aldershot, 1985); D. Buchanan and D. Boddy, *Organisations in the Computer Age* (Farnborough, 1983); Willman, *New Technology*; McLoughlin and Clark, *Technological Change*; Martin, 'Technological Change'; Daniel, *Technical Change*.

96. B. Jones, 'Work and Flexible Organisation in Britain', *Work, Employment and Society* 2 (1988); E. Batstone, S. Gourlay, H. Levie, and R. More, *New Technology and the Process of Labour Regulation* (Oxford, 1987).

97. C. Lane, *Management and Labour In Europe* (1989), Chapters 6 and 7.

98. Daniel, *Technical Change* and Willman, *New Technology*.

99. A. Sorge, G. Hartman, M. Warner, and I. Nicholson, *Microelectronics and Manpower in Manufacturing* (Aldershot, 1983); N. G. Attenborough, 'Employment', p. 18; J. Northcott and P. Rogers, *Microelectronics* (1984); Daniel, *Technical Change*.

7 INDUSTRIAL RELATIONS: CHALLENGES AND RESPONSES

1. Ministry of Labour, *Written Evidence to the Royal Commission on Trade Unions and Employers' Associations* (1965), para. 48.

2. G. S. Bain and R. Price, *Profiles of Union Growth* (Oxford, 1980), p. 40.

3. Ministry of Labour and National Service, *Report for the Years 1939-46* (Cmd 7225, 1947), p. 276.

4. The Order also prohibited strikes and lock-outs and referred disputes to compulsory arbitration. It continued in effect until 1951.

5. See Chapter 9. H. F. Gospel, 'Employers' Organisations: Their Growth and Function in the British System of Industrial Relations 1918–1939', Ph.D. thesis (London, 1974), pp. 262–73; K. G. J. C. Knowles and D. J. Robertson, 'Earnings in Engineering 1926–1948' *Bulletin of the Oxford University Institute of Statistics*, 13 (1951).

6. Academic commentators, both British and foreign, joined practitioners in seeing the system as stable, mature, and successful. See, for example, A. M. Ross and P. T. Hartman *Changing Patterns of Industrial Conflict* (New York, 1960); M. Derber, 'Adjustment Problems of a Long-established Industrial Relations System: An Appraisal of British Engineering, 1954–61', *Quarterly Review of Economics and Business*, 3 (1963); A. Fox, *History and Heritage: The Social Origins of the British Industrial Relations System* (1985), pp. 368–72.

7. Bain and Price, *Profiles*, pp. 40–2. Non-union employers included firms such as D. C. Thomson and American firms such as IBM and Mars.

8. H. A. Clegg, *The Changing System of Industrial Relations in Great Britain* (Oxford, 1979), p. 52; A. I. Marsh and E. E. Coker, 'Shop Steward Organisation in the Engineering Industry', *British Journal of Industrial Relations* 1 (1963).

9. H. A. Clegg, *The System of Industrial Relations in Great Britain* (Oxford, 1970), pp. 15–16.

10. See, for example, K. G. J. C. Knowles and D. J. Robertson, 'Earnings in Engineering 1926–1948'; K. G. J. C. Knowles and D. J. Robertson, 'Some Notes on Engineering Earnings', *Bulletin of the Oxford University Institute of Statistics*, 13 (1951); G. Evans 'Wage Rates and Earnings in the Cotton Industry from 1946 to 1951', *Manchester School* 21 (1953); H. A. Turner, 'Wages: Industry Rates, Workplace Rates and the Wage-drift', *Manchester School* 24 (1956); K. G. J. C. Knowles and T. P. Hill, 'The Variability of Engineering Earnings', *Bulletin of the Oxford University Institute of Statistics* 18 (1956); D. J. Robertson, *Factory Wage Structures and National Agreements* (Cambridge, 1960); E. H. Phelps Brown, 'Wage Drift', *Economica* 29 (1962); S. W. Lerner and J. Marquand, 'Workshop Bargaining, Wages Drift and Productivity in the British Engineering Industry', *Manchester School* 28 (1960). In part the increase in gap may be attributable to an increase in overtime: the earnings series should therefore be adjusted to take out real (but not fictional) overtime.

11. B. J. McCormick, 'Methods of Wage Payment, Wage Structures and the Influence of Factor and Product Markets', *British Journal of Industrial Relations*, 15 (1977). W. Brown, *Piecework Bargaining* (1973).

12. It is difficult to show this in detail, but it is suggested by the fact that where there was collusion, as in electrical contracting or baking, it continued to exist; in industries where there was strong competition, as in engineering, employer solidarity declined. See A. J. McIvor 'Employers' Associations and Industrial Relations in Lancashire 1890–1939', Ph.D. thesis (Manchester, 1983) Appendix 3; Gospel, 'Employers' Organisations', on the cases of electrical contracting and flour milling.

13. For a management survey of this see J. P. Lowry, *Greener Grass?* (1970), p. 45.

14. In the late 1930s the gap was modest; by the mid-1960s there was a growing divergence. See Gospel, 'Employers' Organisations', Chapter 7.
15. Even when overtime was taken out. See Royal Commission on Trade Unions and Employers' Associations (Donovan Commission), *Report* (Cmnd 3623, 1968), Appendix 5; S. W. Lerner and J. Marquand, 'Workshop Bargaining, Wages Drift and Productivity in the British Engineering Industry'; Knowles and Robertson, 'Some Notes on Engineering Earnings'.
16. For a survey of these see Gospel, 'Employers' Organisations', p. 268.
17. Knowles and Hill, 'The Variability'; D. Robinson (ed.), *Local Labour Markets and Wage Structures* (1970): D. I. Mackay *et al.*, *Labour Markets Under Different Employment Conditions* (1971); S. Tolliday, 'High Tide and After' in B. Lancaster and T. Mason (eds.), *Life and Work in a Twentieth Century City: The Experience of Coventry* (Coventry, 1986). See also the differences between the British motor car companies and the American-owned Ford and Vauxhall with their tighter control systems.
18. H. A. Turner, 'Wages: Industry Rates, Workplace Rates and the Wages Drift', *Manchester School* 24 (1956); Donovan *Report*, Appendix 5.
19. See Gospel, 'Employers' Organisations' Chapter 7, for a discussion.
20. The war effort during the Second World War was probably more popular than during the First World War, among ordinary workers and certainly among trade union activists, especially after the entry of Russia into the war in 1941. See R. Croucher, *Engineers at War 1939-1945* (1982) and F. Zweig, *Productivity and Trade Unions* (Oxford, 1951), p. 21.
21. See, for example, R. K. Brown and P. Brannen, 'Social Relations and Social Perspectives Amongst Shipbuilding Workers – A Preliminary Statement', *Sociology* 4 (1970); R. K. Brown, *et al.*, 'The Contours of Solidarity: Social Stratification and Industrial Relations in Shipbuilding', *British Journal of Industrial Relations* 10 (1972); G. Roberts, *Demarcation Rules in Shipbuilding and Shiprepairing* (Cambridge, 1967); A. J. M. Sykes, 'Unity and Restrictive Practices in the British Printing Industry', *Sociological Review* 8 (1960); K. Sissons, *Industrial Relations in Fleet Street: A Study in Pay Structures* (Oxford, 1975).
22. H. A. Turner *et al.*, *Labour Relations in the Motor Industry* (1967) and S. Tolliday and J. Zeitlin, *The Automobile Industry and Its Workers* (1986).
23. H. Beynon, *Working for Ford* (1973).
24. A. Flanders, *The Fawley Productivity Agreements: A Case Study of Management and Collective Bargaining* (1964); D. Gallie, *In Search of the New Working Class* (Cambridge, 1978).
25. E. Owen Smith, *Productivity Bargaining: A Case Study of the Steel Industry* (1971); *Report of a Court of Inquiry into the Causes and Circumstances of a Dispute at Stewart and Lloyds Limited at Corby* (Cmnd 3260, 1967); National Economic Development Office, *Manpower in the Chemical Industry: A Comparison of British and American Practices* (1967).
26. E. G. Whybrew, *Overtime Working in Britain*, Royal Commission Research Paper 9 (1968); H. A. Clegg, *The System*, pp. 182-5; D. Leslie, 'Hours and Overtime in British and United States Manufacturing Industries: A Comparison', *British Journal of Industrial Relations* 14 (1976); National Board for Prices and Incomes, *Hours of Work, Overtime and Shift Working*, Report 161 (Cmnd 4554, 1970).

27. R. Hyman and T. Elger, 'Job Controls, the Employers' Offensive, and Alternative Strategies', *Capital and Class*, 15 (1981). The authors do admit to a real problem for British management.
28. Of course, not all firms recognised this. F. Zweig, *Productivity and Trade Unions* (1951), points out that 'some firms may have adapted themselves so well to the practice that they do not feel it at all or do not realise its existence' p. 19. See also A. Aldridge, *Power, Authority and Restrictive Practices* (Oxford, 1976). A. Fox, *A Sociology of Work in Industry* (1971), p. 33 refers to the low aspirations and standards of many managements until goaded by increasing competition.
29. Official trade unions sometimes condemned them. See Clegg, *The System.* p. 8.
30. Flanders, *Fawley.* p. 251.
31. Quoted in P. Pagnamenta and R. Overy, *All Our Working Lives* (1984), p. 92.
32. National Board for Prices and Incomes, *Wages, Costs and Prices in the Printing Industry* (Cmnd. 2750, 1965), p. 16.
33. T. Lupton, *On the Shop Floor*, (Oxford, 1963).
34. W. Brown, *Piecework Bargaining*; W. Brown, 'A Consideration of "Custom and Practice"', *British Journal of Industrial Relations* 10 (1972).
35. Department of Employment, *British Labour Statistics: Historical Abstract 1886-1968* (1971) p. 396; J. W. Durcan *et al.*, *Strikes in Post-War Britain* (1983).
36. Durcan, *Strikes* Chapters 3 and 4. This increase was not concentrated in a few industries, but was spread throughout the economy.
37. Department of Employment, *Labour Statistics*; figures for official and unofficial strikes only exist from 1960 onwards. See Durcan, *Strikes*, p. 130; Donovan, *Report*, paras. 367-70.
38. E. H. Phelps Brown, *The Origins of Trade Union Power* (Oxford, 1983), Chapter 10; Durcan *et al.*, *Strikes*, Chapter 12.
39. A. I. Marsh, *Disputes Procedures in British Industry*, Royal Commission Research Paper 2 (1) (1966); A. I. Marsh and W. McCarthy, *Disputes Procedures in Britain*, Royal Commission Research Paper 2 (2) (1968); N. Singleton, *Industrial Relations Procedures*, Department of Employment Manpower Paper 14 (1975), p. 64.
40. Marsh, *Disputes Procedures*; Marsh *Engineering*, Chapter 5; R. Hyman, *Disputes Procedures in Action* (1972) stresses procedure as an extension of bargaining.
41. Turner *et al.*, *Motor Industry*, p. 258.
42. Marsh, *Disputes Procedures*, para 78; Singleton, *Procedures*.
43. Turner *et al.*, *Motor Industry*, p. 258.
44. C. T. B. Smith *et al.*, *Strikes in Britain: A Research Study of Industrial Stoppages in the United Kingdom*, Department of Employment, Manpower Paper 15 (1978), show that only 0.25 per cent of all manufacturing plants accounted for a quarter of all strikes and two-thirds of all days lost p. 55; Durcan *et al.*, *Strikes*, pp. 425-8.
45. D. C. Smith, 'Trade Union Growth and Industrial Disputes', in R. E. Caves and L. B. Krause (eds.), *Britain's Economic Performance* (Washington, 1980), p. 144.

46. Lowry, *Greener Grass*, p. 47.
47. R. C. O. Matthews, C. H. Feinstein, and J. C. Odling-Smee, *British Economic Growth 1856-1973* (Oxford 1973), p. 485; National Economic Development Council, *Britain's Industrial Performance* (1985), pp. 22-9.
48. Various attempts have been made to measure trade union wage power and pressure. There are those who have looked at the proportion of the labour force unionised e.g. A. G. Hines, 'Trade Unions and Wage Inflation in the United Kingdom: 1893-1961' *Review of Economic Studies* 31 (1964) and A. G. Hines, 'The Determinants of the Rate of Change of Money Wage Rates and the Effectiveness of Incomes Policy' in H. G. Johnson and A. R. Nobay (eds.) *The Current Inflation* (1971). There are those who have included strike frequency e.g. L. G. Godfrey, 'The Phillips Curve: Incomes Policy and Trade Union Effects' in *ibid.* and D. Laidler, 'Inflation: Alternative Explanations and Policies; Tests and Data Drawn from Six Countries' in K. Brunner and A. Metzler (eds.) *Institutions, Policies and Economic Performance* (New York, 1976). Others have looked at the trade union mark-up over non-union wage rates e.g. R. Layard *et al.*, 'The Effect of Collective Bargaining on Relative and Absolute Wages', *British Journal of Industrial Relations* 16 (1978). In the case of the latter, the relative wage advantage of union over non-union labour steadily increased from the early 1960s onwards. M. B. Stewart, 'Relative Earnings and Individual Union Membership in the UK', *Economica* 50 (1983) probably provides the best estimate of the differential at around 8 per cent.
49. Matthews, Feinstein, and Odling-Smee, *Economic Growth*, pp. 177-97; S. Pollard, *The Development of the British Economy 1914-1980* (1983), pp. 323-4; A. Glyn and R. Sutcliffe, *British Capitalism, Workers and the Profits Squeeze* (1972); J.R. Sargent, 'Productivity and Profits in UK Manufacturing', *Midland Bank Review* (1979); M. Panic and R. E. Close, 'Profitabilty and British Manufacturing Industry', *Lloyds Bank Review* (1975).
50. Matthews, Feinstein, and Odling-Smee, *Economic Growth*, pp. 300-3, 390; National Economic Development Council, *Britain's Industrial Performance*, pp. 6-7.
51. G. S. Bain and R. Price, 'Union Growth: Dimensions Determinants, and Destiny', in G. S. Bain (ed.) *Industrial Relations in Britain* (Oxford, 1983), pp. 5-9.
52. S. Courtauld, *Ideal and Industry* (Cambridge, 1949), p. 8.
53. E. Wigham, *The Power to Manage: A History of the Engineering Employers' Federation* (1973), Chapter 8; J. P. Lowry, 'The Future of National Wage Bargaining', pamphlet based on speech to IPM conference (1968), p. 8.
54. H. A. Clegg and R. Adams, *The Employers' Challenge*, (Oxford, 1957); Wigham, *Power to Manage*, pp. 178-88.
55. Wigham, *Power to Manage*, pp. 190-3.
56. In the case of the engineering industry there were Courts of Inquiry in 1948, 1954, and 1957; the National Incomes Commission reported on the 1963 engineering agreement in 1964 and 1965; and the National Board for Prices and Incomes produced three reports in 1967, 1968, and 1969. See *ibid.* Chapters 8 and 9. B. C. Roberts 'Is Nation-wide Bargaining Desirable?', *The Listener* (11 April 1957); B. C. Roberts, *National Wages Policy in War and Peace* (1958), pp. 170-6; E. H. Phelps Brown, 'The Importance of

Works Agreements', *Personnel Management* (March 1960); D. Robertson, *Factory Agreements*, Chapters 11 and 12.

57. Lowry, 'National Wage Bargaining', pp. 5-8; Commission on Industrial Relations, *Employers' Organisations and Industrial Relations*, Report 1 (1972).

58. National Joint Industrial Council for the Rubber Manufacturing Industry, *Productivity Bargaining* (1967) and Rubber Economic Development Council, *Plant Bargaining* (1968).

59. Chemical Industries Association and Various Unions, *Joint Agreement on Principles and Procedures of Productivity Bargaining* (1968).

60. W. Brown and M. Terry, 'The Changing Nature of National Wage Agreements, *Scottish Journal of Political Economy*, 25 (1978).

61. Flanders, *Fawley*.

62. R. B. McKersie and L. Hunter, *Pay, Productivity and Collective Bargaining* (1973); M. Nightingale, 'UK Productivity Dealing in the 1960s', in T. Nichols (ed.), *Capital and Labour* (1980); N. Cooper, 'The British Productivity Agreements: Some Reflections Based on Action at BOC', an address to the OECD International Management Seminar (Paris 26-29 September 1967).

63. Nightingale, 'Productivity'.

64. National Board for Prices and Incomes, *Productivity Agreements*, Report 123 (Cmnd 4136, 1969); Royal Commission on Trade Unions and Employers' Associations, *Productivity Bargaining*, Report 4 (1) (1967). McKersie and Hunter, *Pay*; Nightingale, 'Productivity'.

65. Donovan, *Report*.

66. *Ibid.* pp. 12-13, paras 46, 50, 52.

67. *Ibid.* pp. 120-1, para 454.

68. *Ibid.* p. 262, para 1014.

69. *Ibid.* pp. 41-2, paras 168-71 and p. 45 para 182.

70. *Ibid.* p. 45, para 182.

71. *Ibid.* pp. 262-4, especially para 1025. Change, it felt, should be brought about voluntarily without legal compulsion, but it recommended a standing Industrial Relations Commission to advise and guide employers and trade unions.

72. Inflation and Employment (1971) cited in *Industrial Relations Review and Report*, (September 1971).

73. Donovan *Report* pp. 38-40, paras 156-61. See also H. A. Turner, 'The Royal Commission's Research Papers', *British Journal of Industrial Relations* 6 (1968), p. 359.

74. P. Geroski and K. G. Knight, 'Corporate Merger and Collective Bargaining in the UK', *Industrial Relations Journal* 15 (1984); P. Marginson, 'The Multidivisional Firm and Control Over the Work Process', *International Journal of Industrial Organisation* 3 (1985).

75. H. A. Turner et al., *Management Characteristics and Labour Conflict: A Study of Managerial Organisation, Attitudes and Industrial Relations* (Cambridge, 1977); E. Batstone, 'What Have Personnel Managers Done for Industrial Relations' *Personnel Management* 12 (June 1980).

76. For some statistical information on this see W. Brown (ed.), *The Changing Contours of British Industrial Relations: A Survey of Manufacturing Industry* (Oxford, 1981) pp. 5-31.

77. Donovan Commission, Minutes of Evidence, 59, para 9384 (1966).

78. *Ibid.*, 20, para 2843 (1966).

79. Cadbury's *Board Minutes* 307, 18 December 1967, and Board File re Minute 61, 25 March 1968.

80. D. McIntyre, 'Inquest on the Engineering Dispute and the Future of Two-tier Bargaining', *Personnel Management* (December 1979).

81. Wigham, *Power to Manage*, pp. 253-40; Clegg, *Changing System*, p. 88: a new procedure was agreed in 1976 which allowed for one external stage in local conference.

82. Brown *et al.*, *Contours*, pp. 19-23; Commission on Industrial Relations, *Employers' Organisations*.

83. Along with Brown *et al. Contours* and Daniel and Millward, *Workplace Industrial Relations*, see W. W. Daniel *Wage Determination in Industry* (1976); A. Marsh, *Employee Relations Policy and Decision Making* (Aldershot, 1982), Chapter 6; N. J. Kinnie, 'Bargaining Structure and Management Control of Industrial Relations', Ph.D. (Warwick, 1980); N. J. Kinnie, 'Single-employer Bargaining', *Industrial Relations Journal* 14 (1983); P. B. Beaumont *et al.*, 'Bargaining Structure', *Management Decision* 18 (1980); P. Marginson *et al.*, *Beyond the Workplace* (Oxford, 1988).

84. Brown *et. al.*, *Contours*; Daniel and Millward, *Workplace Industrial Relations*; B. Willey, *Union Recognition and Representation in Engineering* (1986).

85. W. Brown *et al.*, 'Factors Shaping Shop Steward Organisation in Britain' *British Journal of Industrial Relations* 16 (1978); M. Terry, 'Shop Stewards Through Expansion and Recession', *Industrial Relations Journal* 14 (1983); Clegg, *Changing System*, pp. 51-53.

86. See some discussion in P. Willman, 'Leadership and Trade Union Principles', *Industrial Relations Journal* 19 (1981).

87. W. E. J. McCarthy, *The Closed Shop in Britain* (Oxford, 1964); Brown *et al.*, *Contours*, pp. 54-59; Daniel and Millward, *Workplace Industrial Relations*, Chapter 3; S. Dunn and J. Gennard, *The Closed Shop in British Industry* (1984).

88. Daniel and Millward, *Workplace Industrial Relations*, p. 74.

89. W. Brown, 'Britain's Unions: New Pressures and Shifting Loyalties', *Personnel Management*, 15 (October 1983).

90. Office of Manpower Economics, *Measured Daywork* (1973); A. Flanders, 'Measured Daywork and Collective Bargaining', *British Journal of Industrial Relations* 11 (1973).

91. By 1978 50 per cent of all manufacturing establishments were using work study techniques, Brown *et al.*, *Contours*, pp. 113-14.

92. Flanders, 'Measured daywork'. The National Board for Prices and Incomes, *Job Evaluation* (Cmnd 3772, 1968) reported that 23 per cent of all employees in manufacturing were covered by job evaluation. Brown *et al.*, *Contours*, reported that 55 per cent of manual and 56 per cent of non-manual are covered, p. 111. Daniel and Millward, *Workplace Industrial Relations*, put

234 Notes to pages 144–145

the figure lower at 23 per cent for all plants, but rising in size to 53 per cent in plants employing 500 or more, p. 204.
93. Turner *et al.*, *Management Characteristics* and Batsone, 'What Have Personnel Managers Done' make this point.
94. M. Terry, 'The Inevitable Growth of Informality', *British Journal of Industrial Relations* 15 (1977).
95. Department of Employment, *British Labour Statistics*, p. 396, and P. K. Edwards, 'The Pattern of Collective Industrial Action', in G. S. Bain (ed.), *Industrial Relations in Britain* (Oxford, 1983). Turner *et al.*, *Management Characteristics* suggests that formalisation caused a higher incidence of strikes; Batsone, 'What Have Personnel Managers Done', suggests that the increase in the number of personnel managers and the formalisation they created led to strikes; for a more sceptical view see P. Joyce and A. Woods, 'The Management of Conflict: A Quantitative Analysis', *British Journal of Industrial Relations* 22 (1984).
96. Durcan *et al Strikes*, Chapter 5; P. K. Edwards, 'Britain's Changing Strike Problem', *Industrial Relations Journal* 13 (1982); Smith *et al.*, *Strikes*.
97. H. A. Clegg, *Trade Unionism Under Collective Bargaining* (Oxford, 1976), p. 12. The spurt in unionisation from the late 1960s onwards was due to a number of factors – white-collar workers' fears that their relative economic position and status were threatened and government support for recognition. G. S. Bain, *The Growth of White Collar Unionism* (Oxford, 1970).
98. Commission on Industrial Relations, *Recognition of White-Collar Unions in Engineering and Chemicals*, Study 3 (1973). G. S. Bain, 'Management and White-Collar Unionism', in S. Kessler and B. C. M. Weekes (eds.), *Conflict at Work* (1971).
99. See, for example, S. Creigh and P. Makeham, 'Strikers' Occupations: An Analysis', Department of Employment, *Gazette* (March 1980), pp. 237–39.
100. B. C. M. Weekes *et al.*, *Industrial Relations and the Limits of the Law: The Industrial Effects of the Industrial Relations Act 1971* (Oxford, 1975); M. Hart, 'Why Bosses Love the Closed Shop', *New Society* (15 February 1979); But see S. Dunn, 'The Law and the Decline of the Closed Shop in the 1980s' in P. Fosh and C. Littler, *Industrial Relations and the Law in the 1980s* (Aldershot, 1985).
101. Committee of Inquiry on Industrial Democracy (Bullock Committee), *Report* (Cmnd 6706, 1977).
102. There have been various proposed EEC Company Law Directives, among which the Fifth Directive on employee participation on company boards was first proposed in 1972 and the so-called Vredeling Directive on information and consultation rights for employees was first proposed in 1980.
103. Brown, *et al.*, *Contours*, p. 76.
104. On company initiatives see J. Elliott, *Conflict or Cooperation?* (1978); J. Elliott, *Financial Times* (31 January 1978); Confederation of British Industries, *Current Employee Involvement Practice in British Business* (1981); M. J. Dowling *et al. Employee Participation: Practice and Attitudes in North West Manufacturing Industry*, DE Research Paper 27 (1981); P. Cressey *et al.*, *Industrial Democracy and Participation: A Scottish Survey*, DE Research Paper 28 (1981); Institute of Personnel Management, *Practical Participation and Involvement* 5 Volumes (1981–82); Daniel and Millward, *Workplace*

Industrial Relations, found that 40 per cent of organisations, public and private, reported some form of participation, however embryonic.

105. D. R. Deaton and P. B. Beaumont, 'The Determinants of Bargaining Structure: Some Large-scale Survey Evidence for Britain', *British Journal of Industrial Relations* 18 (1980); Brown, *et al., Contours,* pp. 7-13; Daniel and Millward, *Workplace Industrial Relations,* pp. 177-91.

106. L. Hannah, 'Visible and Invisible Hands in Great Britain', in A. D. Chandler and H. Daems (eds.), *Managerial Hierarchies: Comparative Perspectives on the Rise of the Modern Industrial Enterprise* (Cambridge, Mass., 1980) p. 69; Size Report, *British Companies,* C. & D. Partners (1979), quoted in W. Brown and K. Sissons, 'Industrial Relations in the Next Decade: Current Trends and Future Possibilities', *Industrial Relations Journal* 14 (1983), p. 10.

107. See, for example, J. Gennard, *Multinational Corporations and British Labour: A Review of Attitudes and Responses* (1972); J. Gennard and M. D. Steuer, 'The Industrial Relations of Foreign-owned Subsidiaries in the United Kingdom', *British Journal of Industrial Relations* 9 (1971); J. Hamil, 'Labour Relations in Foreign-owned Firms in the UK', Ph.D. thesis (Paisley College, 1982); P. J. Buckley and P. Enderwick, *The Industrial Relations Position of Foreign-Owned Firms in Britain* (1985); Brown *et al., Contours,* passim; Daniel and Millward, *Workplace Industrial Relations,* passim.

108. D. Marsden and M. Thompson, 'Flexibility Agreements and Their Significance in the Increase in Productivity in British Manufacturing Since 1980', *Work, Employment and Society,* 4 (1990) and P. Ingram, 'Changes in Manufacturing in British Manufacturing Industry in the 1980s', *British Journal of Industrial Relations,* 29 (1991).

109. For a good review see P. Edwards and K. Sissons, 'Industrial Relations in the UK: Change in the 1980s', ESRC Research Briefing (Warwick, 1979).

110. Brown, *et al. Contours,* pp. 7-13; Daniel and Millward, *Workplace Industrial Relations,* using a wider sample, put single-employer bargaining lower, p. 187.

8 EMPLOYMENT RELATIONS IN THE POSTWAR PERIOD

1. C. Kerr, 'The Balkanisation of Labour Markets', in E. W. Bakke (ed.), *Labor Mobility and Economic Opportunity* (Cambridge, Mass., 1954); L. Reynolds, *The Structure of Labor Markets* (New York, 1951); A. M. Ross, 'Do We Have a New Industrial Feudalism', *American Economic Review* (1958); P. B. Doeringer and M. J. Piore, *Internal Labor Markets and Manpower Analysis* (Lexington, Mass., 1971).

2. Doeringer and Piore, *Internal Labour Markets.*

3. R. Edwards, *Contested Terrain: The Transformation of the Workplace in the Twentieth Century* (New York, 1979); D. M. Gordon, R. Edwards, and M. Reich, *Segmented Work, Divided Workers: The Historical Transformation of Labor in the United States* (Cambridge, 1982).

4. See E. F. Lazear, 'Agency, Earnings Profiles, Productivity, and Hours Reductions', *American Economic Review,* 71 (1971), and J. M. Malcolmson, 'Work Incentives, Hierarchy, and Internal Labour Markets', in G. A. Akerlof

and J. L. Yellen, *Efficiency Wage Models and the Labour Market* (Cambridge, 1986).

5. R. Edwards, *Contested Terrain: The Transformation of the Workplace in the Twentieth Century* (New York, 1979); D.M. Gordon, R. Edwards, and M. Reich, *Segmented Work, Divided Workers: The Historical Transformation of Labor in the United States* (Cambridge, 1982).

6. Elements of this are to be found in Doeringer and Piore *Internal Labour Markets*, and S. M. Jacoby, *Employing Bureacracy: Managers, Unions, and the Transformation of Work in American Industry, 1900-1945* (New York, 1985).

7. R. C. O. Matthews, C. H. Feinstein, and J. C. Odling-Smee, *British Economic Growth* (Oxford, 1982), pp. 81-95.

8. *Ibid.*, pp. 88-89; R. R. Neild, *Pricing and Employment in the Trade Cycle*, National Institute of Economic and Social Research, Occasional Paper 21 (Cambridge, 1964).

9. J. Bowers, D. Deaton, and J. Turk, *Labour Hoarding in British Industry* (Oxford, 1982).

10. J. Nissim, 'An Examination of the Differential Pattern in the Cyclical Behaviour of the Employment, Hours, and Wages of Labour of Different Skills: British Mechanical Engineering 1963-78', London School of Economics, Centre for Labour Economics Discussion Paper 139 (1982). Note also differences between industries in labour hoarding reflecting two-dimensional labour markets and firms. S. McKendrick, 'An Inter-industry Analysis of Labour Hoarding in Britain 1953-72', *Applied Economics* 7 (1975).

11. The British Institute of Management published figures of labour turnover between 1949 and 1950. Various issues of the *Journal of the Institute of Personnel Management* contain turnover figures. See, for example, 30 (1948) pp.84-88 and 232-36. The Ministry of Labour series begins in 1948 and was published in the *Gazette*. See also G. Thomas, *Labour Mobility in Great Britain 1945-1949*, Ministry of Labour and National Service Report 134, undated; A. K. Rice, J. M. M. Hill, and E. L. Trist, 'The Representation of Labour Turnover as a Social Process' *Human Relations* 3 (1950); J. R. Long, *Labour Turnover Under Full Employment* (Birmingham, 1951); J. R. Greystoke, G. W. Birks and T. Murphy, 'Surveying Labour Turnover in the Sheffield Area', *Yorkshire Bulletin of Economic and Social Research* 3 (1951); J. R. Greystoke, G. F. Thomason and T. J. Murphy, 'Labour Turnover Series', *Journal of the Institute of Personnel Management*, 34 (1952); H. Behrend, 'Absence and Labour Turnover in a Changing Economic Climate', *Occupational Psychology* 27 (1953); H. Silcock, 'The Phenomenon of Labour Turnover', *Journal of the Royal Statistical Society* 117 (1954). (Turnover after the Second World War was not as high as after the First World War, however it was higher than in the 1950s, Long, *Labour Turnover*, p. 35).

12. See, for example, B. O. Pettman, *An Annotated Bibliography of Labour Turnover Studies* (Bradford, 1970); see also the bibliography in B. O. Pettman (ed.), *Labour Turnover and Retention* (Aldershot, 1975); A. L. Dooley and R. Watson, 'Labour Turnover and Cost', *Times Review of Industry*, 2 (February 1948), p. 9; H. G. Knight, 'The Social Cost of Labour Turnover', *The Cost Accountant* 29 (1951); 'The Cost of Labour Turnover',

The Economist (7 July 1951); P. H. Cook, 'Labour Turnover as a Measure of Control', *The Cost Accountant* 29 (1951): P. H. Cook, 'Labour Turnover Research', *Journal of the Institute of Personnel Management* 33 (1951); F. T. Pearce, *Financial Effects of Labour Turnover* (Birmingham 1954); British Institute of Management, *The Cost of Labour Turnover* (1959).

13. Rice, *et al.*, 'Labour Turnover'; Long, *Labour Turnover*; Greystoke, Birks, and Murphy, 'Surveying'; R. James, 'Human Waste: An Analysis of Labour Turnover in Industry', *Economic Journal* 59 (1949).

14. James, 'Human Waste', p. 122.

15. Long, *Labour Turnover*, p. 16.

16. British Institute of Management, 'Turnover', p. 42.

17. The engagement and leaving rates are annual averages of four four-weekly rates. They refer to the number of engagements and separations per 100 employees at the beginning of the four-week period. Total turnover is understated since neither engagements nor leavings include those who were hired or left *within* the four-week period. Department of Employment and Productivity, *British Labour Statistics: Historical Abstract 1886-1968*, Table 147 and Department of Employment *Gazettes* for January, April, July and October. See also D. R. Jones, 'Redundancy, Natural Turnover and the Paradox of Structural Change', *Bulletin of Economic Research* 37 (1985).

18. Thomas, *Labour Mobility*, p. 59; *Journal of Institute of Personnel Management* 30 (1948), pp. 84-88, 232-36; J. Shorey, 'An Analysis of Quits Using Industry Turnover Data', *Economic Journal* 90 (1980); Jones, 'Redundancy'.

19. Rice *et. al.*, 'Representation'; Long, *Labour Turnover*; Greystoke, Birks, and Murphy, 'Surveying'; D. I. MacKay, 'Wages and Labour Turnover' in D. Robinson (ed.) *Local Labour Markets and Wage Structures* (1970).

20. See, for example, P. S. Florence, *The Economics of Sociology and Industry* (1964), p. 118.

21. B. G. M. Main, 'The Length of a Job in Great Britain', *Economica* 49 (1982).

22. A. I. Harris *Labour Mobility in Great Britain 1953-63* (1966), p. 5, shows that over the ten years 1953-63 56 per cent of men had one job only. Main's figures for 1968 suggest that 69 per cent had jobs that did not end before 1978, p. 329. See also Silcock, 'Labour Turnover' and G. N. Gilbert, S. Arber, and A. Dale, 'General Household Survey Office of Population Censuses and Surveys, 1973' (University of Surrey, Guildford, mimeo 1980). For a good review of the comparative literature, see D. Metcalf, 'Labour Market Flexibility and Jobs', Centre for Labour Economics, Discussion Paper 254 (1986).

23. J. H. Richardson, *An Introduction to the Study of Industrial Relations* (1954), p. 49; E. F. L. Brech *et al.*, *The Principles and Practice of Management* (1953), pp. 470-71.

24. Rice *et al.*, 'Labour Turnover'; J. M. M. Hill, 'The Representation of Labour Turnover as a Social Process' in B. O. Pettman (ed.), *Labour Turnover*, p. 93.

25. Acton Society Trust, *Redundancy: A Survey of Problems and Practices* (1958); Ministry of Labour, *Security and Change: Progress in Provision for Redundancy* (1961); International Labour Organisation, *Dismissal Procedures in Nine Countries*, (Geneva, 1959), Chapter 5; F. Meyers, *Ownership of Jobs: A Comparative Study* (Los Angeles, 1964), pp. 33-43.

238   Notes to pages 153–155

26. H. A. Turner, G. Clark, and G. Roberts, *Labour Relations in the Motor Industry* (1967), Chapter 4; E. Wigham, *The Power to Manage* (1973), pp. 208–9.
27. Ministry of Labour, *Dismissal Procedures. Report of a Committee of the National Joint Advisory Council on Dismissal Procedures* (1967); S. D. Anderman, 'Voluntary Dismissal Procedures and the Proposed Legislation on Unfair Dismissal', *British Journal of Industrial Relations* 8 (1970).
28. Ministry of Labour, *Positive Employment Policies* (1958), and *Security and Change* (1961).
29. P. E. Leighton and S. L. Dumville, 'From Statement to Contract – Some Effects of the Contracts of Employment Act 1972' *Industrial Law Journal* 6 (1972).
30. A part of the redundancy payment comes from a central Redundancy Fund and the remainder is paid by the employer. The proportions have varied over time, but the average amount paid by the employer had been about five weeks earnings.
31. Reinstatement is, however, seldom awarded.
32. W. Brown, *The Changing Contours of British Industrial Relations* (Oxford, 1981), pp. 115–17; Jones, 'Redundancy'.
33. W. W. Daniel and E. Stilgoe, *The Impact of Employment Protection Laws* (1978).
34. W. W. Daniel and N. Millward, *Workplace Industrial Relations in Britain* (1983), p. 163; L. Dickens, M. Jones, B. Weekes, M. Hart, *Dismissed: A Study of Unfair Dismissal and the Industrial Tribunal System* (Oxford, 1985); for an overview of the Redundancy Payments Act see P. Lewis, *Twenty Years of Statutory Redundancy Payments in Great Britain*, Leeds and Nottingham Occasional Papers in Industrial Relations, No.8 (1985).
35. B. Hepple, 'A Right to Work', *Industrial Law Journal*, 10 (1981) and Dickens, *Dismissed.*
36. See also the Sex Discrimination Act 1975, Equal Pay Act 1970, Race Relations Acts 1968 and 1975, Health and Safety at Work Act 1974, Employment Protection Acts 1975 and 1978. S.J. Nickell, 'Fixed Costs, Employment, and Labour Demand over the Cycle', *Economica* (1978); R. Layard and S. Nickell, 'The Performance of the British Labour Market', paper for conference on the British Economy, White House Conference Centre, Isle of Thorn, Sussex, May 1985; Daniel and Stilgoe, *The Impact*; W. W. Daniel, 'The Effects of Employment Protection Laws in Manufacturing Industry', *Department of Employment Gazette* (June 1978).
37. B. Hepple, 'A Right to Work', *Industrial Law Journal* 10 (1981). Only in some of the ports, as a result of post war decasualisation of the docks, did the law provide job security, pp. 74–75; G. Phillips and N. Whiteside, *Casual Labour: The Unemployment Question in the Port Transport Industry 1880–1970* (Oxford, 1985). However, the National Docks Labour Board was abolished by the Conservative government in 1989.
38. There were some earlier examples. The railway companies conceded a kind of guaranteed week agreement at the end of the First World War.
39. A. Bullock, *The Life and Times of Ernest Bevin*, Volume II (1967), p. 274.
40. Incomes Data Service, *The Guaranteed Week*, Study 235 (1981), p. 1.

41. I am indebted to J. Richards and E. Szyszczak for this information. See in particular their 'Guaranteed Week Agreements in the Vehicle Industry', Short-Time Working Project, Working Paper Number 13, University of Kent (1984), and 'Short-time Working in Great Britain: Historical Developments and the Decline of Unemployment Benefit for Short-time Compensation', Working Paper Number 15, (1985). In this area legislation and government policy have also lent some support to voluntary arrangements. The Employment Protection Act 1975 introduced statutory guaranteed payments subject to a maximum amount and maximum period. Between 1978 and 1984, in a series of ad hoc measures aimed at averting redundancies and the payment of unemployment benefit, governments operated a state-funded system of short-time compensation.

42. National Institute of Industrial Psychology, *The Foreman: A Study of Supervision in British Industry* (1951), p.40; R. M. Blackburn and M. Mann, *The Working Class in the Labour Market* (1979), pp. 279-80.

43. On the USA see, for example, Meyers, *Ownership of Jobs* and Jacoby, *Employing Bureaucracy.* For Japan see A. Gordon, *The Evolution of Labour Relations in Japanese Heavy Industry 1853-1955* (Cambridge, Mass., 1985). For Germany see W. Streck, *Industrial Relations in West Germany* (1984).

44. L. C. Hunter, G. L. Reid, and D. Boddy, *Labour Problems of Technical Change* (1970), pp. 171, 179.

45. Mackay 'Wages', pp. 302-21; Robinson (ed.), *Local Labour Markets,* Chapters 1,2,7,8. A 1953-63 survey of labour mobility showed that 17 per cent of men had changed their jobs within the enterprise during that period, Harris, *Labour Mobility,* pp. 52-54.

46. A. Egan, 'Women in Banking: A Study in Inequality', *Industrial Relations Journal* 13 (1982); J. D. Mace, 'Internal Labour Markets For Engineers in British Industry', *British Journal of Industrial Relations* 17 (1979), pp. 50-63.

47. Mackay, 'Wages'; K. Dunnell and E. Head, *Employers and Employment Services,* Office of Population Censuses and Surveys (1974); and G. Courtney and S. Hedges, *A Survey of Employers' Recruitment Practices,* Social and Community Planning Research (1977), show increased internal recruitment of manual workers over this time period. J. Ford, T. Keil, A. Bryman, and A. Beardsworth, 'Internal Labour Market Processes', *Industrial Relations Journal* (1984).

48. G. Becker, *Human Capital* (New York, 1964).

49. Of course, though it may be optimal for the employer, such training may be insufficient to provide a national labour force and the government will need to provide general training and to train those not attached to firms.

50. G. D. H. Cole, 'General Education and Vocational Training in Great Britain', *International Labour Review* 72 (1953).

51. M. M. Postan, *British War Production* (1952); H. M. D. Parker, *Manpower in War* (1957) p. 388.

52. Royal Commission on Trade Unions and Employers' Associations (Donovan Commission), *Report* (Cmnd 3623, 1968), p. 87, para 337. See pp. 85-93 for a summary of the kinds of criticism. For a different interpretation, see D. Lee, *British Journal of Industrial Relations,* 1979.

240   Notes to pages 157–159

53. D. C. Thompson, *Training Worker Citizens* (1949); C. H. Northcott, *Personnel Management: Its Scope and Practice* (1945) pp. 106–7; National Institute of Industrial Psychology, *Training Factory Workers* (1956).
54. Ministry of Labour, *Training for Skill: Recruitment and Training of Young Workers in Industry* (1958); G. Williams, *Recruitment to Skilled Trades* (1957); (1963); S. Vickerstaff, 'The Limits of Corporatism: The British Experience', Ph.D. thesis (Leeds, 1984).
55. By 1972 there were 27 industrial training boards covering 15 million workers. See Department of Employment, *Training for the Future: A Plan for Discussion* (1972), pp. 11, 52.
56. *Ibid.* p. 52. This also claimed that over time the industrial training boards came to favour more firm-specific training, p. 59. M. Oakey argues that firms training in firm-specific skills got a double pay off from the levy-grant system in that they received a direct return from their investment and were also paid a grant towards the cost of that investment. M. Oakey, 'The Economics of Training With Respect to the Firm', *British Journal of Industrial Relations* 8 (1970). Matthews, Feinstein, and Odling-Smee, *Economic Growth*, pp. 108–11. Increased automation and the extension of machine-minding jobs meant non-apprenticed training at least was more firm specific. See also G.D.H. Cole, 'General Education', p. 179.
57. See, for example, Department of Trade and Industry, *First Report of the Skills Shortage Committee* (1984).
58. The Employment and Training Act 1973 modified the levy-grant system and in 1982 and 1983 the number of industrial training boards was substantially reduced.
59. Department of Employment, *Unqualified, Untrained, Unemployed* (1974), Table 5; Department of Employment, *Gazette* (November 1983), p. 489; Engineering Industry Training Board, *Economics and Industrial Monitor* (14 November 1983), section 9 and Annex A. The total number of apprentices has been falling since 1969.
60. See, for example, S. J. Prais, 'Vocational Qualifications of the Labour Force in Britain and Germany', *National Institute Economic Review*, 98 (1981); S. J. Prais, *Productivity and Industrial Structure* (Cambridge, 1981); National Economic Development Council and Manpower Services Commission, *Competence and Competition – Training and Education in the Federal Republic of Germany, the United States, and Japan* (1984); Coopers and Lybrand for the Manpower Services Commission and National Economic Development Council, *A Challenge to Complacency: Changing Attitudes to Training* (1985).
61. The proportion of manual workers paid by results rose from 25 per cent in 1938 to 32 per cent by 1951. Thereafter, for a time, the proportion remained fairly constant having risen to only 33 per cent ten years later. National Board for Prices and Incomes, *Payment by Results*, Report Number 65, Cmnd 3627 (1968), p. 76; Ministry of Labour, *Gazette* (September 1961).
62. McCormick, 'Methods of Wage Payment' p. 249; Daniel and Millward, *Workplace Industrial Relations*, p. 207; A. R. Swannack, *Wage Payment Structures* (1980), Chapter 2.

63. F. R. J. Jervis and W. F. Frank, *An Introduction to Industrial Administration* (1962), Chapter 4; National Board for Prices and Incomes, *Payment by Results*; McCormick, 'Method of Wage Payment'. There has, however, been some increase in lighter industries and in the public sector.

64. See, for example, the famous case of the Glacier Metal Co. W. Brown, *Piecework Abandoned* (1962).

65. Office of Manpower Economics, *Measured Daywork* (1973), pp. 10, 12, 22; M. White, *Payment Systems in Britain* (Aldershot, 1981), p. 96.

66. National Board for Prices and Incomes, *Job Evaluation*, p. 10; for an early example at Carreras Ltd see E.M. Pepperell, 'Why and How We Introduced a Job Evaluation Scheme', *Journal of the Institute of Personnel Management*, 30 (1948), pp. 16–19.

67. National Board for Prices and Incomes, *Job Evalutation*, p. 4; Brown *et al.*, *Contours*, p. 111. Brown found that 43 per cent of plants had job evaluation; Daniel and Millward, *Workplace Industrial Relations*, found that 42 per cent of plants with 50 or more employees had job evaluation, p. 207.

68. Office of Manpower Economics, *Daywork*, p. 15; National Board for Prices and Incomes, *Job Evaluation*, p. 10; White, *Payment Systems*, pp. 57, 96, 106; Brown, *et al. Contours*, pp. 111–13; Daniel and Millward, *Workplace Industrial Relations*, p. 205; P. Enderwick and P.J. Buckley, 'Industrial Relations Practices in Britain: A Comparative Analysis of Foreign- and Domestically-owned Firms', *Labour and Society* 8 (1983).

69. White, *Payment Systems*, p. 117; Institute of Personnel Management, *Job Evaluation in Practice* (1976). More critical commentators have claimed that it serves as a management weapon to 'divide and rule' workers. T. Cliff, *The Employers' Offensive* (1970), Chapter 6; T. Nichols and P. Armstrong, *Workers Divided* (Glasgow, 1976).

70. White, *Payment Systems*, p. 117. Both the Institute of Personnel Management, *Job Evaluation* and National Board for Prices and Incomes, *Job Evaluation*, Report Number 83, Cmnd 3772 (1968) refer to better employee relations, higher morale, and lower turnover.

71. Confederation of British Industry, *Incentive Payment* (1985); White, *Payment Systems*, pp. 16, 77.

72. Their spread may predate the Finance Acts of 1978, 1984, and 1989. See Daniel and Millward, *Workplace Industrial Relations*, p. 212; S. Creigh, N. Donaldson and E. Hawthorn, 'A Stake in the Firm – Employee Financial Involvement in Britain', Department of Employment, *Gazette* 89 (May 1981); M. Poole, 'Profit Sharing and Share-ownership Schemes in Britain', paper presented at British Universities Industrial Relations Association, Bath, July 1986.

73. White, *Payment Systems*, pp. 45, 75; Industrial Relations Review and Report, 'Courage Brewery Opts For Novel Job Evaluation Technique', *Report*, Number 241 (February 1981) pp. 2–4; Pilkington Brothers PLC, 'Pilkington Flat Glass: Greengate Workers: The Factory and the Jobs' (1980) p. 3; D. Gregson and K. Ruffle, 'Rationalising Rewards at Rogerstone', *Personnel Management* (October 1980); D. Martin and B. Groom, 'Slow Move Towards a Unified Structure', *Financial Times* (18 March 1985); D. Thomas, 'The Pressure for Unification', *Financial Times* (28 March 1986); A.

Whitaker, 'Cadbury Limited Chirk: People, Tasks and Technology: A Study in Consensus' (University of Lancaster, undated).
74. D. J. Robertson, *Factory Wage Structure* (Cambridge, 1960); D. Robinson (ed.), *Local Labour Markets and Wage Structures* (1970); D.I. MacKay, D. Boddy, J. Brack, and N. Jones, *Labour Markets Under Different Employment Conditions* (1971); W. Brown, *Piecework Bargaining* (1973).
75. External comparisons are taken into account by comparing certain 'benchmark' jobs with those in the external labour market.
76. P. Nolan and W. Brown, 'Competition and Workplace Wage Determination', *Oxford Bulletin of Economics and Statistics* 45 (1983). See also earlier studies in Robinson (ed.) *Local Labour Markets*, and Mackay, *et al.*, *Labour Markets*, which also show that earnings for a particular class of labour show very wide variations within a locality. Nolan and Brown suggest that the firm-specific effect on pay is increasing over time.
77. Office of Manpower Economics, *Incremental Payment Systems* (1973), pp. 4, 14; R. M. Blackburn and M. Mann, *The Working Class in the Labour Market* (1979), Chapters 3 and 4; P. Collier and J. B. Knight, 'Seniority Payments, Quit Rates and Internal Labour Markets in Britain and Japan', *Oxford Bulletin of Economics and Statistics* (47) 1985.
78. G. C. Cameron, 'The Growth of Holidays With Pay in Great Britain' in G. L. Reid and D. J. Robertson (eds.), *Fringe Benefits, Labour Costs and Social Security* (1965).
79. G. L. Reid, 'Sick Pay', in Reid and Robertson, *Fringe Benefits*; Ministry of Pensions and National Insurance, *Enquiry into the Incidence of Incapacity to Work*, Part II, (1964); Ministry of Labour, *Sick Pay Schemes* (1964), p. 5. By 1974 74 per cent of manual men and 55 per cent of manual women were members of employer-based sick-pay schemes. Department of Health and Social Security, *Report on a Survey of Occupational Sick Pay Schemes* (1977).
80. L. Hannah, *Inventing Retirement: The Development of Occupational Pensions in Britain* (Cambridge, 1986), p. 145.
81. By 1975 about 11.5 million workers or just over half the total number were in occupational pension schemes. Some 5.2 million or about 40 per cent of manual employees were covered compared with 6.3 million or around 60 per cent of non-manual employees. There were also significant differences between men and women (75 and 25 per cent respectively) and between public and private (74 and 38 per cent respectively). Government Actuary, *Occupational Pension Schemes* 1975, Fifth Survey by the Government Actuary (1978).
82. Hannah, *Inventing Retirement*, pp. 106-11. There has been a spread of schemes based on final year's pay.
83. Department of Employment, Labour Cost Surveys. See also R. A. Hart, *The Economics of Non-Wage Labour Costs* (1984), Chapters 3 and 10.
84. W. Oi, 'Labour as a Quasi-fixed Factor', *Journal of Political Economy* 70 (1962).
85. This is the conclusion of Hannah, *Inventing Retirement* and F. Green, 'Occupational Pension Schemes and British Capitalism', *Cambridge Journal of Economics* 6 (1982), on pensions. See also G. L. Reid and D. J. Robertson, 'Introduction', in Reid and Robertson, *Fringe Benefits*, p. 30.

86. F. Green, G. Hadjimatheou, R. Smail, *Unequal Figures* (1984) and Advisory Conciliation and Arbitration Service, *Developments in Harmonisation*, Discussion Paper 1 (1982).
87. R. Price, 'The Decline and Fall of the Status Divide?', in K. Sisson (ed.), *Personnel Management in Britain* (Oxford, 1989); A. Russell, *Employee Benefits in Historical Perspective: The Changing Pattern of Workplace Inequality in the Twentieth Century*, Chapter 6 (forthcoming).
88. H. Mulis and G. Grist, *Towards Single Status* (1975); Institute of Manpower Studies, *Staff Status for Manual Workers*, Company Manpower Commentary No. 9, (1981); Industrial Relations Review and Report, *Staff Status*, No. 248 (May 1981); Incomes Data Services, *Harmonisation of Conditions*, No. 273 (September 1982); Advisory Conciliation and Arbitration Service, *Harmonisation*; C. Roberts, *Harmonisation* (1985).
89. Advisory Conciliation and Arbitration Service, *Harmonisation*, p. 2; Russell, *Employee Benefits*; T. Robinson, *Staff Status for Manual Workers* (1972); Enderwick and Buckley, 'Industrial Relations Practices'.
90. Advisory Conciliation and Arbitration Service, *Harmonisation* p. 2; Russell, *Employee Benefits*
91. Advisory Conciliation and Arbitration Service, *Harmonisation* p. 4; Incomes Data Service, *Harmonisation.*
92. J. Rubery, 'Structured Labour Markets, Worker Organisation and Low Pay' *Cambridge Journal of Economics* 11 (1978).
93. T. Lawson, 'Paternalism and Labour Market Segmentation Theory', in F. Wilkinson (ed.), *The Dynamics of Labour Market Segmentation* (1981); N. Bosanquet and P. B. Doeringer, 'Is There a Dual Labour Market in Great Britain?', *Economic Journal* 83 (1973).
94. C. Hendry, 'The Corporate Managment of Human Resources Under Conditions of Decentralisation', *British Journal of Management*, 1 (1990).
95. *Ibid.*; P. Townsend, *Poverty in the United Kingdom* (1979) pp. 77–79; A. B. Atkinson, *The Economics of Inequality* (1975), Chapter 6.
96. G. Pscacharopoulos, 'Labour Market and Income Distribution: The Case of the UK', in W. Krelle and A. F. Shorrocks (eds.), *Personal Income Distribution* (Amsterdam, 1978); K. Mayhew and B. Roswell, 'Labour Market Segmentation in Britain', *Oxford Bulletin of Economics and Statistics* 41 (1979); R. McNabb and G. Pscacharopoulos, 'Further Evidence on the Relevance of the Dual Labour Market Hypothesis for the UK', *Journal of Human Resources* 16 (1981).
97. See, for example, J. Rubery and F. Wilkinson, 'Outwork and Segmented Labour Markets', in Wilkinson (ed.), *The Dynamics*; National Economic Development Office, *Changing Patterns of Work: How Companies Introduce Flexibility To Meet New Needs* (1986); A. Pollert, 'The Flexible Firm: Fixation or Fact?', *Work, Employment and Society*, 2 (1988).

9 MARKETS, FIRMS, AND THE MANAGEMENT OF LABOUR

1. J. MacInnes, *Thatcherism at Work* (Milton Keynes, 1987); P. Beaumont, *Change in Industrial Relations* (1990); D. Metcalf, 'Water Notes Dry Up: The Impact of the Donovan Reform Proposals and Thatcherism on Labour

244 Notes to pages 177-182

Productivity in British Manufacturing Industry', *British Journal of Industrial Relations*, 27 (1989); P. Nolan and P. Marginson, 'Skating on Thin Ice: David Metcalf on Trade Unions and Productivity', *British Journal of Industrial Relations*, 28 (1990); J. Storey and K. Sisson, 'Limits to Transformation: Human Resource Management in the British Context', *Industrial Relations Journal*; D. Guest, 'Human Resource Management: Its Implications for Industrial Relations and Trade Unions', in J. Storey, (ed.), *New Perspectives on Human Resource Management* (1989).

2. O. Williamson, *Markets and Hierarchies* (New York, 1975), Chapter 8.
3. H. Braverman, *Labour and Monopoly Capitalism* (New York, 1974).
4. W. W. Daniel and N. Millward, *Workplace Industrial Relations in Britain* (1983); N. Millward and M. Stevens, *British Workplace Industrial Relations 1980-1984* (1986); P. Marginson *et al. Beyond the Workplace* (Oxford, 1988).
5. L. Mackay and D. Torrington, *The Changing Nature of Personnel Management* (1981).
6. M. Jaces and B. Roberts, 'Labour Costs in 1988', Department of Employment *Gazette* (September 1990).
7. Storey and Sisson, 'Limits to Transformation'; Marginson *et al.*, *Beyond the Workplace*; D. Guest, 'Human Resource Management in the UK', in B. Towers (ed.), *Handbook of Human Resource Management* (Oxford, 1991).
8. This is similar to Mintzberg's distinction between *intended* and *enacted* strategy, where the former refers to desired goals, the latter to actual patterns of behaviour. Mintzberg suggests that enacted strategies are the most important and that research should concentrate on these. See *The Nature of Managerial Work* (New York, 1973).
9. For a general argument on these lines see A. D. Chandler, *Scale and Scope: The Dynamics of Industrial Capitalism* (Cambridge, Mass., 1990). For a review of the argument that British management failed to develop effective marketing strategies see National Economic Development Office, *Industrial Performance: Trade Performance and Marketing* (1981).
10. W. Kennedy, *Industrial Structure, Capital Markets and the Origins of British Economic Decline* (Cambridge, 1987); S. Pollard, *The Wasting of the British Economy* (1986) pp. 130-5 and *The Development of the British Economy* (1983), p. 348.; L. Rostas, *Comparative Productivity in British and American Industry* (Cambridge, 1948); R.E. Caves, 'Productivity Differences among Industries', in R. E. Caves and L. B. Krause (eds), *Britain's Economic Performance* (Washington, D.C., 1980); M. E. Blume, 'The Financial Markets' in *ibid.*; R. W. Bacon and W. A. Eltis, *The Age of UK and US Machinery* (1974); N. Crafts, 'British Economic Growth Before and After 1979', Centre for Economic Policy Research, Discussion Paper 292 (1988), pp 20-21.
11. L. Ulman, 'Collective Bargaining and Industrial Efficiency', in R. E. Caves (ed.), *Britain's Economic Prospects* (1968), p. 327.
12. The evidence on the economic effects of trade unions in Britain is rather contradictory. For some historical studies, see J. Pencavel, 'The Distributional and Efficiency Effects of Trade Unions in Britain', *British Journal of Industrial Relations*, 15 (1977); P. J. Hilditch and A. Reid, 'Trade Unions and Labour Productivity: The British Shipbuilding Industry, 1870-1950',

Department of Applied Economics, Cambridge, Working Paper 8907 (1989). For the contemporary debate, see Metcalf, 'Water Notes'; Nolan and Marginson, 'Skating on Thin Ice'; S. Wadhwani, 'The Effects of Unions on Productivity Growth, Investment and Employment: A Report on Some Recent Work', *British Journal of Industrial Relations*, 28 (1990); N. Oulton, 'Labour Productivity in UK Manufacturing in the 1970s and 1980s', *National Institute Economic Review*, 132 (1990).

13. R. E. Caves, 'Productivity Differences', p. 170. There is an argument that the concentration of strike activity in large plants adversely affected the operations. See, for example, S. Prais, *Productivity and Industrial Structure* (1985); P. K. Edwards, 'The Strike-Proneness of British Manufacturing Industry', *British Journal of Industrial Relations* 19 (1981); S. W. Davies and R. E. Caves, 'Inter-Industry Analysis of UK-US Productivity Differences', National Institute for Economic and Social Research, Discussion Paper No. 61, Industry Series No. 13 (1983).

14. See, for example, R. Dore, *British Factory – Japanese Factory* (1973); D. Gallie, *In Search of the New Working Class* (Cambridge, 1978), Chapter 5; B. Holz, 'Productivity Differences and Industrial Relations Structures: Engineering Companies in the United Kingdom and Federal Republic of Germany', *Labour and Society* 7 (1982).

15. P. J. Buckley and P. Enderwick, *The Industrial Relations Position of Foreign-Owned Firms in Britain* (1985).

16. Recent work by S. Prais and his colleagues at the National Institute has stressed how deficiencies in the education and training systems in Britain have led to the less effective organisation of production and inferior work performance.

17. See E. F. Lazear, 'Agency, Earnings Profiles, Productivity, and Hours Reductions', *American Economic Review*, 71 (1971), and J. M. Malcolmson, 'Work Incentives, Hierarchy, and Internal Labour Markets', in G. A. Akerlof and J. L. Yellen, *Efficiency Wage Models and the Labour Market* (Cambridge, 1986). The conclusions are somewhat similar to human capital theory, but without the emphasis on training and firm-specific skills.

18. S. Zweig, *Productivity and Trade Unions* (Oxford, 1951), p. 20.

19. This term is taken from G. B. Richardson, 'The Organisation of Industry', *Economic Journal*, 83 (1972).

20. A. M. Ross, 'Do We Have A New Industrial Feudalism?', *American Economic Review*, 47 (1958).

21. For a similar argument see H. Ramsay, 'Cycles of Control', *Sociology* 11 (1977).

22. M. Wiener, *English Culture and the Decline of the Industrial Spirit, 1850–1980* (Cambridge, 1981); R. Locke, *The End of Practical Man: Entrepreneurship in Germany, France and Great Britain* (Greenwich, Conn., 1984).

23. For the US see D. Nelson, *Workers and Managers: Origins of the New Factory System in the United States, 1880–1920* (Madison, WI, 1975); S. M. Jacoby, *Employing Bureaucracy: Managers, Unions and the Transformation of Work in American Industry 1900–1945* (New York, 1985); H. J. Harris, *The Right to Manage: Industrial Relations Policies of American Business in the 1940s* (Madison, WI, 1982). For Japan see W. M. Fruin, *Kikkoman*:

Company, Clan and Community (Cambridge, Mass., 1983); K. Taira, *Economic Development and the Labor Market in Japan* (New York, 1970); D. Gordon, *The Evolution of Labor Relations in Japanese Heavy Industries 1853-1955* (Cambridge, Mass., 1985). For Germany see W. Streck, *Industrial Relations in West Germany: A Case Study of the Car Industry* (1984).

Index

Printed in the United States
By Bookmasters